COSMOPOLITAN IMAGINARIES AND INTERNATIONAL DISORDER

COSMOPOLITAN IMAGINARIES AND INTERNATIONAL DISORDER

Aaron C. McKeil

UNIVERSITY OF MICHIGAN PRESS

Ann Arbor

Published in the United States of America by the
University of Michigan Press
First published March 2025

A CIP catalog record for this book is available from the British Library.

Library of Congress Cataloging-in-Publication Data

Names: McKeil, Aaron, author. | Michigan Publishing (University of Michigan), publisher.
Title: Cosmopolitan imaginaries and international disorder / Aaron McKeil.
Other titles: Configurations (Ann Arbor, Mich.)
Description: Ann Arbor : University of Michigan Press, [2025] | Series: Configurations :
    critical studies of world politics | Includes bibliographical references (pages 159–185)
    and index.
Identifiers: LCCN 2024046652 (print) | LCCN 2024046653 (ebook) | ISBN 9780472076062
    (hardcover) | ISBN 9780472056064 (paperback) | ISBN 9780472903405 (ebook other)
Subjects: LCSH: Cosmopolitanism. | Globalization. | International relations.
Classification: LCC JZ1308 .M44 2025 (print) | LCC JZ1308 (ebook) | DDC 327.1—dc23/
    eng/20250107
LC record available at https://lccn.loc.gov/2024046652
LC ebook record available at https://lccn.loc.gov/2024046653

DOI: https://doi.org/10.3998/mpub.12794206

An electronic version of this book is freely available, thanks in part to the support of libraries
working with Knowledge Unlatched (KU). KU is a collaborative initiative designed to make
high quality books Open Access for the public good. More information about the initiative
and links to the Open Access version can be found at www.knowledgeunlatched.org.

The University of Michigan Press's open access publishing program is made possible
thanks to additional funding from the University of Michigan Office of the Provost
and the generous support of contributing libraries.

Front cover image: *The Great Day of His Wrath*, by John Martin (1851–53, oil on canvas).
Tate, purchased 1945. Photograph by permission of Tate Museum.

Authorized Representative: Easy Access System Europe, Mustamäe tee 50, 10621 Tallinn,
Estonia, gpsr.requests@easproject.com

The world would have the appearance of a large republic; men
would live everywhere like brothers, and each individual be a citizen
of the universe. That this idea should be but a delightful dream! yet
it flows from the nature and essence of man. But disorderly passions, and private and mistaken interest, will for ever prevent its
being realized.

 —Emer de Vattel
  (*The Law of Nations*, Book II, Chap. I, §16)

Contents

Foreword

Aaron McKeil's book pushes the discussion of global cosmopolitanism in new directions, fueled by a commitment to explanation rather than to just normative analysis. McKeil asks why, despite a number of visions of global unity that many have found compelling in principle over the centuries, nothing like a unitary global polity has yet emerged. His answer is that part of the reason for the absence of such a polity can be found in the contestation of the narratives supporting such a polity—contestation on behalf of advocates of more particularistic identities. In a way, his book is an excavation of the cultural preconditions of a global polity, and in that way is a rejoinder to the conventional wisdom in international studies that a global polity would require a global hegemonic power; even if such a dominant power were to arise, McKeil suggests, in the absence of a compelling and relatively uncontested cosmopolitan narrative, material power enough would be insufficient.

McKeil sets up his detailed discussion of different cosmopolitan visions with an investigation of the most all-encompassing near-global polities in history, namely, the Roman and Han empires (which thought of themselves as in fact controlling the whole world). He demonstrates not that a shared narrative of a global identity was the most important factor in their success, but instead, that we cannot explain their successes without reference to such narratives. This makes a cosmopolitan imaginary a key part of the configuration of elements driving a unitary global polity. The argument here is thus appropriately configurational and not based on any kind of estimate of the independent impact of a narrative vis-à-vis other elements; what matters here is the *combination*, and in particular, the way that a cosmopolitan narrative knits together other aspects of a polity and (as Max Weber might put it) transmutes raw domination into more or less legitimate authority. McKeil then uses this ideal-typical investigation of ancient empires to organize a discussion of contemporary cosmopolitan visions, assessing each with respect to their capacity to perform the legitimating task that a global polity would require.

Because McKeil's account emphasizes the ways that past cosmopolitan projects have foundered on the exclusionary narratives and practices of particular polities, it might appear that he is ultimately presenting us with a pessimistic view of the possibilities of a genuinely inclusive global order. But McKeil's argument, to the contrary, helps us get a better grasp on just what a successful cosmopolitan project would entail, at the same time as his careful tracing of cosmopolitan traditions reminds us that the notion of unification beyond sovereign states has always been part of the general discourse of international affairs broadly understood. In the face of climate change and given the continued exploitation of social and cultural differences for short-term political gain all around the globe, clear thinking about a future cosmopolitan order is arguably one of the most important tasks facing us. Aaron McKeil's insightful account helps us to do just that.

Patrick Thaddeus Jackson
Series Editor, Configurations

Acknowledgments

This book reconciles the literature of cosmopolitan politics with the failures of attempts to construct alternative cosmopolitan global orders in modern international history. I began researching this topic in the context of Brexit and Donald Trump's presidency. I found that these events were not unprecedented and that they reveal something important about the limits and patterns of international orders in modern international experience. Martin Wight's celebrated lectures on international theory have provided an instrumental framing device for this study, helping to organize cosmopolitanism broadly defined. His writings have also been a source of inspiration. The epilogue considers Wight's own evaluation of his category and I owe a debt of thanks to the LSE Wight archives librarians and staff.

This book owes intellectual debts to colleagues present and former in the Department of International Relations at the London School of Economics and Political Science, where I conducted the PhD studies that formed the basis of this book, and to colleagues at LSE IDEAS, where I have conducted further research, especially Christopher Coker, and Peter Wilson and Mark Hoffman for PhD supervision, as well as Kirsten Ainley, Maggy Ainley, Chris Alden, Stuart Austin, Michael Banks, Tarak Barkawi, Martin Bayly, David Brenner, Chris Brown, Barry Buzan, William Callahan, Ilaria Carrozza, Michael Cox, Andrew Delatolla, Ida Danewid, Robert Falkner, Marian Feist, Kerry Goettlich, Annissa Haddadi, Scott Hamilton, Liane Hartnett, Alvina Hoffman, Chris Hughes, Sidharth Kaushal, Mark Kersten, Paul Kirby, Nicholas Kitchen, Mathias Koenig-Archibugi, Saniya Kulkarni, George Lawson, Margot Light, Gustav Meibauer, Jens Meierhenrich, James Morrison, Jeppe Mulich, Christopher Murray, Tristen Naylor, Iver B. Neumann, Andreas Aagaard Nohr, Dave Rampton, Adrian Rogstad, William Rook, Emma Saint, Alireza

Shams-Lahijani, Giogio Shani during his time at the LSE Centre for International Studies, Dimitrios Stroikos, Bjornar Sverdrup-Thygeson, Joanne Yao, and Asad Zaidi. Andrew Linklater and Chris Brown provided comments on the PhD thesis. I also wish to acknowledge debts and thanks for comments and conversations with William Bain, Craig Calhoun, Filippo Costa-Buranelli, Tad Daly, Richard Falk, Oliver Kessler, and participants of a book workshop at the University of Erfurt, Cornelia Navari, Inderjeet Parmar, Yannis Stivachtis, Hidemi Suganami, and R. B. J. Walker. I am grateful for the thoughtful and helpful comments received from anonymous peer reviewers and the series editor, Patrick Thaddeus Jackson. This book is indebted above all to the patient support of my wife and family.

—A. C. M.
London

Introduction

The idea of a cosmopolitan order embracing all humankind is ancient, but in the post–Cold War world it was widely believed to be an emerging future. In practice, this idea was the hope and promise of enthusiast architects of neoliberal globalization, humanitarian advocacy groups, progressive international lawyers, and Silicon Valley utopians. In theory, academics produced a wave of literature on cosmopolitan globalization. This large and for a time influential literature argued that increasing global interdependence and interaction were generating the structural transformation of world politics into a new kind of post-Westphalian cosmopolitan order.[1] These ideas have been dramatically contradicted by the revolt against globalism, the decline of cosmopolitanism, and an increasingly divisive and unstable international order. World politics is now more divided and in more ways than before, even while technologies continue to increase interaction capacities and material security interdependencies. This reversal revives the problem of international order in practice but also poses a general puzzle for International Relations theory. Why have anticipated and advocated cosmopolitan orders struggled to emerge in the modern global world? Why, moreover, have attempts to construct a cosmopolitan order tended to be followed by new and greater forces of division and disorder?

The argument I make in this book is that cosmopolitan order projects in the modern global world have encountered and been overwhelmed by hierarchy legitimation conflicts and recognition struggles reasserting modern state power and remobilizing exclusionary nationalist identities, especially when intensified in contexts of international instability and economic turmoil. Advocating cosmopolitan ordering in practice (be it by signaling internationalist cosmopolitan obligations or by calling for cosmopolitan institutions) implies formal or informal hierarchical relations of some states, authorities, and groups over others, hence the challenge of legitimation. Mixed in with this is the process whereby claims to the existence of a cosmopolitan community virtually always generate recognition struggles with identities not finding themselves included and not "fitting in" the supposedly all-embracing cosmopolitan vision. Legitimating cosmopolitan hierarchies and managing recognition struggles are steep hurdles to any cosmopolitan ordering project. This argument does not explain the collapse of globalism, the rise of populism, and deglobalization as such, which have their own growing literatures.[2] My argument instead understands these destabilizing trends as contexts intensifying ongoing hierarchy legitimation conflicts and recognition struggles that have embroiled and repeatedly overwhelmed cosmopolitan politics in the modern world.

This argument has implications for the theory of international order and for advocates and critics of cosmopolitan order alternatives in practice. For theory, this argument clarifies the explanation and understanding of the limits of cosmopolitan ordering in the modern global world. It explains why increasing "dynamic densities" of globalizing interdependence and interaction capacities have been insufficient to generate global solidarity and stabilize a cosmopolitan order.[3] It also offers a counterargument to realists who suggest that the return of great power politics and the collapse of globalism have vindicated their theoretical assumptions. Conventional "realist" explanations of persistent global disunity remain unconvincing and misleading.[4] Contrary to these realist theories, I make the case that cosmopolitan and national belonging have been coconstitutive in the modern international experience, that nations are not latent or preexisting obstacles to internationalist cosmopolitanism as realists assume, but are instead reconstituted as exclusionary in processes of recognition struggle and the reassertion of nation-state authority. Contrary to realist thinkers, moreover, it is not simply the continued diffusion of power that matters, but the social processes of hierarchy legitimation conflicts and recognition struggles that have reconstituted a socially and politically divided international society.[5] These theoretical arguments are not good news for advocates of cosmopolitan politics in practice, but they at least clarify the hurdles of hierarchy legitimation and recognition struggles in practice.

My aims in this book are twofold. The first aim is conceptual and philosophical, to clarify how cosmopolitan belonging and cosmopolitan ordering are not exclusively a liberal Kantian category, offering a wider conceptual map of cosmopolitan thought and practice in the modern international experience. The second aim is more sociological and historical, to explore how and why these varied cosmopolitan imaginaries have struggled to be realized as cosmopolitan orders. In this introductory chapter, I first outline my main concepts and definitions of cosmopolitanism and cosmopolitan order in theoretical terms, then convey the transformations in cosmopolitan imagination and its paradoxes in the modern global world. In chapter 1, I develop my ideal type concept of cosmopolitan order and contrast orders in ancient versus modern contexts. Chapters 2, 3, 4, and 5 then each explore the rise and retreat of different cosmopolitan waves in the modern experience, the liberal Kantian, world communist, postcolonial, and green cosmopolitan imaginaries. These cases, overlapping in time and space, in broad cosmopolitan waves, worked through different political actors advancing distinct and often competing visions of cosmopolitan order. Chapter 6 considers cosmopolitan politics in the increasingly divisive and disorderly times of emergent geostrategic competition. The conclusion reiterates my main argument and its implications for cosmopolitan theory and practice in a divided and disorderly world.

Absent Cosmopolis

The rise and fall of cosmopolitanism in the post–Cold War world was the most recent in a series of cosmopolitan waves in the modern international experience.[6] Revolutionary internationalist cosmopolitanism swept the Atlantic world in the 18th and 19th centuries, for instance, with radical cosmopolitan visions anticipated by leading intellectuals of the age, not least Immanuel Kant and Karl Marx. In the wake of the First World War, cosmopolitan ideas again became popular demands. The ordering decisions embodied in the Covenant of the League of Nations did not include the more ambitious and radical transformative ordering calls of numerous advocates, including Japan's racial equality principle, or the demands of the Women's International League for Peace and Freedom, the Pan African Congress, and not least the revolutionary demands of Vladimir Lenin's new Soviet Union.[7] The 1920s experienced considerable activism calling for more radical cosmopolitan ordering alternatives, but in the wake of the Great Depression and the instabilities of the 1930s, the forces of remobilized exclusionary nationalism and state power redivided international society more deeply than perhaps it had been for centuries.[8]

Out of the depths of the Second World War, calls emerged again for radical cosmopolitan order alternatives. A large literature advocating world federation emerged, including Clarence K. Streit's *Union Now* (1939) and Emery Reeves's *The Anatomy of Peace* (1945).[9] Public intellectuals, such as Albert Einstein, Niels Bohr, and Bertrand Russell, proposed the establishment of world government to manage a nuclear world.[10] Even the realist Hans Morgenthau gestured to the importance of David Mitrany's planned world peace system.[11] It is little remembered today how widely discussed and seriously debated these ideas were at the time.[12] Presidential candidate Wendell Wilkie coined the phrase "one world" after his tour of service in the Second World War, and proposed a more conciliatory postwar world order.[13] In January 1945, emerging from the Second World War, Franklin D. Roosevelt declared in his fourth inaugural address, "We have learned to be citizens of the world, members of the human community."[14] Roosevelt's envisioned United Nations was not so ambitious as the radical transformative order visions on offer at the time, but it was universal, and even his allies Joseph Stalin and Winston Churchill were terrified by the ambition of Roosevelt's envisioned universal order. Calls for a more radical transformation of international society soon became impossible and forgotten, however, with Stalin's redivision of Europe—as a part of his own revolutionary strategy—and the deepening divides of the global Cold War. World communism, up to its abandonment and dissolution, was itself a kind of cosmopolitan wave broadly defined, containing a radical world order vision, albeit one opposed by as many millions as supported it.

In the post–Cold War world, the last of these historical episodes and the most immediate in our memory, the wave of neoliberal commercial cosmopolitanism promised liberal prosperity, peace, and freedoms in principle for all humankind. Some cosmopolitan voices were more ambitious than even this, calling for global democracy and cosmopolitan expansions of humanitarian international law and authority.[15] This cosmopolitan wave always struggled to constrain war, as liberal and humanitarian interventionism morphed into a global war on terror. And when strained and stressed by economic turbulence in the wake of the global financial crash, the wave was completely broken. In the revolt against globalism, cosmopolitan ideas have been attacked and seemingly cast into the wasteland of history. Against neoliberal cosmopolitanism, antiglobalization movements organized resistance, in protests of World Trade Organization proceedings, but the post–Cold War neoliberal cosmopolitan wave was not overturned until it was opposed by the reassertion of modern state power, following the populist upheavals of 2016, remobilizing exclusionary nationalist identities, in a new antiglobalism. This outcome is not entirely surprising, at least in hindsight, because the character of neoliberal cosmopolitanism made it difficult for its believers to understand nonliberal identities or to sympathize with deep inequalities. In the wake of neoliberal cosmopolitanism, however, international society is again experiencing an era of deepening division and disorder, one that is likely to continue into the foreseeable future.

In each of these and intervening episodes, cosmopolitan waves obviously encountered a range of immediate political and strategic obstacles in the existing conflicts that these same cosmopolitan politics paradoxically aimed to overcome. Across international society, deep political and strategic conflict balance huge military and political forces, be it in the longstanding conflicts in the Korean Peninsula, Kashmir, and Israel-Palestine, or in emerging arms races and strategic arenas constraining states from in many cases even the cessation of hostilities, let alone some supposed cosmopolitan unity. Obviously, these existing strategic and political challenges in every region pose practically impossible hurdles to legitimating *structurally* integrative cosmopolitan orders. More puzzling, however, is why even calls for nonstructural *internationalist* cosmopolitan solidarities aiming to conciliate and ease these very tensions have been so widely resisted and rejected. The argument is that even where cosmopolitan politics is not advocating new political authorities or structures, when connected to foreign policies they implicitly threaten the real or imagined informal de facto hierarchies of some states, populations, and groups over others, generating legitimation conflicts and with few exceptions struggles for recognition. Narratives of cosmopolitan belonging are particularly prone to recognition struggles, precisely because they aim to be all-embracing.

In theoretical terms, by hierarchy legitimation conflicts, I mean contestation over the legitimacy of political authorities and social and economic inequalities.[16] By recognition struggles, I mean conflicting and contested demands for acknowledgment of self-defined identities, individual or collective.[17] My conception of "recognition" is closer to an understanding of it as relationally constituting discourses and practices of the self. My argument in these terms is that, in the modern international experience, cosmopolitan ordering projects have not emerged because they have encountered and been overwhelmed by hierarchy legitimation conflicts and recognition struggles that reassert the diffuse sources of modern state power and exclusionary national identities. In contexts of geopolitical stress and economic strain, these tensions and sources of conflict have tended to become intensified by political actors not least due to heightened political stakes, resulting in the balancing of force and the political and social redivision of humankind, both *vertically* between states and *horizontally* across groups and classes.

In the modern international experience, calls for cosmopolitan order alternatives have tended to express responses to the injustice and dangers posed by global modernity's contradictions. Contradictions between loyalties to sovereigns and obligations to humankind, contradictions between sovereignty and capital, tensions between nuclear stability and species survival, and tensions between capital and climate have all generated calls for cosmopolitan order alternatives. The breadth of these calls and the seriousness of the common responsibilities that they aim to address have been insufficient time and time again to overcome the countervailing reassertions of modern state power and exclusionary nationalist identities in hierarchy legitimation conflicts and recognition struggles.

Cosmopolitan Order and Belonging

Nations have been important sources of meaning and community in the modern global world, but their division of humankind has also inspired and characterized the imagination of cosmopolitan belonging and alternative orders.[18] "Cosmopolitanism" narrowly defined refers to a tradition of imagining humankind as a universal moral community, from ancient thinkers Zeno and Diogenes to Kant and contemporary Kantians.[19] I distinguish this tradition of upper "C" Cosmopolitanism from lower "c" cosmopolitanism, broadly defined as ways of imagining belonging in a community of humankind, including Kantianism but also traditions beyond it.[20] In this book, I am primarily interested in the broadly defined category of cosmopolitan thought. Martin Wight's celebrated lectures on international theory, for instance, categorized cosmopolitans broadly as "revolutionaries," even though not all cosmopolitans seek the revolutionary unification of international society.[21] *Moral* cosmopolitans tend to advocate internationalist solidarity, while *institutional* cosmopolitans tend to advocate political world unity.[22]

By cosmopolitan order, as an ideal type concept,[23] I mean a kind of international order transcending international society, by (*a*) forming some sense of imagined cosmopolitan belonging embracing all humankind, with (*b*) an ability to mobilize resources for common interests to some degree, via (*c*) either *institutionally* unifying international society with legitimated cosmopolitan authorities or via legitimated *internationalist* cosmopolitan solidarity and nonstate actor coordination.[24] Cosmopolitan orders, as international orders, are also a kind of political order, which among other purposes manage political violence between communities, structure political relations, and legitimate types of political authorities through institutionalized discourses and practices.[25] As emergent and ongoing processes, "orders are fashioned within particular cultural and material milieus, with their constitutional structures being profoundly conditioned by prevailing social imaginaries and geopolitical contexts."[26] International orders as such have a wide range of configurations and modes of imagination.[27] The idea of a cosmopolitan order in this sense is a radically transformative type of international order, often supposed in the modern world to possibly emerge in a remote future.[28] Partial cosmopolitan configurations of this ideal type are possible in practice too, however. Because international orders are layered and include differentiated suborders, it is possible to develop "cosmopolitan" orders within some suborders, such as the humanitarian order, without a complete cosmopolitan transformation of the order's central institutions of sovereignty and security as such.[29] International orders at a regional level moreover can develop "cosmopolitan" order configurations, most approximately in the European Union for instance, without equivalent global level and inter-great-power configurations.

The idea of international society, as early as Hugo Grotius and Francisco de Vitoria, has been claimed to rest upon an underlying moral community of humankind, a *civitas maxima*. If this moral community of humankind exists, then international society has struggled to meet what moral obligations it has.[30] International society has had considerably little cosmopolitan solidarity, relative to such moral demands, and what cosmopolitan institutions have been constructed are so limited and weak that to say international society is a cosmopolitan order would be to quite misrepresent it. Kant's criticism of Grotius's *civitas maxima* as "cold comfort" for the victims of war and injustice is still true today.[31]

The legal fiction of a *civitas maxima* has little parallel sociological sense of cosmopolitan belonging. By cosmopolitan belonging, I mean a sense or feeling of "fitting in" and identifying with humankind. Belonging as "fitting in" and togetherness, in this sense, is expressed in narratives and performed in practices that nest geographically disparate people and groups into larger imagined communities. A feeling of belonging ideally hangs together with and is affirmed by a mutual feeling of being understood by members of that community, in everyday life, because of how one "fits in" by sharing these common horizons of understanding and some basic everyday practices that perform it.[32] Ideal typically speaking, a cosmopolitan community and sense of cosmopolitan belonging has qualitative differences in the way it is imagined and constituted from national communities. The difference is not simply one of scale. Cosmopolitan belonging and the idea of a cosmopolitan community is in principle all-embracing, against the idea that humankind is a set of discreet "in-groups" with "us" against "them" dynamics. It is often overlooked how the idea of the cosmopolitan community is older than that of the national community.[33] In important respects, the idea of the national community was developed in modern demands for recognition of collective identities distinct and discreet from larger and older cosmopolitan modes of political community. Cosmopolitan and national identities are both imagined communities, in a mutually constitutive relationship in the modern world, the construction of each affecting and reshaping the imagination of the other.[34]

Modern Cosmopolitan Imaginaries

By "cosmopolitan imaginaries," I mean the taken-for-granted assumptions people hold about what cosmopolitan belonging can possibly mean, and what it can possibly mean for all humankind to form a political community.[35] Exploring the predominant hegemonic discourses, images, and vaguer notions commonly held about what a cosmopolitan order and mode of belonging can possibly mean helps clarify its social form in the modern world, both enabled and constrained by these predominant discourses and practices. Identifying these imaginaries also helps clarify the wider variation and range of cosmopolitan thought and practice beyond its predominant liberal Kantian imaginary.

The imagination of a cosmopolitan community, moral or political, oftentimes experienced intuitively, other times expressed in narratives and practices of universal solidarity, tends to arise from the feeling that a world of sequestered loyalties and competing interests is not the world humankind needs or deserves. According to Catherine Lu, "In both the ancient and modern worlds cosmopolitan ideas have developed alongside, if not directly in response to, the posited social, political, economic and ethical imperatives of a divided world."[36] It was in the context of the city-states of ancient Greece, for instance, that the philosopher Zeno of Citium first imagined a world city, the *cosmopolis*. Confucius imagined a vision of *da tong* (Grand Harmony or Grand Unity) in the warring states era of ancient China.[37] Modern philosophers with a cosmopolitan imagination, such as Kant and Marx, articulated their sweeping cosmopolitan visions in a context of emerging sovereign states and international thought, but also globalizing travel and interdependence.[38]

As an ancient and global idea, cosmopolitan imagination has transformed along with humankind, across world history. *Ancient* and *medieval* cosmopolitan imaginaries tended to assume that world unity is cosmic, timeless, divinely ordained, and coinciding hierarchically with universal empire. Zeno's *cosmopolis* imagined a universal moral order, and sources such as *Antigone* express this idea, without universal empire, against Thrasymachus' idea of justice as that of the stronger.[39] These non-imperial cosmopolitan ideas may have been more of an exception in the ancient world, however, as ideas of universal conquest as universal "peace" were widespread in ancient empires.[40] The Cyrus cylinder records the oldest extant expression of the imaginary of universal conquest, "I am Cyrus, king of the universe." In the legend of Alexander the Great's meeting with the philosopher Diogenes, who imagined himself a "citizen of the world," Diogenes dismissed Alexander's audience, having no need or interest in world empire. Aristotle, however, in a purported letter to Alexander, saw benefits for humankind in world empire, "Happy is he who sees the resplendence of that day when men will agree to constitute one rule and one kingdom. They will cease from wars and strife, and devote themselves to that which promotes their welfare and the welfare of their cities and countries."[41] Dante Alighieri's *De Monarchia* also made a case for universal monarchy for universal peace. In the context of the conquest of the "New World," Vitoria articulated the Christian imaginary of a universal community underlying international society, *universalis civitas humani generis*.[42]

Modern cosmopolitan imaginaries have increasingly cast the idea into progressive futures, in material ways more than spiritual. For the 19th century political theorist Henri Saint-Simon, "The imagination of poets has placed the golden age in the infancy of the human race, amidst the ignorance and coarseness of ancient times.... The golden age of the human race is not behind us; it lies before us, in the perfection of the social order."[43] For

Saint-Simon, perfecting modernity meant the construction of a rational, scientific, commercial, and pacific world federation. The ancient idea of the *cosmopolis* became the Enlightenment image of a global collaborative order in the future, rationally conforming to increasingly discovered universal Newtonian laws.[44] Kant, although himself never having left his local hometown, Königsberg, gave the cosmopolitan imagination the inflection of worldliness by imagining diversity increasingly connected and mixed by expanding travel in the modern global world.[45] For Kant, these trends were producing a "cosmopolitan condition," to be more fully realized in the future.

Tennyson's "Locksley Hall" is still the definitive expression of the modern way of imagining world unity:

For I dipt into the future, far as human eye could see,
Saw the Vision of the world, and all the wonders that would be;

Saw the heavens fill with commerce, argosies of magic sails,
Pilots of the purple twilight, dropping down with costly bales;

Heard the heavens fill with shouting, and there rain'd a ghastly dew
From the nations' airy navies grappling in the central blue;

Far along the world-wide whisper of the south-wind rushing warm,
With the standards of the peoples plunging thro' the thunder-
   storm;

Till the war-drum throbb'd no longer, and the battle-flags were furl'd
In the Parliament of man, the Federation of the world.

There the common sense of most shall hold a fretful realm in awe,
And the kindly earth shall slumber, lapt in universal law.[46]

Tennyson's later poem, "Locksley Hall Sixty Years After" (1886), written in his later life, held out hope for a future peace, "When the schemes of all the systems, Kingdoms and Republics fall, / —Something kindlier, higher, holier—all for each and each for all?"[47]

Because modern cosmopolitan imaginaries tend to occupy the future, science fiction literature is full of them. H. G. Wells's futures were the most popular and imaginative of his generation. His *Anticipations*

(1901), *A Modern Utopia* (1905), *The World Set Free* (1914), *The Peace of the World* (1915), *The Open Conspiracy* (1928), and *The Shape of Things to Come* (1933), to name only a few, all assumed a world federation of sorts would exist somewhere beyond the near future.[48] In his *Outline of History* (1920), Wells speculated that into the future, having so joined together, humankind will stand up, "upon the earth as upon a footstool, and stretch out . . . amidst the stars."[49] Dystopian depictions of totalitarian futures and evil galactic empires were also popular tropes of this literature. The "One State" of Yevgeny Zamyatin's *We* (1920) depicts everyone working in *unison* like industrial automatons under a totalitarian world state.[50]

Paradoxes of Cosmopolitanism

Cosmopolitan politics in the modern global world is riddled with paradox. For Jacques Derrida, if cosmopolitan law is a Kantian moral imperative transcending states, how could states possibly make or apply it correctly?[51] Stranger is how cosmopolitanism is an ancient idea about an existing universal moral order, that moderns—not least Kant—have imagined as a utopia to be realized in the future.

Emer de Vattel supposed that if voluntary international law were made to coincide with natural law, then a kind world republic would emerge, although he doubted its possibility. For Vattel,

> the world would have the appearance of a large republic; men would live everywhere like brothers, and each individual be a citizen of the universe. That this idea should be but a delightful dream! yet it flows from the nature and essence of man. But disorderly passions, and private and mistaken interest, for ever prevent its being realized.[52]

In reaching this conclusion, Vattel was technically working with a Hobbesian concept of individual interests, adopted from Christian Wolff, who sought to apply Hobbes' ideas to international society. Earlier, the Abbé Saint-Pierre also attempted to extend Hobbes's thought to the international, but drew opposite conclusions, calling for a federative peace. Jean-Jacques Rousseau found Saint-Pierre's proposed federation to be nearly impossible to achieve, "except by a revolution," while Rousseau also expressed mixed views about its desirability, that it might "do more harm" than the harm it would prevent.[53] Insofar as peace proposals such as Saint-Pierre's or Kant's rely on a "domestic analogy" (presuming that order between states is not categorically different from order between individuals), the challenge of cosmopolitan political theory has been one of imagining a cosmopolitan order fit to constrain states as such so to respect the rights of individuals, or to imagine the conditions of one cosmopolitan world state, although it is possible to conceive a wide range of world order models with mixed ordering arrangements including individuals and states, some of which we might describe as "cosmopolitan."[54]

The modern society of states and imagination of cosmopolitan alternatives has been defined by these productive tensions and contradictions, at once practical and moral, between loyalties to states, the society of states, and humankind.[55] Rousseau was perhaps the most eloquent, in his paradoxes that "Man is born free, everywhere he is in chains" and "in joining a particular group of men, we have really declared ourselves the enemies of the whole race?" Thomas Paine's *The Rights of Man* used Diogenes' contradictory phrase "my country is the world." For Marx and Engels' *Communist Manifesto*, "The working men have no country," insofar as countries did not work for workers. For Virginia Woolf's *Three Guineas*, "As a woman I have no country. As a woman I want no country. As a woman, my country is the whole world." Modern cosmopolitan thinkers, in imagining a larger community of humankind, in contradiction with international society, built up tensions and a wish for revolutionary change.

Cosmopolitan change has been far more limited in the modern world than its cosmopolitan thinkers have expected and anticipated. Martin Wight's LSE lectures suggest this outcome is unsurprising, because, for Wight, "the central paradox of the successive waves of Revolutionist and counter-Revolutionist doctrine that they aim at uniting and integrating the family of nations but in practice divide it more deeply than it was divided before."[56] The pattern, for Wight,

> was embodied in the three successive waves of Revolutionist ideology that had divided modern international society on horizontal rather than vertical lines: that of the Protestant Reformation, that of the French Revolution and that of the Communist Revolution, of our own times. But it was also embodied, he thought, in the Counter-Revolutionist ideologies to which each of these affirmations of horizontal solidarity gave rise: that of the Catholic Counter-Reformation, that of International Legitimism and that of Dullesian Anti-Communism.[57]

Paradoxically, for Wight, revolutionary and counterrevolutionary attempts to forge a unified cosmopolitan world order have tended to only divide it more deeply and more bitterly than before.[58] Wight did not fully explain or untangle this pattern, although his writings are peppered with insights. His lecture on "International Revolution" suggested two reasons, first that revolutionary cosmopolitanism tends to excite fanatical passions, and second that it tends to slide into imperialism.[59] With variation, in the "age of extremes," it was the counterrevolutionary resistance that drove revolutionaries to extremes as much as it was the extremes of the revolutionaries that drove the resistance, in cycles of mass political violence.[60] Wight's unfinished and posthumously published essay, "The Disunity of Mankind," also suggests that the ancient idea of human unity "has repeatedly suffered shipwreck from two causes. One is the moral heterogeneity of mankind. The other is their social heterogeneity."[61] Against these hurdles, the Christian missionary imaginary of unifying human by teaching its overarching spiritual unity has always struggled to become universal on earth. By imagining humankind's spiritual unity, its political, moral, and social disunity became possible to imagine as problematic. Like Wight, his contemporaries such as Eric Voegelin understood modern revolutionary ideologies of progressive futures as secularized religious narratives.[62] Paradoxically, by drawing on intellectual sources from the ancient and medieval past, these ideas sought to envision the future.[63] Others instead imagined *retrotopias*, seeking to recover spiritual unity in a disenchanted world.[64] In doing so, these visions tended to reflect their own times and context, rather than any real or possible future.

Daniel Nexon's study of the Protestant Reformations suggests that "religion need not be seen as categorically different from discursive frameworks of the kinds associated with Marxism, secular nationalism, or other ideologies."[65] The crisis of the medieval world, in the reformations and counterreformations, as Nexon argues, was not due to any essential content of the ideas themselves. Instead "they resulted from the intersection of heterogeneous religious movements with ongoing patterns of collective mobilization."[66] Edmund Burke's own account of the Reformations is illuminating:

> The spirit of proselytism expanded itself with great elasticity upon all sides: and great divisions were everywhere as a result. These divisions, however, in appearance merely dogmatic, soon became mixed with the political: and their effects were rendered much more intense from this combination. . . . These principles of

internal as well as external division and coalition are but just now extinguished.[67]

Burke was surprised to see these divisive forces return in a secular form in the French Revolution, now in the cause of liberty and political equality.

In the modern global world, contradictions between the globalization of stratified capital and multiplication of sovereignty, best expressed by Marx, have been a consistent source of calls for alternative orders and wider modes of belonging.[68] So have recurrent great power wars. In the 20th century, international organization in the League of Nations and the United Nations was considered the ersatz of a cosmopolitan global order.[69] As UN Secretary-General Dag Hammarskjöld argued, "It is because world community does not exist at a time when world interdependence has become a reality, that world organization has become a necessity as a bridge which may help us to pass safely over this period of transition."[70] In practice, however, international organization has tended to provide a new forum in which statespersons draw attention to their divisions; between democratic and authoritarian states, developed and underdeveloped states, and so on.[71] Globalization in the post–Cold War world further mixed cosmopolitanism as a *normative* aspiration with the notion of its emerging *sociological* reality in a staggering output of literature.[72] The rise of universal human rights discourse gave cosmopolitanism both a moral language and aspirational practice in a disorderly world.[73]

In this study, I find utility in Wight's terms of "vertical" divisions between states (lines of sovereignty) and "horizontal" divisions across them (lines of class, race, creed). For Wight, "to borrow Arthur Koestler's language, "horizontal forces" shake and distort "the vertical structure of competing national egoisms."[74] Wight explains, "The word horizontal is useful since it allows us to avoid the ambiguities of the word 'international.'"[75] These terms help conceptualize the simultaneity and cross sections of interstate and transnational relations. For instance, W. E. B. Du Bois used the concept of the global "colour line" mainly in its vertical sense, but also in a horizontal sense.[76] These terms in these ways help clarify the inherent tensions of humankind's constructed horizontal and vertical divisions.

In eras of revolutionary politics, horizontal and vertical divisions tend to destabilize, but international society has demonstrated remarkable durability. Fred Halliday's *Revolution and World Politics* took Martin Wight's paradox of the divisiveness of revolutionary waves to be the intellectual starting point and crux of the problem of international order.[77] Halliday suggested that the multistate structure of the international system produced a kind of "lock-in" effect, constraining revolutionary action.[78] David Armstrong's earlier *Revolution and World Order* argued that revolutionary states have tended to become constrained by international society and, over time, socialized into conformity.[79] Essentially, both Halliday's and Armstrong's arguments explain the constraints on revolutionary agency through the structure of international society. I suggest that revolutionary cosmopolitan waves encounter and recede against processes of hierarchy legitimation conflicts and recognition struggles reasserting modern state power and remobilizing exclusionary national identities.[80] International society as such is reconstituted in these processes but also changes, just not in ways cosmopolitan revolutionaries expect or hope.[81] I am not interested in explaining specific revolutions, or revolution as such, however.[82] I am interested in the broader pattern of cosmopolitan global order projects in the modern international system, including but not limited to broadly defined cosmopolitan revolutionary and counterrevolutionary waves.

The initial paradox that this book explores is the contradiction between a large literature on the emerging cosmopolitan transformation of international society and the collapse of globalism in recent decades. In International Relations theory, the idea of an emerging cosmopolitan global order gained interest in the post–Cold War era of globalization. Particularly influential was J. G. Ruggie's idea of increasing "dynamic densities," which suggested that the higher density of interaction in a globalizing world would generate positive socialization with wider scales of solidarity. The revolt against "globalism" and retreat of cosmopolitan politics in recent years has evinced more negative socialization and division than anticipated. This poses the question of why Ruggie's interaction processes are insufficient, so easily derailed, and contradictory in practice. Why for instance have world politics become increasingly *anticosmopolitan* and exclusionary, rather than more demanding of a properly inclusive and equitable cosmopolitan politics? I also argue that these contradictory trends in practice of revived nationalism and deepening geopolitical divisions are not the vindication of realist theory. Variants of "realist" theory—especially neorealist theory—are based on misconceptions of states and nations as unitary and substantive bodies, rather than relationally constituted.[83] Cosmopolitan and national identities are mutually constitutive imagined communities, with the reconstruction of each affecting and reshaping the imagination of the other.[84] It is the divisive reconstitution of exclusionary national identities and remobilization of nationalist forces that requires explanation. The alternative argument I offer does not explain the rise of populist nationalism or the collapse of globalism as such but instead makes a more general argument about why cosmopolitan ordering projects have been so divisive and repeatedly overwhelmed in the modern global world.

An Outline of the Book

This book has a three-part organization. Part I, chapter 1, explores cosmopolitan orders in theory and world history, offering an ideal type concept of cosmopolitan order, and considering its conditions of possibility. I consider the theoretical literatures of cosmopolitan globalization and speculative cosmopolitan futures, finding limitations in each, given the contradictory evidence of deglobalization for constructivist theory of "dynamic densities" and interdependence socialization, but also conceptual and theoretical flaws and limitations in the explanations offered by structural realist theory. Following case studies contrasting the conditions of the ancient and modern global world, I advance an alternative theory. I suggest that a cosmopolitan order's conditions of possibility include a combination of social and material forces, stabilizing new hierarchical authorities through practices mobilizing power and resources, and their legitimation through the social construction of imagined collective identities congruent with a cosmopolitan order. Given these steep conditions, I suggest that the ensuing hurdles of hierarchy legitimation conflicts and recognition struggles have overwhelmed past attempts to construct a cosmopolitan order.

In part II, I explore four prominent and influential ways in which broadly understood cosmopolitan belonging and order has been imagined in the modern global world: Kantian cosmopolitanism, world communism, postcolonial cosmopolitanism, and emerging green cosmopolitan imaginaries. These cosmopolitan waves overlap in time and space but have had distinct and often conflicting cosmopolitan order visions. Kantian cosmopolitan narratives and practices of universal human rights emergent in the 1940s and into the 1970s were followed by the rise of neoliberal commercial cosmopolitanism in the 1980s. This wave I find continually encountered hierarchy legitimation conflicts with a range of states and recognition struggles with illiberal societies. At their height in the post–Cold War world, emergent Kantian cosmopolitan narratives and practices were overwhelmed in the upswell of populism mobilizing exclusionary nationalist identities, in combination with illiberal forces, and by the reassertion of modern state power. Turning then to explore the rise and fall of the Marxian imaginary of a universal proletariat, I find that it struggled with internal schisms and encountered hierarchy legitimation conflicts and recognition struggles with liberal societies mobilizing counterrevolutionary forces and ideas of belonging, eventually overwhelming all Marxian thought and practice in the post–Cold War world. Postcolonial cosmopolitan narratives and practices I find rose to a pitch in the 1970s, and then encountered hierarchy legitimation conflicts and recognition struggles with developed liberal powers deploying the beginnings of neoliberal globalization. Lastly, I find that the green cosmopolitan narratives and practices of planetary belonging have encountered and become embattled by persistent and fierce hierarchy legitimation conflicts and recognition struggles with forces of nationalist climate denialism.

Part III then considers the configuration of the emerging global disorder as the liberal cosmopolitan wave recedes against rising illiberalism. I suggest that people do not need or want a return to neoliberal cosmopolitanism, which generated destabilizing inequality and struggled to achieve its aims or legitimacy as states and populations have mobilized against it. I make the case that although cosmopolitan order is virtually impossible in the foreseeable future, cosmopolitan concerns and action are likely to emerge and possibly serve a minimal ordering role where growing extremes of crisis and injustice arise in a dividing and disorderly world.

The book concludes by reflecting on the long story of cosmopolitan waves in the modern international experience and revisits its implications for international order theory and practice.

PART I

ONE

"Cosmopolitan" Order in Theory and World History

In this chapter, I aim to further clarify the ideal type concept of a cosmopolitan order and to convey the challenges and hurdles for cosmopolitan orders in the modern global world. I find that the literatures of cosmopolitan globalization and speculative world federation and global democracy to be full of insights, but also find limitations in their explanation of the absence of the cosmopolitan order that they often have anticipated. Literatures on cosmopolitan globalization struggle with contradictory evidence, and realist theory misleads with mistaken assumptions, while the more futurological literature of possible cosmopolitan futures is often unduly speculative. The ideal type concept of a cosmopolitan order that I offer follows constructivist and English School contributions, but makes conceptual modifications and theoretical qualifications to underlying assumptions about the role of power, while advancing concepts of hierarchy legitimation conflict and recognition struggle to make sense of evidence contradicting much of this literature.

This discussion first offers my ideal type concept of cosmopolitan order, then examines the literature of cosmopolitan globalization, and the literature on speculative cosmopolitan futures, before exploring the contrasting conditions of the ancient and modern worlds.

Cosmopolitan Order, an Ideal Type

By cosmopolitan order, as an ideal type concept,[1] I mean a kind of international order transcending international society, by (A) forming some sense of imagined cosmopolitan belonging embracing all humankind, with (B) an ability to mobilize resources for common interests to some degree, via (C) either *institutionally* unifying international society with legitimated cosmopolitan authorities, or via legitimated *internationalist* cosmopolitan solidarity and nonstate-actor coordination.[2] Cosmopolitan orders, as international orders, are also a kind of political order, which among other purposes manage political violence between communities, structure political relations, and legitimate types of political authorities through institutionalized discourses and practices.[3] As emergent and ongoing processes, "orders are fashioned within particular cultural and material milieus, with their constitutional structures being profoundly conditioned by prevailing social imaginaries and geopolitical contexts."[4] International orders as such have a wide range of configurations and modes of imagination.[5] The idea of a cosmopolitan order in this sense is a radically transformative type of international order, often supposed in the modern world to possibly emerge in a remote future.[6] Partial cosmopolitan configurations of this ideal type are possible in practice, too. Because international orders are layered and include differentiated suborders, it is possible to develop "cosmopolitan" orders within some suborders such as the humanitarian order, without a complete cosmopolitan transformation of the order's central institutions of sovereignty and security as such.[7] International orders at a regional level moreover can develop "cosmopolitan" order configurations, most approximately in the European Union (EU), for instance, without equivalent global level and inter-great-power configurations.

In theoretical terms, my argument is that transnational political movements and foreign policies that have sought to construct "cosmopolitan" global orders in the modern age have encountered and been overwhelmed by hierarchy legitimation conflicts and reactionary recognition struggles reasserting the sources of modern state power and remobilizing exclusionary nationalist identities. By hierarchy legitimation conflicts, I mean contestation over the legitimacy of political authorities and social and economic inequalities.[8] By recognition struggles, I mean conflicting and contested demands for acknowledgment of self-defined identities, individual or collective.[9] My conception of "recognition" is closer to an understanding of it as relationally constituting discourses and practices of the self. My argument in these terms is that in the modern international experience, cosmopolitan ordering projects have not emerged because they have encountered and been overwhelmed by hierarchy legitimation conflicts and recognition struggles reasserting the diffuse sources of modern state power and exclusionary national identities.[10] In contexts of geopolitical stress and economic strain, these tensions and sources of conflict have tended to become intensified by political actors not least due to heightened political stakes, resulting in the balancing of force and the political and social redivision of humankind, both *vertically* between states and *horizontally* across groups and classes.

Cosmopolitan Order and Globalization

The majority of the literature on the cosmopolitan transformation of world politics produced in the last few decades has emphasized the structural transformations underway in globalizing forces. Highly influential in this literature is Ruggie's argument that Durkheimian "dynamic densities" (increased interactions) produce "organic solidarities," which in a globalizing world were theorized to be producing a new "world polity" formation.[11] The denser the global interactions, the more emergent global solidarity, so the Durkheimian theory goes.[12] The pattern from an organic anarchy to organic solidarity that Ruggie speculated about has not emerged in a structurally transformative way in the modern world. To the contrary, we have seen emergent fracturing and remobilization of non-integrationist nationalist identities, even while interaction capacities and security interdependencies continue to increase.

Similar to Ruggie's leading arguments, Barry Buzan proposed that the globalization of modern "liberal logics" resistant to state hierarchies, working through vanguard nonstate actors, could potentially constitute the emergence of a "world society" (as a structural transformation of international society in which nonstate actors share a "thin" *Gesellschaft* identity and are granted recognition and differentiated status alongside states).[13] Martin Shaw also argued that the contradictions between the state system and globalization were incrementally generating political unification through a web of international organizations forming a global "conglomerate state" and "global society."[14] A large sociological literature theorized an emergent cosmopolitan world society, but not its political reordering as such.[15] The global civil society literature found tensions in the limitations of civil society actors in practice, and conceptual critiques of a "global" civil society in the absence of global institutions.[16] Other thinkers recognized the rising number and activity of nonstate actors in global governance while also being aware of the limits and possible pitfalls of emergent cosmopolitan solidarities.[17] Today, this literature appears to have held a somewhat misplaced optimism, and that history has taken an unexpected turn. Buzan's proposed "vanguard" theory or norm entrepreneur theory would suggest that liberal civil society advocates and cosmopolitan norms were simply insufficient in number and advocacy intensity to overcome countervailing norms and illiberal politics. My argument instead works to unpack the generative processes that have reasserted the modern sources of state power and reconstructed exclusive nationalist identities.

Among the most interesting contributions to this literature are those that argue that the emergence of a cosmopolitan global civil society and a fledgling global polity was an extension of globalizing state power, and not its diminution, as other cosmopolitan and globalization thinkers supposed.[18] Taking the concept of power seriously, Iver Neumann and Ole Jacob Sending have made the case that through power over subjectivities in disciplining discourse and practice, "globalist" subjectivities were in the process of being constructed, not to constrain states so much as to extend their reach into globalizing foreign markets and to a transnational global level.[19] Gramscian-inspired literature also suggested a similar argument that new ideas of a globalizing world community were the reflection of emergent hegemonic thinking in a global market civilization.[20] What is puzzling here is why the supposedly powerful forces of market capitalism and modern state power over subjectivities have been dramatically disrupted. Part of the answer is that the power over subjectivities exercised by globalizing neoliberal states should not be exaggerated on a global scale, given their highly limited impact on illiberal societies that mobilize counteridentities. The other aspect of the answer is that the hierarchy legitimation conflicts and recognition struggles that neoliberal discourse and practice encountered became intensified and overwhelming in the wake of the global financial crash. Intensified by economic turmoil and international instability, these processes generated the reassertion of modern state power and reconstruction of exclusionary nationalist identities, dramatically enough in global capitalism's core, the United States.

The global constitutionalism literature offers another theoretically sophisticated and nuanced emphasis on the emergence of a constitutive normative order underpinning international and transnational legal and institutional integration, understood as an ongoing process of constitutional norm contestation and interpretation.[21] Regional integration theory has diverging strands, while constructivist integration theory has made important contributions to how large regional identities are socially constructed and how regional orders fit into interregional social processes.[22] Connecting regional integration and global governance literatures also highlights denationalization patterns in legitimation conflict processes.[23]

Postfunctionalist integration theory also interestingly points to exclusionary identities as imposing obstacles and sources of resistance to integrative projects.[24] In this literature, domestic-level interests in dis-integration can also include the economic incentives of groups and classes, alongside and reinforcing exclusive social identities. My argument emphasizes the *reconstruction* of exclusionary nationalist identities through processes of hierarchy legitimation conflicts and recognition struggles, which tend to be intensified in contexts of worsening economic turmoil and insecurity.

The facilitating conditions of the possibility of a stabilized global cosmopolitan unifying process as such are theoretical and counterfactual, but crucial for understanding and explaining the struggle for a cosmopolitan order to emerge in the modern global world. Bruce Cronin, for instance, argued that transnational communities emerge when people sharing common characteristics, experiences, and positive interdependence form political consciousness through the identification of collective selves and others.[25] Amitai Etzioni, interested in political hierarchies as well as identities, instead proposed more demanding state-like preconditions for the emergence of "supranational communities" including the "legitimate control of the means of violence, which must exceed that of the member units; allocation of resources among the member units; and command of political loyalties that exceed those accorded to member units."[26] In this sense, Cronin and Etzioni differ on the degree of power concentration considered to be a necessary condition for unification.[27] My argument does not dramatically depart from these literatures but emphasizes the hurdles to large-scale integration, chiefly hierarchy legitimation conflicts and recognition struggles as driving processes that require legitimation strategies against counterforces. Contrary to realist approaches, I do not see the modern nation-state as a solid and preexisting obstacle, but rather one that is continually reproduced and socially reconstructed in ongoing processes of political conflict and struggles for recognition.

Speculative Cosmopolitan Theory

Alongside this literature of cosmopolitan globalization there was a revival of interest in the possibility of world government and a parallel literature on global democracy. This literature is highly normative and almost inherently speculative, theorizing distant futures and radically different global political orders.[28] The most widely accepted view is that a world government is virtually impossible to create and would be impossible to sustain under its own weight, even if it had cosmopolitan characteristics. Kenneth Waltz for instance argued that a centralized hierarchical international system would generate its own destruction:

> As hierarchical systems, governments nationally or globally are disrupted by the defection of major parts. In a society of states with little coherence, attempts at world government would founder on the inability of an emerging central authority to mobilize the resources needed to create and maintain the unity of the system by regulating and managing the parts. The prospect of a world government would be an invitation to prepare for world civil war.[29]

Waltz's line "mobilize the resources needed to create and maintain the unity of the system" suggests that only a staggering concentration of power would be sufficient.[30] The more important line in Waltz's passage above is the idea of "a society of states with little coherence." For English School theory, it is the construction of social, cultural, and political coherence that would make a powerful world state less necessary, while constructivism emphasizes power in this process of social construction.

John J. Mearsheimer argues that the self-determination preferences of nation-states rule out the possibility of a supranational state:

> There is not going to be a world state anytime soon. For starters, there is virtually no chance that any nation with its own state will voluntarily give it up. And it is hard to imagine that those nations clamoring for a state will abandon that aspiration. Nations are obsessed with self-determination and thus unlikely to be willing to put their fate in the hands of a superstate over which they have at best limited control.[31]

Mistaking nations for latent and preexisting bodies, rather than socially constructed identities, this thinking misses the processes by which larger collective identities are constructed, and the further processes by which exclusionary national identities become reconstructed against them. There are many cases of large-scale multinational federations, and regional scale unions, such as the European Union, for example. What is interesting about Brexit, for instance, is how exclusionary national identities were remobilized in what I conceptualize as hierarchy legitimation conflicts and recognition struggles.

Joseph Parent has the interesting argument that voluntary unification in world politics emerges in such cases as the United States where common threats and active domestic actors with sufficient resources can mobilize unification against external threats.[32] The argument goes on to suggest that on a global scale therefore unification has not emerged in the modern international system because there has been no global scale threat (except for those threats such as nuclear weapons or climate change that are posed by the divisions of humankind). In principle, this is another and even more highly speculative argument, whether an extraglobal threat might produce global unity. Who is to say, if such a scenario is so outlandish?[33] Essentially, the scenario Parent is suggesting is the subsumption of world politics into a large international system of security interaction. It may be a categorically different question, then, if conceptually speaking the unification of a unit *in* a system, even one as large as the United States, has categorical qualitative differences from the unification *of* a system into a single unit. The mode of belonging, the kinds of necessary political structures, the conditions of stabilization—these are categorically different things in a radically different type of reconfiguration of world politics.[34]

Alexander Wendt argues that the construction of a world state will eventually emerge (in 100 years) out of the modern anarchical international system, as a response to global security interdependencies posed by nuclear weapons.[35] For Wendt, the "logic of anarchy" generates struggles for social recognition of subjectivities, which can produce progressive "cultures of anarchy."[36] On this basis, he argues that in a modern context of nuclear proliferation actors will eventually become compelled to recognize one another and thereby transcend anarchy through a "world society" collective identity and Weberian world state.[37] First, I take issue with Wendt's ontology of a world state "as person," because a states are not made "real" like a beehive in the process, as Wendt argues, and identities do not dissolve into a single identity, as Wendt suggests, but instead would ideal-typically speaking be "nested" and overlapping in ongoing processes of constitution.[38] Second, I also am skeptical of Wendt's Weberian monopoly on the legitimate use of force conception of the configuration of a world state. Because a "world" state in principle is a different type of political configuration, radically transcending states, I am unconvinced it necessarily would have a configuration strictly conforming to the modern state that it transcends. Third, the main issue with Wendt's argument is the anticipation of a global solidarity achieved through positive socialization. It is a problem for Wendt's argument that the modern global international system has not yet developed more positive socialization and integrated global-level political structures in response to global-level challenges such as nuclear weapons, as Wendt suggests it will in future. Why should it emerge in 100 years, if it has not emerged yet, after over seventy years of nuclear proliferation?[39] At what threshold of nuclear proliferation does Wendt's recognition socialization take place? It is unconvincing that more nuclear weapons will do the trick. Finally, the further obvious issue in Wendt's argument is that it is unduly speculative. In the remote long-term future, Wendt's teleological argument is neither convincing nor unconvincing. In 100 years, what is likely or unlikely is unduly speculative to suppose in political matters. It is more reasonable to anticipate that too many unanticipated events will arise on such a timescale.[40] My question in this book, however, is not exactly when or if world unification will emerge, but rather why cosmopolitan order projects have been so fruitless and divisive in the modern global world.

The modern global world remains far away from an *institutionally* integrated cosmopolitan order, while the fledgling aspects of an *internationalist* cosmopolitan order are in decline in an increasingly dividing and disorderly world. In the remote long-term future, pushing the evolution of modernity forward upwards of 100 years, the constellation of the sources of power and prevailing social imaginaries may realign, transform, and give way to conditions for what Barry Buzan calls a planetary "species empowerment" future with the "possibility of transition to eras beyond modernity (Star Trek [TV series]; the 'Culture' novels of Iain M. Banks)."[41] If speculating on a future so remote, the derailment of humankind, in "species suicide" and "species replacement" by artificial intelligences, are possible outcomes too. In either case, my argument suggests that the consolidation of a cosmopolitan order stabilizing Buzan's Wellsian speculative "species empowerment" future would require meeting steep legitimation demands for emergent planetary hierarchies and ongoing recognition struggles over "species being."

Most world government thinkers have proposed a gradualist pathway, understood to be punctuated by moments where steps of further integration are taken.[42] A hurdle to any step in that direction is hierarchy legitimation conflict between a democratic world federation and authoritarian states.[43] How to integrate political systems that in principle contradict? World federalist thinkers facing this challenge have recommended functionalist-style mechanisms integrating international law and economies, attempting to permit authoritarian and democratic state membership.[44] The original motto of the United World Federalists movement was "unity and diversity."[45] Paired with this idea is the functionalist-style proposal to integrate global economies in critical industries and supranational economic arrangements bridging.[46] These mechanisms in themselves offer not a legitimation strategy so much as they aim to dodge the problem of political differences, and not convincingly, especially in a fracturing world. Because divisive geopolitics stymie reform, United Nations insider Mark Malloch-Brown has suggested that a new "San Francisco moment" is required to achieve it, but geopolitical tensions present no "moment" foreseeable in the future.[47] The cosmopolitan order alternatives offered by the World Order Models Project were more thoroughly pluralistic, but their feasibility in transition strategies of planned integration and popular "bottom up" pressure remain doubtful, at least without considerable modification and updating.[48] On the idea of world federalism, Jawaharlal Nehru—who himself once considered it—suggested, "The mechanical part of it [world federation] is not so very difficult. The real difficulty is how to tackle the psychological and to some extent economic barriers that come in our way."[49]

In his classic lectures on international theory, Martin Wight suggested three ways international society could be transformed into the "domestic politics of the universal *civitas*," citing "doctrinal uniformity, doctrinal imperialism, and cosmopolitanism."[50] By doctrinal uniformity Wight meant the domestic ratification of a *civitas maxima* across international society. By doctrinal imperialism Wight meant its coercive imposition. And, by the third, "cosmopolitanism," Wight meant the dissolution of international society itself, into a structurally transformative cosmopolitan order, "which over-rides nations or states . . . This is cosmopolitanism: *cosmopolis* equals world city equals *civitas maxima*."[51] None of these pathways appear remotely plausible, although Wight only vaguely describes them. Hedley Bull classically suggested three pathways by which a world government could come about: (1) a "knockout tournament," (2) "a social contract among states [forming] a universal republic or cosmopolis founded upon some form of consent or consensus," or (3) "it may be thought of as arising gradually, perhaps though accretion of the powers of the United Nations."[52] From these three pathways, the idea of a violent "knockout tournament" is not really a plausible pathway, because a nuclear punch-up would be a planetary "knockout."[53] A limited nuclear war if possible would be less destructive and may produce a global outcry and demand for arms control or disarmament, but these demands may be limited too, because the issues or miscalculations leading states into a limited nuclear war may not apply to the rest of the nuclear powers. Bull's second pathway, social contracting a cosmopolis, has highly unclear conditions, and Bull's third pathway, a gradual evolutionary transformation of international society, has failed to emerge and is contradicted by divisive trends disrupting and destabilizing international society today.

The global cosmopolitan democracy literature is primarily normative, but includes sophisticated theoretical consideration of whether such an order is possible, even if unlikely.[54] Global cosmopolitan democracy, as a speculative ideal type concept, in practice could include a wide range of configurations, just as nation-state democracies do. A global cosmopolitan democracy configuration is conditional on processes of social and structural integration. As a democracy, such a political formation implies that it would necessarily require a *demos* with a sense of *global* belonging, plus a *kratos*, which implies some degree of power, for enforceable legislative and judicial authorities.[55] A cosmopolitan global democracy is in this sense an *institutional cosmopolitan order*. The conditions of a cosmopolitan global democracy as such are far steeper, relative to its steeper formal hierarchies. The concentration of power for an institutional cosmopolitan global democracy is not necessarily a global monopoly on the use of force, however, although the precise degree of power concentration needed is unclear.

It is evident that dynamic densities and interdependence imperatives have not been sufficient to socialize humankind into wider solidarities as Ruggie and other constructivists have anticipated. In my view, this outcome is not simply a lack of sufficient socialization *agency*, because processes of hierarchy legitimation conflicts and recognition struggles concatenate and are subject to the mobilization of political power, with more powerful groups of actors tending to dominate outcomes. This again does not validate alternative structural realist theory as a satisfactory explanation. It is not the self-help anarchical structure of the modern international system that is preventing the emergence of a cosmopolitan order better fitted to address common interests, because international systems vary in their historical condition and social patterning (the constructed condition of anarchy can be competitive or cooperative, and stabilized or destabilized, regardless of polarity under anarchy). In the theoretical picture I am conveying, it is the hierarchy legitimation conflicts mixed with recognition struggles that cosmopolitan politics encounter which overwhelm them, especially in intensified contexts of economic turmoil and international instability that drive political actors to reassert the modern sources of state power and remobilize exclusionary nationalist identities. The conditions of possibility for the emergence of a cosmopolitan order as such are not simply a material-structural shift from an anarchical multiplicity of power to a hierarchical concentration of power. Its conditions of possibility instead are a combination of social and material forces, including the stabilization of new hierarchical authorities through practices mobilizing power and resources, their legitimation through discursive action, and the social construction of larger "nesting" collective identities congruent to a cosmopolitan order.

In these terms, the management of hierarchy legitimation conflicts and recognition legitimation strategies of discursive action and organization of power in practices are critical for meeting these conditions of possibility, but they also create unwieldy hurdles for any such project. In abstract terms, a few more words on the idea of collective identity formation on a systemwide scale are needed. Such a process ideal typically includes "top down" and "bottom up" discursive action applying narratives of collective identity to an entire global system of relational social networks.[56] Deployed in contexts of political practices, collective identities have a discursive "narrative structure," as they are composed of stories about the past, present, and future of systems of relations.[57] They are messy and stochastic in application, not necessarily used consistently, and are subject to meaning contestation. The process of collective identity constitution in this sense is close to the concept of a speech act, but in an iterative ongoing process of constitution and combined with associated practices.[58] These narratives and practices in this sense are deployed in appeals and legitimation strategies and contestation by both super- and subordinate actors in social networks.[59] These narratives can also be deliberately "polyvalent" and "multivocal" to manage contestation and legitimacy conflicts.[60] Importantly, collective identity formation in this process does not dissolve identities, especially those mobilized in recognition struggles, but instead nests overlapping identities in a total relational network identity. Lastly, as combined processes of ideational discourse and material practice, this is not to say that these identities become real or solid, but rather their ongoing stabilization in discursive action and performative practices over longer timescales can become taken for granted background imaginaries. Various large-scale identities populate the modern global world, in religions and civilizations, but there is no clear discursive narrative content to the vaguer identity called "humankind."

Ancient "World" Empires

Hedley Bull once suggested that "there has never been a government of the world, but there has often been a government supreme over much of what for those subjected to it was the known world."[61] The sprawling "world" empires of antiquity are often alluded to by world state thinkers,[62] but my argument is first that the way cosmopolitan order is imagined in the modern global world is essentially antithetical to these ancient imperial cosmopolitan orders, and second, that the countervailing forces of the modern sources of power and pervasive forms of belonging are not conducive to either form of cosmopolitan order.

The literature of the comparative study of international systems developed a large body of research indicating the wide variation in the configurations of international systems in world history.[63] Toynbee's and Wight's early studies referred to ancient imperial orders as "suzerain" systems, and suggested that most international systems in world history have eventually fallen into this category, under "world" empires.[64] In the 1940s and 1950s, Reinhold Niebuhr and Frederick Schuman also pointed toward the Roman experience to suggest that a stable world state or world federation would require a preponderance of power, as well as some kind of world community feeling.[65] The contemporary literature on international systems in world history has vastly expanded the comparative study of the "imagined worlds" of large-scale imperial orders in world history, marking wide-ranging variation of configurations and hierarchy legitimation practices.[66]

Exploring ancient imaginaries and legitimated "collective beliefs" clarifies by way of contrast radically different orders and ways of imagining belonging, while offering illustrative empirical evidence contrasting the ancient and modern worlds. In this discussion, I offer a comparative exploration of imperial integration processes in the Roman Empire and the Han dynasty, which I then contrast with the divisive processes, transformed social imaginaries, and diverging conditions of the modern global world. These ancient cases demonstrate what are essentially state-formation processes but on vast scales approximating nearly entire regional international systems. In each case, imperial political ideology of a universal order and elite network collective identity emerged as imperial legitimation devices.

The Roman World

At its height, the Roman Empire was a world of cities within an imagined world city. The empire, in Ovid's words, was "at once a city (*urbis*) and a world (*orbis*)."[67] This notion was more than a flourish of imperial poets. Belonging in the empire was attained in practice through membership in a city, a *civitas*, which itself fit into the Roman world city, the *civitas maxima*,[68] and notional cosmic city, the *cosmopolis*.[69] Nor was this notion a legal fiction or an obscure religious principle. The imagined world city had a center that could be physically visited, in the city of Rome, imagined simultaneously as the center of the *cosmos*, as the political center of the empire, and as a microcosm of the wider world city. The entire world was imagined to be physically on display and possible to experience in the diversity of Rome's inhabitants, visitors, and goods.[70] It was not simply an integrated structure imagined as a world city, but it also contained—at least for an imperial strata—a sense of Roman belonging, of becoming Roman. In one remarkable example Aelius Aristides claimed for second century Greeks "common ownership for the Roman name."[71]

To explain this world, Clifford Ando's numerous works on the Roman Empire offer an especially insightful combination of sophisticated social theory and classical knowledge. In his *Roman Social Imaginaries*, Ando explains that "Romans understood political belonging principally on a contractualist model: it was voluntary assent to the normative strictures of the community and collaboration in matters of shared utility that made one Roman."[72] This had one sense of Roman social customs and practices, Romanization, but in a more crucial sense "one becomes Roman by becoming juridically Roman."[73] The imagination of Roman belonging was a legal status, in principle, while in a social sense people were also understood to be able act, dress, and speak "as if" they were Romans. What is interesting is how far flung and long lasting this sense of Roman belonging became in the Roman world, although limited mainly to an imperial elite.

It is also remarkable how integrated the Roman world became. Josiah Osgood's *Rome and the Making of a World State* for instance suggests it had world-state-like integration, not only connecting the Mediterranean system in a vast network of roads and a common currency system but also integrating it in a political architecture across virtually an entire international system.[74] It was a joined-up system, at its height, with a political hierarchy centered on Rome's imperial government and administration, drawing on elites across the empire. It was also relatively long-lasting, with social imaginaries deepening overtime. The Roman Empire dominated the entirety of the Mediterranean world for nearly 700 years. Rome's hegemony emerged after defeating its Carthaginian rival in the Third Punic War, 149–146 BCE, which coincided with Rome's domination of Greece through a mix of invitation and imposition, including the military defeat of the Macedonian Empire.[75] Full Roman dominance of the entire Mediterranean system was established roughly by the time of the battle of Actium, 31 BCE, with the incorporation of Egypt into the empire. Asia Minor and Gaul had already been brought under Roman rule by that time. The Roman Empire, while relatively vast, integrated, and long-lasting, also encountered numerous rebellions and local bids for independence such as in the Roman Jewish War.

An interesting aspect of the Roman case is its connection and contrast to the Hellenistic system. Zeno's philosophy of the *cosmopolis* was present and became widely diffused across the Hellenistic system. Greek Stoicism was a personal ethic, not a public doctrine.[76] In their exposure to the Hellenistic world, the idea of the *cosmopolis* was received by Roman elites. Cicero, for instance, philosophized the "fellowship of the human race" and made considerable contributions to the tradition of cosmopolitan thought and the idea of a *civitas maxima*.[77] Much later, the emperor Aurelius asked, if "the universe is a kind of city; in what other common constitution will anyone say that the whole human race shares?"[78] These notions were used as an ethical quasi-political imperial discourse, layered upon others.

Available sources suggest that the integration of an elite Roman identity and concept of belonging is evident in legal, religious, and political practices. Starting with Roman law, cities across the empire held various terms of relations with Rome that could be deepened from the status of friends of Rome, to allies, and eventually bringing whole cities into Roman citizenship. The city-state *civitas* polities of the Roman Empire maintained local laws, *ius civile*, but were also incorporated into Roman law, *ius gentium*, which came to be seen as synonymous with the law of the world city, the common law of humankind.[79] These ideas were connected by Roman elites to discourses of imperial unity and hierarchy: *orbis Romanum*, approximately meaning the Roman command of the world, and the *communis patria*, the paternal community of all humankind. The practice of public acclamations communicating approval between ruling and ruled across the empire has also been suggested to have "invoked imagined visions of the empire as a unified community."[80]

In receiving Roman education and literacy, elites not only adopted Roman practices and attained some legal benefits and responsibilities but also became familiarized with its narratives.[81] Some argue that Roman citizenship was more than a legal status. It was a social and cultural one, requiring literacy and the performance of practices that required concepts of an elite cosmopolitan culture, chiefly the notions of *humanitas* and *Romanitas*, applied to transimperial elite relations.[82] In 212 CE, Roman citizenship was extended to all free males across the empire.[83] By the late empire, irrespective of one's polity of origin, a family could improve its standing in the six levels of imperial citizenship, generation by generation, as each generation could ascend one level, given certain conditions. Senators and even emperors were no longer exclusively from Rome, or Italy, but arose from across the empire.

In public religious practices performed through official public temples, membership in the empire required participation in public religion, through sacrificial rituals, ceremonies, and festivals.[84] Roman emperors, following Augustus, held the role of chief priest of the empire. Performance of public ceremonies and rituals, in the Roman worldview, maintained the favor of the gods. Through religious rituals, pre-Christian Romans did not perform practices of "faith," but instead performed practices based on "knowledge" of the gods that was empirically directed.[85] Roman public temples were not places of assembly or congregation, because they were seen as the physical homes of the gods. Public religious festivals and ceremonies were instead performed outside in public spaces and involved general public participation. It was the elites who paid for these festivals and ceremonies, including paying for the freely distributed bread and minted gold. Knowledge of the Roman gods and other aspects of *Romanitas* was spread to populations through elites.[86] Although an imperial elite emerged across the Roman Empire, they were not mutually integrated, but were instead connected to the imperial core and developed a wide variation of hybrid Roman-local practices across local elite cultural contexts in the vast empire. While empires tend to connect peripheries to the core through intermediaries, they tend to aim to segregate and differentiate peripheries from one another, to keep the conquered divided. In sum, there is evidence of a unifying process in legal, political, and religious contexts within the Roman Empire, but these were fairly limited to elite participation and took on diverse hybrid cultural forms in local contexts. Such practices and discourses nevertheless enabled diverse groups and people across vast distances, with little knowledge of one another, to imagine membership in a larger Roman polity.

The rise of the Christian *ecumene* across the joined-up empire produced a network of power and universal discourse rivaling that of the empire. An influential Christian view was that "Christ had appeared in the reign of Augustus, even as the empire was established, so that his worship might spread more rapidly through a unified world."[87] Christian refusals to sacrifice to the deified emperors and gods in public rituals strained public life and produced bouts of Christian persecution within the empire. The Christian beliefs of soldiers were particularly critical in this period because soldiers played a key role in supporting rival would-be emperors aiming to concentrate power in the system. Christians were still Romans, however, even if criminalized. Tertullian, a Carthaginian Christian Roman citizen, for instance, critiqued "Roman imperialism and its theological underpinning" on the grounds that "we are from your people: Christians are not born but made."[88] This appeal to a shared Roman identity suggests that the idea of Roman unity could be used as an argument and appeal to mitigate coercion. The tension between Christian beliefs and public pagan religion eventually shifted, following the military victories of Constantine over his rivals in 324 CE. In power, Constantine legalized and enthusiastically supported Christianity with the spread of churches across the empire. By the fourth century CE, Christianity had become the official public religion of the empire. The collapse and conquest of the Western Roman Empire effectively reduced Rome to a local although relatively still considerable power. This decline and division essentially ended the Roman Empire's pretense to be, in Virgil's phrase, an "empire without limit." Following its decline and the breakup of the Western Roman Empire, Christianity continued to spread across the region, albeit through multiple and often conflicting sects. The medieval order of Europe that gradually emerged in the wake of the universal empire inherited and developed Roman Catholic integration and the idea of Christendom. Latin texts also continued in use among elites, medieval Christendom could mobilize resources to some degree, and it held a common idea of belonging, legitimating multiple but overlapping political authorities.

The Han Dynasty

Across the world, the Han dynasty was another sprawling empire, and a contemporary to the Roman Empire. The two empires had minimal mutual awareness and only indirect contact through trade, with no diplomatic or strategic interaction.[89] Before the Qin-Han period, during the Spring and Autumn period (770–453 BC) and Warring States period (453–221 BC), the region was a system of multiple states with multiple distinctive cultural identities.[90] The short-lived Qin dynasty was the first to establish a political unification of territorial China through military conquest of the Warring States in 221 BC, bringing the region under "universal domination."[91] Aware of the significance of the military conquest of the region, the first emperor conducted *feng* sacrificial ceremonies to claim "world sovereignty."[92] Having conquered rival states, the Qin dynasty demilitarized the conquered states and initiated projects for the political and infrastructural unification of the disparate and formerly independent states into a vast region-wide state. The system's distant past had experienced the emergence of hierarchies, the historically remote Shang dynasty (1600–1045 BC) conquered by the Zhou dynasty (1045–221 BC), although these dynasties were not system-wide in extent. The Zhou dynasty developed a hierarchy beyond its areas of direct rule through extending feudal kinship relations.[93] Unlike these predecessor dynasties, the Qin dynasty (221–207/6 BC) conquered the region, although it was a short-lived, falling to rebellion and insurrection shortly after the death of the first emperor.

The following Han dynasty would extend and build upon the state-building projects initiated by the Qin dynasty, including that standardization of coinage and script, as well as roadways and infrastructure projects, joining together territories and populations into a vast state-like structure. The Han dynasty (206 BC–220 AD) has two periods, the earlier or Western and the later or Eastern Han dynasty, being divided by the brief interregnum of Wang Mang's short-lived Xin dynasty (9–25 AD). Across this period, the Western Han dynasty emerged as a political and military power on a relatively vast geographical scale, nearly system-wide in terms of its historical context, while notable nearby powers, such as the northern Hsiung-nu polities, balanced against it and engaged in complex diplomatic relations. The Western and Eastern Han dynasties engaged in state-building projects to unify their vast empire, including the establishment of a common currency, writing, travel, and transport systems, joining together the system into a single state-like polity on a vast scale.

The case of the Han dynasty is particularly interesting, however, because it evinces not only a concentration of political and military power and economic and infrastructural integration but also a unifying idea, the Confucian teachings and notion of *da tong*, "Grand Unity." The pre-Han dynasty imperial principle of the "Mandate of Heaven" was a principle of suzerain legitimacy, although some scholars suggest it was not heavily used to legitimate the Han empire until the later or Eastern Han dynasty, after the interregnum of Wang Mang's short-lived Xin dynasty.[94] Secondary and historical sources instead indicates evidence of the elite circulation of "Confucian" moral codes and identities during the Han dynasty, particularly in educational practices and in the emergence of consciously tiered or ranked legal, bureaucratic, and social ordering practices. Confucianism predated the Qin and Han dynasties by centuries, and ancient China included several distinct religious traditions besides, Buddhism and Daoism most prominently.[95] Confucianism in this context was more of an ethic than a religion, however, even though it assumed some spiritual and cosmological principles. In practice, what was considered "Confucian" was also subject to change and context. The term Confucian, *ru* or *rujia*, in the context of the Han dynasty is also somewhat fuzzy and stochastic in practice.[96] The independent polities, north and west, were subject to campaigns of expansion, and were fit into Han dynasty imperial narratives of a Confucian world order imaginary.[97] Confucian narratives, with the idea of *da tong* (Grand Unity) and a body of moral codes, suited imperial legitimation by providing not only an edifying morality but also the idea of a universal order surrounding the imperial state in the cosmos.[98]

When Confucianism became officially adopted by the Han dynasty, its use and spread is evident in educational, legal, administrative-bureaucratic, and social elite networks on a relatively vast scale, over hundreds of years. Recruitment into the higher tiers of imperial society came to require adoption of Confucian principles and practices, as acquired through newly established public schools and institutions, where education for elites became shaped by the state adoption of Confucianism.[99] Confucian "schools of thought" and institutions of preserving Confucian knowledge predated the Qin and Han dynasties by several centuries, but it was in the Han dynasty that their teachings were officially adopted.[100] Graduates could apply to sit an examination to join the governing class of the civil service.[101] Memorization of the classic texts became the main emphasis of education in the Han dynasty, and the examination of one or more became the test for recruitment to the civil service.[102] In the later or Eastern Han dynasty, these requirements and tests became subject to written examination.[103] Appointed officials were expected and in probationary periods required to demonstrate the appropriate qualities and conformity to their education's teachings. The Han dynasty established a vast bureaucratic and administrative system staffed by elites at local and central imperial levels.[104] By the later or Eastern Han dynasty, Confucian narratives prescribing Confucian ethics and social hierarchies had become increasingly pervasive in political practice.[105] The local county-level office of magistrates in the Han dynasty also received training in public schools and were responsible for administering official rituals and monitoring the performance of the local schools.[106] Law in the Han dynasty came to reflect a tiered or stratified order through differentiated rewards and punishments applied to the same crime depending on an individual's status.[107] There were twenty tiers of aristocratic hierarchy in the Han dynasty.[108] Gradually, the scholar-official classes gathered increasing privileges and protections in law.[109]

Michael Nylan argues that the *changing interpretation* of Confucianism gradually created a mismatch between Confucian teachings and imperial order, not the renunciation of Confucianism as such.[110] A declining ability to mobilize resources through imperial administrators, in any case, became a challenge in the later Han dynasty. Public schools also declined relative to private schools. More consequentially, the gradual rise of local warlords and family powers within the empire made them increasingly able to mobilize military forces independently. Warfare in northern territories also exacted a considerable cost on the empire's resources. Ultimately, the Han dynasty succumbed to internal rebellion. The last Han emperor abdicated in 220 AD,[111] after which the empire was divided in the "Three Kingdoms" or Wei-Chin period (220–420 AD). During its rise and before its eventual fall, however, the Han dynasty exhibited considerable state-building processes, on what at the time was a vast scale.

The Modern Global World

The Han dynasty and the Roman Empire are two cases illustrative of highly integrative ancient imperial orders that developed elite imperial identity networks on relatively vast scales and over relatively long timescales. The way cosmopolitan order is imagined in the modern global world, however, is essentially antithetical to these ancient imperial cosmopolitan orders, while the countervailing forces of the modern sources of power and pervasive forms of belonging have been unconducive to a cosmopolitan order. Under such empires, the ancient world nevertheless experienced eras of "globalization" with the increased interaction and movement of people, goods, and ideas.[112] The differences are interesting, however. Ryan Griffiths has argued that ancient international systems like the Roman Empire tended to follow a path from *mechanical anarchies* to *mechanical hierarchies* under empires, which later developed into *organic hierarchies*; whereas modern systems, contrary to Ruggie's anticipations, have instead developed persistent *organic anarchies*, albeit under successive hegemonic hierarchies.[113] By contrast to ancient empires, at the height of its power, in the unipolar moment, US hegemony constructed a hierarchical order some referred to as "new Rome on the Potomac," but systemic integration under US-led globalization was quite different from the ancient world, with neo-imperial economic levers, deterrent constraints, and dramatically different social imaginaries.[114]

The modern global world has experienced considerable integration, with increasing interaction between state and nonstate actors.[115] But the conditions of the modern global world have also been deeply divisive and wracked by recurrent eras of fracture too. The modern international system developed thin and limited "cosmopolitan" configurations around the humanitarian order, including crimes against humanity and the International Criminal Court, but with limited to no great power legitimation of or compliance with the institution.[116] At the regional level, the European Union has developed an approximate "cosmopolitan" configuration, but with limited application to other regions. The political character of the modern cosmopolitan imagination moreover is radically different, typically secular, progressive, in principle anti-imperial, and democratic. Although many optimistic constructivist theorists of globalization anticipated the emergence of a cosmopolitan "post-Westphalian" order through the "dynamic densities" and structural interdependency imperatives of modernity, international society's divisive patterns have persisted, and are likely to continue to persist, into the foreseeable future.[117] The theoretical explanation for this persistent divisive pattern in the modern global world is that cosmopolitan ordering discourses and practices have repeatedly been overwhelmed by hierarchy legitimation conflicts and recognition struggles reasserting modern state power and remobilizing exclusionary nationalist identities, intensified in contexts of international instability and economic turmoil. The prevalence of nationalism and nation-states is not in itself a sufficient explanation for the limited and divisive outcomes of cosmopolitan ordering projects in the modern world, because it is the ongoing reconstitution of nationalism, the recurrent shoring up of state power, and the generative redivision of humankind that requires explanation. Helpful in explaining these patterns are the processes of hierarchy legitimation conflicts generating political resistance and delegitimation, alongside of and mixed with recognition struggles against large collective identity constructs, whereby exclusionary nationalist identities are remobilized and reconstituted.

The conditions of possibility for a cosmopolitan order are relatively steep in the modern global world, which is characterized by state power mobilizing national identities. Recognition struggles pose a demanding hurdle for any cosmopolitan mode of belonging attached to a political project, which are mixed with challenging hierarchy legitimation conflicts. An *institutional* cosmopolitan order is exceedingly challenging because it has steeper hierarchy legitimation conflicts and a degree of power consolidation is assumed to be needed to support its ability to mobilize even a minimal degree of resources for common global purposes. Power consolidation is not assumed to be needed for an *internationalist* cosmopolitan order, however. An internationalist cosmopolitan order has less formally steep hierarchies but nevertheless encounters hierarchy legitimation hurdles in implied and emergent de facto hierarchies. Either kind of order, moreover, also has the facilitating conditions of relative international and economic stability, without which legitimation conflicts and recognition struggles intensify. The conditions of possibility for the emergence of a cosmopolitan order in the modern global world are not simply a material-structural shift from an anarchical multiplicity of power to a hierarchical concentration of power. Its conditions of possibility instead are a combination of social and material forces, including not only the stabilization of new hierarchical authorities through practices mobilizing power and resources, but equally their legitimation through discursive action and the social construction of larger collective identities congruent with a cosmopolitan order. In the modern international experience, no cosmopolitan political movement has remotely approached these conditions, even while capital and new interaction capacities have integrated world politics more deeply than in ages past.

Conclusion

The literatures of cosmopolitan globalization and speculative world federation and global democracy have offered numerous insights but contain limitations in their explanation of the absence of a cosmopolitan order whose emergence their theory often anticipated. While literatures on cosmopolitan globalization struggle with contradictory evidence, and some of the more futurological literature is unduly speculative, realist theory misleads with mistaken assumptions. The ideal type concept of a cosmopolitan order that I offer draws on constructivist and English School contributions, but makes modifications and theoretical qualifications to underlying assumptions about the role of power, while advancing concepts of hierarchy legitimation conflict and recognition struggle to make sense of evidence contradicting much of this literature. This ideal type concept of cosmopolitan international order that I advance includes distinct *internationalist* and *institutionalist* configurations, whose conditions of possibility include challenging legitimation strategies, combining relative stabilization of new hierarchical authorities through practices mobilizing power and resources, with their legitimation through discursive action, and the social construction of collective identities congruent to a cosmopolitan order. Given these steep conditions of possibility, it is unsurprising that a cosmopolitan order, even of a thin internationalist configuration, has not taken shape.

PART II

TWO

Kantian Cosmopolitanism

Kant reimagined the ancient idea of cosmopolitan belonging for the modern global world. Advancing the largely Western cosmopolitan tradition, Kant imagined a universal moral order and notion of being a citizen of the world for an age of global travel and transformation.[1] His philosophy mixed the old ideas with new notions of "worldly" cosmopolitan attitudes and dispositions of being open to the company of foreigners and having worldly interest in languages and cultures in an age of global navigation.[2] This Kantian cosmopolitan tradition has been the predominant form of cosmopolitan politics in the modern global world.[3] For Kant and Kantians, humankind not only shares a universal moral order, with claims to world citizenship, but in a globalizing world, Kant also speculated that humankind would "gradually be brought closer and closer to a cosmopolitan constitution," in a "cosmopolitan condition."[4] Kant's perpetual peace proposal, moreover, offered a model for realizing a cosmopolitan federation.

What is interesting is not only why this kind of cosmopolitan vision has not been more realized, but why and how it is so often resisted, dismissed, and rejected. In the modern international experience, the human rights regime is the most influential expression of this Kantian way of imagining global belonging, but it is highly limited in its depth of ordering and breadth of compliance. Kantian liberal legacies have also been credited with inspiring international organization, from the League of Nations to the United Nations, but these are hardly cosmopolitan orders, and what sphere of democratic peace exists is highly limited.[5] In a dividing and disorderly world, moreover, history does not plausibly appear to have a cosmopolitan purpose. Why have lofty Kantian ideas calling for a cosmopolitan order for the modern globalizing world proven to be so limited in their achievements? Why, moreover, have they been so divisive?

My argument in this chapter is that liberal Kantian cosmopolitan narratives and practices, which were most clearly expressed in the universal human rights regime rising in the 1940s and into the 1970s and post–Cold War world, continually encountered hierarchy legitimation conflicts with a range of states as well as recognition struggles with illiberal societies. At their height in the post–Cold War world, these cosmopolitan discourses and practices were overwhelmed and delegitimated by the upswell of populism reasserting modern state power and mobilizing exclusionary nationalist identities, in combination with illiberal political forces.

Universal Human Rights and Its Critics

In modern international thought, Kantian cosmopolitanism is so predominant it is often taken to be synonymous with cosmopolitan politics itself, narrowly defined. Martin Wight's lectures for instance used Kant and Kantianism to name and express the entire category of revolutionary thought, even though it includes a wide range of cosmopolitan traditions.[6] Although Kantian cosmopolitanism is itself a broad, internally diverse, and adaptive tradition, its discourse tends to tell a distinct kind of story about a universal moral order that forms a moral cosmopolitan community.[7]

Kantian cosmopolitan thought manifest in several waves in the modern international experience. The call for "liberty" as universal "natural rights" became a popular revolutionary movement across the globalizing Atlantic world, in the 18th and 19th centuries, calling for *internationalist cosmopolitan* solidarities.[8] The upheavals of the American, French, and Haitian Revolutions are also often considered to be the era in which modern ideas of universal rights to liberty and freedom started to transform world politics. The abolition movement, importantly, was a part of this cosmopolitan wave.[9] Pamphlets, newspapers, and books (the printed word) were the medium of these revolutionary cosmopolitan ideas in the 18th and 19th centuries. Thomas Paine was among the most prolific and famous writers at the time, in his revolutionary texts including *Common Sense* and *The Rights of Man*, defending the legitimacy of revolution if waged on the basis of universal natural rights.

Amid these revolutionary times, a more fully realized cosmopolitan order was increasingly imagined in the future. Kant, not least, offered his speculative history. The cosmopolitan dream of universal liberty was a popular idea, however, not limited to philosophical discourse. Among the first science fiction novels ever written for instance was Louis-Sébastien Mercier's *L'An 2440*, published in 1771 (published in English as *Memoirs of the Year Two Thousand Five Hundred*, in 1772). This novel was inspired by the new cosmopolitan imagination of liberty and the spirit of progress.[10] It invented a new genre of future utopian fiction, and created the science fiction trope of the character who falls asleep, by some accident, to awaken in the remote future, in Mercier's case, the year 2440.[11] In Mercier's *L'An 2440*, the protagonist awakens from extended sleep in a future Paris. There he soon encounters a statue of a black man labeled "the Avenger of the New World." Liberties had transformed world politics in the future, so the story presumed. Mercier's *L'An 2440* was among the most popular books of the 18th century, selling over 60,000 copies. George Washington and Thomas Jefferson reportedly each owned copies.[12]

Although widespread, the ideas of an internationalist cosmopolitan order with universal liberties and democracy at the time deeply divided international society in counterrevolutionary struggles. This revolutionary age generated recognition struggles with an aristocratic elite against the new liberal internationalist cosmopolitanism, and its upheavals threatened imperial political hierarchies, while the Napoleonic Wars threatened hegemonic supremacy of Europe.[13] Napoleon was no cosmopolitan. His empire betrayed the revolutionary calls for democratic liberties and freedoms. His defeat was more a victory for the liberty of states than that of peoples, however. The counterrevolutionaries of the 19th century are traditionally portrayed as deeply conservative, if not enemies of freedom, and their post-Napoleonic order as retrogressive,[14] but it had its own modern features and the character of the Holy Alliance was all the more possible having waged its struggle against an enemy with the character of Napoleonic France.[15] Klemens von Metternich, for instance, had studied Kant, and sought not a purely retrogressive retrotopian order, but a modified and even modern order with more management capabilities, for the perception of a changing, busier world.[16] Lord Castlereagh not only sought a counterhegemonic kind of order but also sought the abolition of the slave trade and slavery.[17] The order was transformative of European politics in many ways,[18] but the fear of a new revolutionary power nevertheless did gather the victors into an oppressive counterrevolutionary posture, organized—among other purposes—to restore empires and suppress uprisings, limiting the possibility of anything more radical for some time. We might remember Percy Bysshe Shelley's 1819 poem "The Mask of Anarchy," "written on the occasion of the massacre at Manchester," in which cavalry was deployed against protesters. Hearing the news, away in Italy, the Romantic thinker and poet Shelley wrote a call to revolution, for "justice," for "liberty" . . . "I met murder on the way—He had a mask like Castlereagh" . . . "Rise like Lions after slumber—In unvanquishable number."[19] Shelley, like William Godwin and other Enlightenment thinkers who became radical Romantics, believed that humankind could master its destiny and find universal harmony if freed from existing political orders and given proper and sufficient moral guidance. The political orders of the time had their own masters, however. The counterrevolutionary character of the post-Napoleonic order was arguably itself a contributing factor in the revolutionary upheavals of 1848, but also much of what gave it its durability against them.[20]

Into the late 19th century, the international peace movement became increasingly active, calling for arbitration and related peace mechanisms, but also for social and distributive justice as peace requisites. In the wake of the First World War, these demands gained a new urgency and popular support in a moment of opportunity in the hands of the victors. The ordering decisions embodied in the Covenant of the League of Nations did not include the more ambitious and radical transformative ordering calls of numerous advocates, including Japan's racial equality principle, or the demands of the Women's International League for Peace and Freedom, the Pan African Congress, and not least the revolutionary demands of Lenin's new Soviet Union.[21] The 1920s experienced considerable political activism for more radical cosmopolitan ordering alternatives, but in the wake of the Great Depression and the instabilities of the 1930s, the incomplete and limited League of Nations' order destabilized.[22] The forces of remobilized exclusionary nationalism and state power redivided international society once more.[23]

The next major opportunity for revolutionary cosmopolitan change emerged in response to the depths and divisions of the Second World War. The widespread call for human rights was initially an answer to the Holocaust, to prevent another in the future.[24] The Universal Declaration of Human Rights had a symbolic aspect, as a declaration, but it is a significant document. It is significant that Western and non-Western statespersons contributed to its language and that the majority of states have ratified it.[25] Article 1 of the Universal Declaration of Human Rights states, "All human beings are born free and equal in dignity and rights. They are endowed with reason and conscience and should act towards one another in a spirit of brotherhood."[26] This kind of language of rights, "reason," and "conscience" clearly speaks to the cosmopolitan tradition and its idea of universal moral law.[27] The rise of "crimes against humanity" and international criminal law in this era also contributed to elements of an *internationalist cosmopolitan* legal order of a liberal character.[28] The growth of this legal order has been limited by great power reluctance to accept constraints on their use of force, but it is a significant development.[29]

Although not without considerable achievements, the transformation of the order was nevertheless quite limited, relative to the ambitious calls for radical change at the time. In January 1945, in his fourth inaugural address, Franklin D. Roosevelt declared, "We have learned to be citizens of the world, members of the human community."[30] Roosevelt's envisioned United Nations was not as ambitious as the radical transformative order visions on offer, and cannot be called cosmopolitan, but it was universally internationalist, and even his allies Stalin and Churchill were terrified by its ambition. Stalin's redivision of Europe—as a part of his own revolutionary strategy—quieted the more hopeful while the emergence of the global Cold War redivided international society more widely. A huge literature exists exploring how the divisions among the allies were emergent in their postwar planning, and whether the Soviet occupations were avoidable.[31] More on this in the next chapter.

On the story of human rights, as the divided world became deadlocked, well into the 1970s and 1980s, liberal cosmopolitanism experienced another wave, with relatively lasting influence.[32] Samuel Moyn's *The Last Utopia* describes this wave most clearly:

> As a number of its partisans in the 1970s were well aware, human rights could break through in that era because the ideological climate was ripe for claims to make a difference not through political vision but by transcending politics. Morality, global in its potential scope, could become the aspiration of humankind.[33]

Through NGOs such as Amnesty International and numerous groups and movements, advocates advanced an alternative moral language with which to challenge states. Soviet dissidents, too, in this era, used the language of human rights to critique the failures and abuses of the Soviet Union. Divisions between communist and liberal conceptions of human rights essentially formed recognition struggles between competing visions of modernity, limiting their transformative potential even in an internationalist cosmopolitan register. The Carter administration's adoption of a human rights foreign policy marked a major public shift, although brief and all but abandoned following the Iranian Revolution. This reversal suggested to many that promoting human rights as foreign policy principles tended to instigate militancy abroad, and that such principles moreover should be prudentially superseded by hierarchical geopolitical interests in US foreign policy.[34] The Reagan administration later subsumed human rights discourse into a neoliberal cosmopolitan conception of individual rights, within a foreign policy of liberal democracy promotion.[35] The rise of liberal human rights advocacy in this era had considerable relatively lasting influence, but still fairly limited genuine transformative impact.

In the post–Cold War world, human rights gained new wind in calls for internationalist cosmopolitan solidarities, democratic peace, "human" security, and emergent humanitarian norms of the responsibility to protect.[36] Perhaps most critical for a fledging structural transformation was how liberal cosmopolitan humanitarian interventionism undermined or threatened to revise domestic–international distinctions.[37] The creation of the International Criminal Court and the United Nations Human Rights Council aimed to institutionally embed ideas of universal human rights into international society.[38] The European Convention on Human Rights has also been described by legal scholars as contributing to the emergence of a Kantian "cosmopolitan legal order."[39] The normative power ambitions of the European Union project were closely linked to human rights promotion, directed through the United Nations. The impression of an emerging liberal internationalist cosmopolitan order with embedded moral human rights obligations became widely discussed.[40]

Public intellectuals and political philosophers urged on this post–Cold War cosmopolitan wave too. Martha Nussbaum, for instance, made one of the clearest influential appeals for cosmopolitan foreign policy in her essay "Patriotism and Cosmopolitanism." For Nussbaum, nationalism and cosmopolitanism can and should be reconciled, by instilling societies with universal ethical horizons through means of public education, legislation, and institutional reform.[41] Nussbaum admitted that "world citizenship . . . places exacting demands on the imagination," and that "to be sure, the imagination is not enough."[42] Hence her call for educational, legal, and institutional reforms to realize world citizenship in practice, combining patriotism and cosmopolitanism. Nussbaum continues to defend the central claims of this essay.[43] Jurgen Habermas and Jacques Derrida argued that European states should pursue a common Kantian cosmopolitan foreign policy, to "inspire the Kantian hope for a global domestic policy."[44] The political philosopher Seyla Benhabib also argued that "Kant's cosmopolitan legacy" in world politics includes Kant's distinctions between levels of rights, which have enabled an evolution in the global human rights regime to cover crimes against humanity and further refugee, asylum, and immigration norms.[45] For the Kant scholar Garrett Wallace Brown, Kant's cosmopolitan theory in a globalizing world creates "normative requirements for a constitutional global order."[46]

This wave of Kantian cosmopolitans always had its detractors too, however. Most forceful were authoritarian states. It is often argued that the rejection of liberal human rights and democracy is a rhetorical strategy of authoritarian states seeking to buttress their weak legitimacy, and by implication this would mean it has little to do with genuine demands for recognition.[47] In cases of weak authoritarian military dictators leaning heavily on coercion to maintain domestic authority and order, their rejection of liberal ideas of human rights and democracy is obviously a matter of political convenience, without any genuine recognition objections. These are cases more purely about power political hierarchy conflict, although most cases included mixed political and cultural elements. Critics also questioned the selective political utility of human rights discourse for Western states, and whether there is a concept of "humanity" that can be genuinely nonexclusive and not subject to political manipulation.[48]

Critics of human rights tend to see them as political tools of liberal Western elites, championing secularized universal Christian values. Stephen Hopgood argues that "humanism (the cultural precondition for Human Rights) was a secular replacement for the Christian god."[49] Attempts to reduce human rights discourse to minimal conceptions such as dignity have been unsuccessful in overcoming resistance and disagreement.[50] Human rights advocacy in effect has not provided humankind with agreed moral codes so much as it has provided a discourse about moral practices subject to recognition struggles between different moral cultures and political ways of life.[51] The "Asian values" debate for instance, now past, was mainly about claims to cultural distinctiveness. The Bangkok Declaration of 1993 contrasted collective approaches to rights from individual, civil, and political approaches, in ways similar to how the Soviet Union once emphasized collective rights. The grounds of the Bangkok Declaration were cultural, however, and generated debate over the sources of human rights and the priority of different rights in different cultural contexts. Singapore's prime minister Lee Kuan Yew spoke openly of Asian values in contrast to Western human-rights-based values as a matter of cultural differences. Today, this debate has subsided, but China and other states still regularly reject human rights discourse as culturally Western-centric and politically self-serving. What is interesting, however, is that the entire "Asian values" debate would likely not have taken place without the strong liberal rights advocacy made in the post–Cold War era, because political leaders articulating Asian values would have found it unnecessary to do so. The construction of divisive "Asian values" was itself shaped by the de facto hierarchies threatened and recognition demands produced by the rise of liberal human rights perceived as expressions of "Western values."

The post–Cold War cosmopolitan wave of universal human rights sought to constrain sovereigns, spread democracy, and legitimate humanitarian intervention, but always struggled against its critics and detractors.[52] Advocates of human rights might insist that it is the regime-stability interests of authoritarian regimes that has limited human rights, not their demand by actual populations, suggesting that societies currently under authoritarian regimes would embrace human rights, if given the opportunity. This seems to be a delusional notion in a context where liberal societies themselves have become increasingly in danger of sliding into illiberalism, however. In the wake of the revolt against globalism, democracy and human rights are now in retreat today.

Neoliberal Cosmopolitanism

The rise of universal human rights in the post–Cold War world was parallel to the rise and fall of a neoliberal commercial cosmopolitan wave. Neoliberal economic globalization had a cosmopolitan commercialism about it, insofar as it promised the free movement of capital, goods, people, and ideas on a global scale. Gary Gerstle's *Rise and Fall of the Neoliberal Order* suggests that neoliberalism's moral character was multivalent, including a conservative "neo-Victorian" aspect, but also a "cosmopolitan" aspect. The "moral perspective encouraged by the neoliberal order, which I label cosmopolitan, was a world apart from neo-Victorianism. It saw in market freedom an opportunity to fashion a self or identity that was free of tradition, inheritance, and prescribed social roles. . . . Cosmopolitanism was deeply egalitarian."[53] The market globalization of neoliberal cosmopolitanism was unlike the development and distributive cosmopolitanism called for by liberal Rawlsian-inspired cosmopolitans.[54] Many cosmopolitan moral philosophers critiqued neoliberal globalization's distributive disparities as problems of moral obligations.[55]

The neoliberal cosmopolitan wave of hyper deregulation had well-documented sources in Hayekian thought, taken up by Ronald Reagan and Margaret Thatcher, and ascending globally in ideological triumphalism in the wake of communism.[56] The post–Cold War wave of commercial cosmopolitanism in this sense was made possible by a predominant and pervasive "neoliberal" global market cosmopolitan imaginary, liberal in essence but distinct from Kantian cosmopolitanism as a moral code. The neoliberal commercial imaginary had long-standing roots in the liberal tradition, in the laissez-faire ideas of Adam Smith and Richard Cobden, for instance, who connected free trade to peace as well as prosperity. In its neoliberal Hayekian-inspired form, this gilded commercial cosmopolitan imaginary limited the ability of many post–Cold War cosmopolitans to understand different moral cultures abroad and limited their sympathy for increasingly extreme divides between the rich and poor at home. Against neoliberal cosmopolitanism, antiglobalization movements organized resistance (in the World Trade Organization protests in Seattle in 1999, for instance). The global financial crash also deeply damaged the wave of neoliberal cosmopolitanism, but it was not fully overturned until opposed by the reassertion of modern state power, following the populist upheavals of 2016 that remobilized exclusionary nationalist identities in a new antiglobalism. This revolt against globalism combined numerous disaffected and illiberal forces, domestic and international, raising grievances embroiled in recognition struggles and hierarchy legitimation conflicts with the US-led neoliberal order.[57] In the revolt against globalism, neoliberal cosmopolitanism was thoroughly delegitimated.

The backlash against "cosmopolitanism" and the wave of nationalist foreign policies and protectionism, was in important respects a revolt against neoliberal market globalization.[58] "The West's turn toward neoliberalism set in motion forces that would ultimately come back to haunt mainstream parties by weakening public support for the liberal order and opening the door to political parties advancing anti-globalist platforms."[59] This backlash against capitalist "globalism" itself further multiplied and deepened the division of societies toward political extremes, and it clarified perceptions of the divisions in international society between liberal democratic and neo-authoritarian regimes.[60] Rightwing antiglobalists blamed governments for waging too many wars abroad and favoring minorities over majorities at home. Leftwing antiglobalists blamed big corporations and the billionaire elite for neglecting their societal responsibilities.[61] In appeals to voters, both left-wing and right-wing politicians blamed the neoliberal consensus for enabling China to usurp America's manufacturing economy.

This outcome is not entirely surprising, at least in hindsight. The overconfident character of neoliberal cosmopolitanism rooted in its pervasive imaginary made it difficult for its believers to understand nonliberal identities or to sympathize with those subject to deep inequalities. It was blinded by the delusions of its millennialism. "A worldwide free market embodies the western Enlightenment ideal of a universal civilization. That is what explains its popularity—especially in the United States. It is also what makes it peculiarly dangerous at the present time."[62] Hence, legitimation strategies and management of recognition struggles needed to stabilize the order were both difficult for neoliberalism to formulate and dismissed as unnecessary, despite building domestic unrest. "In the 1990s, globalization became the West's new elixir. Those who argued that too much economic integration would trigger a political backlash were dismissed as Cassandras."[63] When eventually confronted with serious economic strain, in the Great Recession, demands for recognition in economic policy by remobilized nationalist identities became politically overwhelming in 2016. In the wake of neoliberal cosmopolitanism, a new geo-economic contest has emerged between "new leviathans" shoring up state power and mobilizing nationalist economies.[64]

Horizons of Cosmopolitan Belonging

Liberal Kantian cosmopolitanism is embattled and will struggle to find support in an increasingly divisive and illiberal world, but cosmopolitans maintain their moral commitments. Martha Nussbaum's *Cosmopolitan Tradition* argues that "the cosmopolitan tradition is flawed, but capable of self-correction" which she suggests can take the form of "a *materialist global political liberalism* based on ideas of human capability and functioning."[65] Essentially, this is a type of distributive moral cosmopolitanism. Why or how might this modified cosmopolitanism make headway in a divided and increasingly illiberal world? Nussbaum lists moral psychology as the first problem facing the realization this modified cosmopolitanism, the challenge of getting populations to have a sense of moral obligation. This is telling. It is a problem for cosmopolitan thinkers that they have advocated universal moral obligations for decades with relatively little interest from states and societies. Encouraging connections and investing in education are Nussbaum's main recommendations for building up moral psychology. I suggest that the real problem, however, is not the lack of sufficient advocacy or moral education, but the legitimation strategy based on moral authority in a world of numerous moral cultures. Kantian cosmopolitan imaginaries of universal moral community have been predominant in the modern global world, but they have always had limited horizons of belonging, tied to the idea of morality as a universal moral order. A legitimation strategy of claiming moral authority for a certain moral order will tend to struggle with demands for recognition from distinct moral cultures, and conflict with existing political authorities. This is not only a theoretical problem for Kantian moral philosophers. It is a practical and political problem, and it is more problematic that cosmopolitan advocates tend to admit.

A critic of cosmopolitanism, Craig Calhoun, has argued that

> cosmopolitan liberals often fail to recognize the social conditions of their own discourse, presenting it as a freedom from social belonging rather than a special sort of belonging, a view from nowhere or everywhere rather than from particular social spaces. The views of cosmopolitan elites express privilege; they cannot do justice to the legitimate claims made on behalf of "communities," and the reasons why "thick attachments" to particular solidarities still matter— whether in the forms of nations, ethnicities, local communities, or religions.[66]

Liberal cosmopolitanism was widespread in the post–Cold War world but was limited by the horizons of a certain Western and liberal and broadly bourgeois way of imagining the social world where altruistic solidarities between individuals can made sense.

In another sense, a precondition of the possibility of universal human rights discourse and practice is the existence of a kind of moral culture in which moral codes make sense.[67] Rawls's political thought, for instance, was "quasi-Kantian,"[68] and came to "broadly "Kantian" conclusions."[69] His later text on international political theory, *The Law of Peoples*, resisted the more ambitious ideas of institutional cosmopolitans and conveyed a picture of international politics not entirely unlike Kant's *Perpetual Peace*, with a collection of "well-ordered" liberal democratic peoples, who Rawls argued ought to tolerate illiberal polities, with some duties of assistance to them.[70] His ideas inspired debate about global justice and facilitated the reimagination of a cosmopolitan moral community in a globalizing world.[71] For Charles Beitz, "the international realm is coming more and more to resemble domestic society in many of the features usually thought relevant to the justification of (domestic) political principles."[72] And, for Thomas Pogge, "a global institutional scheme is imposed by all of us on each of us."[73] What is interesting in these examples is the kind of moral culture in which they make sense, and those where they don't.[74]

If pressed, cosmopolitan advocates tend to insist human rights form a moral imperative in world politics, regardless of hard cases or culturally based objections.[75] If humankind *is* a moral "global community of human beings" then it *ought* to be recognized as such, so the argument tends to go.[76] In principle, it is not impossible to reconcile Kantian morality with cultural plurality.[77] The point is that arguments attempting to legitimate a cosmopolitan order through a position of moral authority are unlikely to persuade those working with different moral cultures, and may more likely generate recognitions struggles, and hierarchy conflicts, if connected to foreign policies. The philosopher Charles Taylor has argued that the idea of universal moral codes and a Kantian vision of moral order is made possible by the construction of a Western cultural history of secularization.[78] The imaginary of an "immanent frame" contingent on a Christian and Western cultural history, as Charles Taylor has described it, underpins modern Kantian cosmopolitan narratives by shaping what they conceive a cosmopolitan morality can possibly be and what it means to form a global community of rights-bearing world citizens.[79] This poses practical problems, because when Kantian ideas are applied to advocacy and foreign policies, these discourses encounter hierarchy legitimation conflicts and recognition struggles with states and illiberal societies.[80] Discursive action relying on moral authority in a Kantian cosmopolitan sense is a problematic legitimation strategy in a diverse global context. It may better serve as justification of unilateral action than as a tool of moral persuasion. "Kantianism can provide one faith" in a globalized world of interacting moral cultures, "but it can no longer pretend to embody the universal matrix of cosmopolitanism."[81]

Nussbaum attempts to deflect the charge that cosmopolitanism is

Western-centric by gesturing toward similar ideas of human unity found in non-Western cosmopolitan traditions such as Buddhism, although this gesture at least concedes that there are multiple cosmopolitan traditions that need to be reconciled.[82] The philosopher Kwame Anthony Appiah also offers a similar argument, in the picture of the "shattered mirror," one reality and in principle one morality with many reflections.[83] Nussbaum also argues that a liberal Kantian tradition of cosmopolitanism is committed to diversity as a matter of principle, which seems like a good place to start.[84] To address the problem of pluralism, Nussbaum suggests philosophers should seek an "overlapping consensus" between diverse moral systems.[85] Taylor himself has proposed this approach for the thorny issue of defining human rights, although the search for consensus on definitions still has a certain framing of morality as a moral code.[86]

Richard Rorty adopted a different legitimation strategy, arguing for liberal cosmopolitanism not on any universal moral foundation, and readily admitting its cultural sources, but asserting its pragmatically "better" politics.[87] Rorty's classic essay "Cosmopolitanism without Emancipation" offered a characteristically confident but unusually imaginative expression of a liberal cosmopolitan future:

> We [liberal cosmopolitans] look forward, in a vague way, to a time when the Cashinahua, the Chinese, and (if such there be) the planets which form the Galactic Empire will all be part of the same cosmopolitan social democratic community. This community will doubtless have different institutions than those to which we are presently accustomed, but we assume that these future institutions will incorporate and enlarge the sorts of reforms which we applaud our ancestors for having made. The Chinese, the Cashinahua, and the Galatics will doubtless have suggestions about what further reforms are needed, but we shall not be inclined to adopt these suggestions until we have managed to fit them in with our distinctively Western social democratic aspirations, through some sort of judicious give-and-take.[88]

As appealing as this picture may be to some liberal thinkers, it is obviously utopian. Rorty's picture of a galactic liberal cosmopolis is all too reminiscent of Gene Rodenberry's *Star Trek*. It is a fantasy, largely an American one. Even this science fantasy however often acknowledges the challenges of cultural conflicts with its imagined liberal future. For instance, an interesting scene from *Star Trek VI: The Undiscovered Country* explores the alien "Klingon" outsider perspective of the "Federation." The scene is a diplomatic dinner, with Klingon and Federation delegations seeking a negotiated reconciliation of their respective interstellar polities. During the slightly stilted discussion, the Federation officer Chekov suggests, "'We [the Federation] do believe all planets have a sovereign claim to inalienable human rights.'" The Klingon delegates are not impressed. One responds, "Inalien. If only you could hear yourselves? 'Human rights.' Why the very name is racist! The Federation is no more than a homo sapiens only club." Then, in the key line of the scene, another Klingon delegate expresses the Klingons' deeper reservation about reconciliation. "In any case," he says, "we know where this is leading, the annihilation of our culture." The scene ends in diplomatic failure, with both delegations departing feeling defeated and worried about future hostilities. Even in fantastical depictions of the distant future, there is an awareness of persistent cultural objections to a universal liberal cosmopolitan order.

The other well-known example of a liberal cosmopolitan imaginary in contemporary science fiction is Iain M. Banks's Culture series. Banks's future "Culture" is an interplanetary anarchical posthuman and postscarcity liberal society with fully automated machine labor leading to a withering away of the interstellar state. In imagining this "Culture," Banks deliberately sought to envision a progressive future, unlike the dystopian galactic empires populating the genre. The quasi-speculative future depicted in his *Consider Phlebas* is still a space opera, however, in the drama of the war between the "Culture" and the "Indirans." What is interesting is the imaginary of what constitutes the Culture and its justification of war. Banks's culture fought for its liberal morality, and the right to have it, where the Indirans are portrayed as religious fanatics, defending their right to it. "The Indirans fought for their Faith; the Culture for its moral right to exist," the novel's jacket explains. The imagination of future liberal cosmopolitan worlds never seems to escape cultural conflict.

Grappling with these challenges, Luis Cabrera's *The Humble Cosmopolitan* suggests that a less morally authoritative approach would potentially prove more useful in practice, toward "an appropriately configured institutional cosmopolitanism."[89] This is a more promising path, in adapting the cosmopolitan tradition, although the emergence of such a cosmopolitan order is highly unlikely in the foreseeable future.

Conclusion

In the modern international experience, with all its trials and upheavals for liberty and human rights, peace has not readily "taken care of itself," as Kant speculated it someday would.[90] Grotius's idea of a universal moral order underlying international society remains "cold comfort," as Kant called it, in a divisive and disorderly world in which war is multiplying and the humanitarian laws of war are regularly ignored. Liberal Kantian cosmopolitanism has been the predominant cosmopolitan imaginary in the modern global world, but its vision of a cosmopolitan future long advocated for and anticipated remains unrealized and faced with considerable resistance. The legitimation strategies of Kantian cosmopolitans to realize a cosmopolitan order have been about assuming positions of moral authority with claims to the existence of unseen webs of moral obligation, binding states and people. Although not uninfluential, internationalist Kantian cosmopolitan politics has been highly limited in its achievements relative to its ambitions. At its height in the post–Cold War world, the liberal cosmopolitan wave was overwhelmed by the upswell of populism reasserting modern state power and mobilizing exclusionary nationalist identities, in combination with illiberal forces. In the wake of the revolt against globalism and pushback against the global West, Kantian cosmopolitanism appears to occupy the past more than any speculative future. It still has advocates, however, and as a tradition with ancient roots is likely to persist for some time yet. Derrida, a political philosopher both sympathetic and critical of the cosmopolitan tradition, grasped the tensions in the historicity of Kantian cosmopolitanism when he asked, "Where have we received the image of cosmopolitanism from? And what is happening to it? As for this citizen of the world, we do not know what the future holds."[91]

THREE

World Communism

World communism imagined a universal proletariat, enabling the connection of revolutionary struggles on a global scale. In the process, these struggles deeply divided world politics. Resistance to revolutionary liberation emerged in parallel, check and countercheck, with equal and often greater force. In their countermovement, Cold War leaders and thinkers reimagined the idea of the "West" and "Western values," as tied to universal values, in a global struggle for modernity. The dream of world revolution, capturing a great power in Russia, and another in China, aimed to overturn international society and construct a world socialist order, but instead further divided it, more deeply than before, and not only militarily but also morally and socially, between contending political ways of life and competing visions of modernity.

Most histories of world communism explore how communist revolutions emerged in every continent, the sources of its internal divisions, and why Soviet communism ultimately collapsed. I am instead more interested in why and how world communism was resisted as much as it was advocated; why it was ultimately more divisive than unifying. The reasons for this are not easily attributable to the modern forces of nationalism, or simply to the material interests and relative power of capitalist states, as realists might suggest; neither are the reasons entirely attributable to the failures of revolutionary strategy, as Marxists might suggest. Instead, I make the case that the social recognition struggles of world communism with Western societies, and political hierarchy legitimation conflicts across international society, including within the communist world, generated the deeper division of international society. Through this process, it produced implacable visions of modernity, mobilized both vertically between superpowers and horizontally across them. In other words, in exploring the rise and fall of the Marxian imaginary of a universal proletariat, I find that world communism struggled with internal schisms and encountered hierarchy legitimation conflicts and recognition struggles with liberal societies mobilizing counterrevolutionary forces and liberal ideas of belonging, which eventually overwhelmed all Marxian thought and practice in the post–Cold War world.

World Revolution

In the words of the political theorist and economist Harold Laski, "the vital fact about him [Marx] is that he found communism a chaos and left it a movement."[1] Marx and his collaborator Engels were theorists of 19th century globalization. For Marx and Engels,

> the bourgeoisie has through its exploitation of the world market given a cosmopolitan character to production and consumption in every country. . . . In place of the old local and national seclusion and self-sufficiency, we have intercourse in every direction, universal inter-dependence of nations.[2]

The insights of Marx and Engels into modern capitalism and class society, in the sociological concepts of base and superstructure, alienation, value, and so on, are theoretically impressive.[3] Their masterstroke, however, that which arguably gave them powerful political purchase, was their horizontalization, in the idea that the proletariat was universal because it along with capital was global. This move made emancipation potentially global, in world revolution. It offered a new way of imagining global belonging in the modern global world. "The proletarians have nothing to lose but their chains. They have a world to win. Working men of all countries, unite!"[4] Marx and Engels were not alone in making this revolutionary call on horizontal lines, however; they were only the most influential in a wave of socialist and communist thinkers calling for world revolution.[5]

In practice, communism as an international revolutionary force found organization in the International Working Men's Association—the First International—counting Marx and Engels as members, based in London from 1864 to 1874, and in the Second International, based in Paris from 1889 to 1914. The Russian Revolution in 1917, however, raised world communism to the international field of states, in the form of a weakened but still great power, "the weakest link in the system of world-wide capitalism."[6] "The World Revolution has begun" declared the communist party newspaper *Pravda*.[7] From Moscow, Lenin promised the world an alternative anti-imperial and internationalist communist order, but the divisions of world politics were immediate, between states, and within societies.[8] Soviet Russia was excluded from the proceedings at Versailles, and initially from the League of Nations and its new world order.[9] Meanwhile, uneasy perceptions of horizontal insecurity fell across Western capitals, before Russia itself fell into civil war and counterrevolutionary struggle between the Russian "Reds" and the "Whites."[10] The world became divided in the moment of world communism's greatest victory. Capturing a great power, communism became wrapped up in great power politics, but it also reconfigured these politics, along horizontal lines.

Communist parties never were widely supported in most Western democracies, where moderate democratic socialist parties had more support.[11] In the 1920s, the vision of modernity offered by the idea of a Soviet-style future nevertheless appealed to many prominent intellectuals. Harold Laski, among the most prominent, was sympathetic, although not uncritical of the USSR, and also a supporter of Roosevelt's "New Deal." Laski's own thinking argued that there should be a priority in Western states to come to terms with the communist world, although in his view war would persist until global capitalism, and its political edifice, the modern sovereign state, were eventually dismantled, toward the establishment of a pluralist global socialist democracy.[12] Other intellectuals such as E. H. Carr, Sydney and Beatrice Webb, and W. E. B. Du Bois wrote at length on the Soviet Union as a new model for civilization.[13] The Webbs also made close company and friendship with Ivan Maisky, the Soviet ambassador to the United Kingdom from 1932 to 1943.[14]

In the fallout of the Great Depression and the return of international instability, the rise of anticommunist fascism in Italy and Germany became an extreme counterrevolutionary wave. Fascist nationalism reconstituted national belonging along racial lines and sought to structure international society on stratified racial hierarchies.[15] Strategically deluded by his own ideology of superiority, Adolf Hitler drove international society into another world war, producing an unlikely alliance between Moscow and the liberal powers, after he betrayed the equally unlikely Nazi-Soviet Pact.[16] World communism centered in Moscow only narrowly survived its struggle against fascism. This victory for communism cemented confidence in its Marxian definition of modernity, but the experience of the Second World War and the Russian Civil War before that made Soviet leadership wary of their revolutionary mission's vulnerability and dangers. In a defensive outlook, Stalin and the Soviet Union preferred to wait for history to take its toll on the internal contradictions of Western capitalism, rather than to risk provoking the Western powers too soon. Stalin's revolutionary strategy, which in principle ultimately aimed to overturn international society as we know it, ended up cementing its emergent divisions.

The Iron Curtain and Reinvention of the West

As Stalin consolidated the Soviet Union's political holdings, leading up to and after 1945, the specter of communism once again spread out horizontally across European capitals and beyond.[17] The redivision of the world in 1945 hobbled new international organization and prospects for a more ambitious order. Unlike the League of Nations, which we might say failed because its aims were pursued even though their conditions were evaporating, the United Nations we might say continued to exist only because the intentions of its original design were not followed. Roosevelt's vision of a UN system with a four-power concert was impossible and essentially blocked and stifled, dramatically enough, in the construction of threat perceptions between the former Soviet and Western allies.

The Cold War was more than arms racing and competition for global hegemony; it involved mobilizing competing meta-narratives of modernity, each demanding, implicitly, recognition of its rightness and superiority. This process emerged early on, leading up to the bitter division of the Cold War. The partition of Germany by the occupying powers in 1945 indicated the dividing lines that would later be formalized. Churchill's "Iron Curtain" speech in March 1946 expressed the fear of a new unappeasable totalitarian threat, intent on expansion.[18] The cause to be defended, however, were the "great principles of freedom and the rights of man which are the joint inheritance of the English-speaking world." The Atlantic Charter was still relatively new, and out of it Churchill summoned his idea of the English-speaking peoples sharing common cause against tyranny. In his "Long Telegram" of February 1946, George Kennan quoted Stalin at length, as evidence of the Soviet intent to wage a long but decisive struggle against the capitalist world. In closing his case, Kennan called for the US to revive itself, and its way of life, because "the greatest danger that can befall us in coping with this problem of communism, is that we shall allow ourselves to become like those with whom we are coping."[19] In office, President Harry Truman marshaled these arguments and reinvented liberal internationalism, with containment and its new liberal internationalist cause for freedom. The Truman Doctrine and the Marshall Plan were his principal instruments, ensuring that the US would support democracies against the looming danger.[20] But containment was not for Truman just a set of forward defenses against a distant adversary. It was meant to be a positive force, in an extension of American values to free peoples, breaking from American isolationism and creating a new internationalism. The "West" had begun to be reimagined as its Cold War self. Around it, various political forces cohered around the globe, seeking support from the United States for security and economic opportunity or need.[21] And so the world divided again, between the Soviet communist world and the new free world.

Soviet leadership viewed US policies as threatening aggression and—according to Soviet Marxist ideology—the return of capitalist imperialism, now that its fascist menace had been defeated. Influential Soviet insider Andrei Zhdanov made an especially fiery and defiant speech in September 1947 on "New Aspects of World Conflict," expressing Soviet perceptions of threat and warning of American intentions:

> America's aspirations to world supremacy encounter an obstacle in the USSR, the stronghold of anti-imperialist and anti-fascist policy. . . . Accordingly, the new expansionist and reactionary policy of the United States envisages a struggle against the USSR, against labour movements in all countries, including the United States, and against emancipationist, anti-imperialist forces in all countries.[22]

It was not just ideological bluster, or a passing diplomatic complaint. States under Soviet occupation were denied participation in Truman's new plan. The construction of threat had become mutual. Parallel claims to legitimate international leadership and finger-pointing accusations of imperial aggression bound them into hostility more and more tightly, and the mobilization of their rival narratives of modern freedom and global belonging became more and more oppositional.

By this time, many intellectuals formerly sympathetic to Stalinist communism had become disillusioned. In his 1940 novel *Darkness at Noon*, the text that made him famous, Arthur Koestler worked to show not only the brutality of Soviet communism but also its contradictions. "They dreamed of power with the object of abolishing power; of ruling over the people to wean them off the habit of being ruled."[23] By 1954, looking back, he wrote, "I went to Communism as one goes to a spring of fresh water, and I left Communism as one clambers out of a poisoned river strewn with the wreckage of flooded cities and the corpses of the drowned."[24] George Orwell, once sympathetic to socialist causes, when made aware of Stalin's purges, published his *Animal Farm* (1945), which made both him and the idea of the betrayed revolution famous in the English-speaking world.[25] The Tehran Conference in 1943, meanwhile, gave Orwell his idea for his later novel, *Nineteen Eighty-Four*, which he described to his publisher as meaning "to discuss the implications of dividing the world up into 'Zones of Influence.'"[26]

The next ripple in this liberal counterwave went further by reinventing "liberal" values and the idea of the "West" itself. In the United States, Arthur Schlesinger's *The Vital Center: The Politics of Freedom* was the most forceful in its convictions. Schlesinger argued that Soviet communism demanded the renewal of America's liberal democratic freedoms to undercut the appeal of its rivals.[27] Karl Popper's *The Open Society and Its Enemies* offers the idea of an "open society" as a Western political way of life, but by tracing its origins through a certain reading of Western history reaching to ancient Greece.[28] In the pages of *Foreign Affairs*, Isaiah Berlin's essay "Political Ideas in the Twentieth Century" both identified the dangers of totalitarian politics and attempted to define the essence of an alternative liberal way.[29] Liberalism seriously changed in the process.[30] The values, history, and character of liberalism itself were being reinvented in its reaction to the new totalitarian threat and its alternative vision of global modernity. The international relations thinker Martin Wight himself contributed to this counterwave, albeit mainly for an academic audience. His essay, "Western Values in International Relations," was unusually policy prescriptive for Wight. Wading into the Cold War, through a highly selective reading of Western history and philosophy, Wight made the case that "Western values" on the international plane were synonymous with the via media values of "international society," which he insisted had a Grotian underpinning.[31] For Wight, Western values threaded extremes and wagered "that moral standards can be upheld without the heavens falling" and that acting through moral values would not weaken but "strengthen the fabric of political life."[32] For Wight, international society has been modified in international history rather than being destroyed and ceasing to exist, because people have been willing to defend its values, with force if necessary.[33] His reading of these values, however, constituted a certain idea of the West, designed for its own times. In practice, the language game of "Western values" itself arose as a Cold War discourse, mostly American, used by American diplomats and presidents in their relations with other Western states. In the renewed and reimagined West, it also expanded to the east, incorporating its twice former enemy Germany, as well as it could, into a larger "Western" security community.[34] The renewal and expansion of "Western civilization" brought with it a narrative of universal human rights and democratic freedoms, but this in the same process gave it its anticommunist character. "The conservative, anticommunist character of 'Western Civilization' was combined with 'a more proactive transnational set of institutions and organizations.'"[35] Aiming to play a long game of waiting for the West to collapse under its own contradictions, the Soviet Union instead encountered a new, more ferocious adversary with an international reach constructed deliberately to oppose it.

This was not merely a propaganda war, although propaganda campaigns mattered. It was a construction of hostility, in two rival interpretations of modernity, each demanding recognition of its superiority. In his essay "Identity and the Cold War," Robert Jervis insightfully argues that "both the United States and the Soviet Union saw themselves as the standard-bearers of progress and modernity."[36] Neither could recognize the other. "American identity, although also looking to the future, was based on a view of what American society actually was (of course an idealized one). Because the Soviet identity represented beliefs about what would develop, it could lead to grave disappointments."[37]

George Orwell wrote in 1945, "Ten or twenty years ago, the form of nationalism most closely corresponding to Communism today was political Catholicism."[38] For Wight, the messianic qualities of communist foreign policy (derived from its theological sources) also shaped the bitterness of the counterrevolutionary wave that rose to face it. For Wight, this extreme divisiveness "explains the diplomatic principle that 'He who is not with us is against us.' This is a Stalinist maxim, and McCarthyite too: you are not pro-American unless violently anti-Russian. It is reflected in Dulles's belief that neutrality was a kind of treason in the war to preserve civilization."[39]

Schisms of Communism

When Khrushchev later sought a policy of "peaceful coexistence," this sounded reasonable only because the divisions had now become hard to unmake, while anticommunism in Western societies had become extreme in some cases. The hardened divisions were both vertical between superpowers and horizontal between real or imagined "fifth columns." World communism was not a single wave; it was a series of struggles and upheavals, transnational in coordination at times, but also national in context and origins, diverse in self-understandings, and often conflicting and competing. The Cold War was global, but also local. Various political groups, liberal-capitalist, Christian, and conservative, aligned against communist politics. Many of the struggles between socialist and capitalist political forces were within societies, and the use of anticommunist rhetoric and politics had specific local sources, taking advantage of, and being swept up by, global-level political divisions. Communist parties across the communist world were national parties, and held national sympathies, but they were also communist internationalists. They played the language game of "comrades" and were able to imagine its narrative of the universal proletariat, while making use of it on local battlefields.

The communist world had divisions all its own, however. Communist revolutionary strategy itself was a source of debate and division among Marxist-Leninists. Stalin followed Lenin's advice to avoid war with capitalist powers, to let them eventually destroy themselves, but he and Leon Trotsky disagreed on the exportation of revolution and other issues. Debates about communist revolutionary strategy were not simply about praxis and political power, however; it also became the Marxists' ideological struggle to explain the paradox of its own failings, and to cast blame. For Fred Halliday, "the delusion of a worldwide revolutionary conflagration has inspired, and deluded, revolutionary leaders."[40] Theory expected that revolutions in the capitalist world would arise, or that the imperial powers would again descend into a war with one another, but the anticipated revolutions and wars never came. Instead, a durable counterrevolutionary alignment emerged, and, in the Sino-Soviet split, the very idea of world revolution suffered damage.[41] "So inexplicable did the split appear from a Marxist perspective that both Chinese and Soviet historians in retrospect would blame the debacle on the other side's betrayal of Marxism."[42] The wave of world revolution was breaking.

Marxian revolutionary strategy and theory tended to struggle to escape the tautology that revolution did not occur more widely because it was not sufficient, be it in breadth or in solidarity. Antonio Gramsci's earlier writings are among the most sophisticated in their explanation of the missing world revolution, that "hegemony" and the bulwarks of the extended state formed a web of indirect but pervasive counterforces, both domestically and internationally.[43] Therefore, the possibility of a revolutionary outcome, for Gramsci, had both a domestic and an international dimension, requiring a strategic constellation of multiple revolutionary states.[44] C. L. R. James's early work *World Revolution* argued that revolutionary leadership was not sufficiently organized, while his later *State Capitalism and World Revolution* argued that the revolutionary workers were not sufficiently organized either. Counterfactually, because the divisions of world politics had become so deeply constructed, even if the world revolution had more supporters and even more victories, capturing one of the capitalist great powers, for instance, the revolution would still have been resisted and rejected by a transnational anticommunist movement, only instead they would have become the rebels.

Contrary to realities, the futures past of Soviet space race propaganda and science fiction assumed a world communist future and depicted its teleological imaginary. Soviet cosmonauts spoke in secular terms of being "citizens of the universe." Stanislaw Lem, the greatest science fiction author from the communist world (most famous for his work *Solaris*), assumed the planetary communist future quietly in the background of his early novel *The Astronauts* (1951). In his later novel *Memoirs Found in a Bathtub* (1961), Lem tells the tale of a future archeological discovery of memoirs from an ancient lost civilization whose records and history were lost after the "Great Collapse." The memoirs are found in a bathtub buried in the ancient ruins of the Pentagon, possibly the "Third Pentagon." Examining the memoirs, the archeologists read how, when "the populace of Ammer-Ka went over to the side of the 'heretics' and joined the Federation, the priests of the Last Pentagon ordered it to be completely sealed off from the outside world."[45] This is a (dys)topian propaganda story, assuming a terminal American society and a communist future world "federation." This assumed future never arrived. The communist world instead encountered a rival modernity in the "West," deliberately reimagined in opposition to it.

Specters of Marx

In December 1989, Mikhail Gorbachev and George H. W. Bush held frank negotiations at a bilateral summit in Malta. Gorbachev stated, "Now let me mention a concept of U.S. origin: The division of Europe should be overcome on the basis of Western values." And Gorbachev continued, "If policy is made on that assumption the situation could become quite messy." Bush replied, "It's not in hostility that 'Western values' is written. I want to be sure of the difficulty you have in our using this term—I don't want to complicate anything."[46] As the post–Cold War world took shape, however, the language of "Western values" declined in US diplomatic discourse, in favor of "universal human rights," as the West attempted to globalize itself. Only recently, some decades later, in the increasingly divided geostrategic present, has the language of the now "global West" and its like-minded values returned.

The construction of the post–Cold War world was initially a revolutionary wave, as populations liberated themselves from the Soviet Union, but importantly not China.[47] In the post–Cold War world, Marxian world communism was abandoned as a world order project, although Marxian thought continued to inspire the critics of neoliberal globalization.[48] In the afterlife of world communism, many critical theorists turned increasingly to immaterial poststructural discursive constructions to reimagine global belonging.[49] As the power of capital extended into a new transnational hegemonic form, anti-globalization activists found common complaint with their new globalizing structural position, and a new sense of global resistance emerged.[50] Popular thinkers such as Michael Hardt and Antonio Negri articulated a language of "empire" to describe the new US-led global capitalist order.[51] Their ideas advanced a vague alternative global order vision, the "commonwealth."[52] Contemporary communist revolutionary strategy, like most things in the digital age, became more diffuse and network-flexible, but not with much more effectiveness.[53] The language of "comrades," which once conveyed the imaginary of a universal proletariat, became abandoned, not least for its negative connotations with the Soviet experience.[54] Today, the language is used in relations between authoritarian North Korea and China, and at times in their dealings with Russia again too. The Cold War in a sense never ended on the Korean peninsula, but China's neo-authoritarian communism is hardly a global revolutionary ideology. World communism and its narratives of the global proletariat are a bygone force in world history, although critics on the left continue to take inspiration from Marx's thought.[55] The language used on the left in the West today tends to be "allies."

Some of the problems of modernity that Marx and Engels gave a global vision for overcoming still exist, even though that Marxian wave is now long past. Thomas Piketty's *Capital in the Twenty-First Century* (2014) and the follow-up *Capital and Ideology* (2020) made a splash into popular discourse during the crisis and collapse of neoliberal globalism. Finding accumulative extreme inequalities, Piketty called for international tax coordination, among other global economic reforms, to hem in inequality and free up hidden offshore wealth.[56] Like most internationalist ideas at this time, it had widespread discussion, and little effect. Politics at the time became more divisive, as the neoliberal center lost legitimacy. The electoral victories of right-wing politicians in Brexit and in the Donald Trump presidency defeated the neoliberal center. But they also defeated more radical left populist politics expressed at the time by politicians such as Bernie Sanders in the US (although Sanders did not get to fully test his presidential electoral chances) and Jeremy Corbyn in the UK. The collapse of globalism went right, not left, and ideas of a possible new far left international wave went with it, at least perhaps for another generation.

Conclusion

In his response to Saint Pierre's *Perpetual Peace*, Rousseau concluded that it was impossible to achieve, "except by a revolution," but he nevertheless also asserted that if "this Plan remains unexecuted, it is not because it is chimerical; it is because men are insane, and because it is a sort of folly to be wise in the midst of fools."[57] Some two centuries later, George Orwell said of H. G. Wells that he was "too sane to understand the modern world."[58] The modern 20th century seems insane, not because its imagined universal orders were not attempted, but because when attempted it was so often with insane means and deeply divisive extremes.

Philosophically, all cosmopolitan imaginaries, ancient and modern, issue from the principal question that Derrida put best: what does it mean to "live together well."[59] Different philosophers, nations, civilizations, and ages offer diverse answers and judgments on this question; each generation must answer it again, but any answer always begs the further question of a wider and more comprehensive togetherness; every answer extends the question, from self to other, neighbors to foreigners, and so forth, logically, and in the modern global world, practically, toward the furthest and widest propinquity, all humankind. Living together as well as being free and equal, according to the tradition of critical theory, is pulled by its own logic to its maximal global application, all humankind and simultaneously and equally all its social subsets. If valid here, among "us," then there too, everywhere, for everyone, equally, the critical thinking goes. The genius of the Marxian imaginary of global belonging as the globally common structural position of the working class, was that it cut across nations, races, and creeds. The legitimation strategy of Marxian internationalists in the pursuit of a world communist order tended to be about justice for the majority and liberation from structural position, backed up by confidence in its historical superiority, and promise of productive future prosperity. The folly of the Marxian imaginary applied to revolutionary strategy, although there were many, was to misunderstand the divisive and equal if not greater counterforces its pursuit would create.

It is debated whether Marx and Engels themselves envisioned a global communist future. Their writings on this topic are vague and speculative. The underlying imaginaries that their work nevertheless inspired were notions of a global belonging and world revolution. Insofar as these futurist imaginaries were considered imminent by revolutionaries, not least by Lenin and Stalin, they contributed to the configuration of revolutionary strategy and foreign policy. The kind of communist "cosmopolitan" order aimed for was in its own ideal an internationalist order. In practice, the Soviet order appeared more like an imperial order, with an elite party network, often relying on force. And, in its external relations, its strategy for a long-term struggle for world revolution deeply divided international society. For Martin Wight, "The most important characteristic of the Communist theory of international relations is that it sharply divides all states—or rather their actual governments—into two categories: the communist (or 'socialist') and the non-communist."[60] The totalitarian character of the Soviet experience and its construction of a threat shaped the character of its new liberal internationalist counterwave in the "West," in a contest of superpower hierarchies, wielding mutually contradictory meta-narratives of modernity. Schisms in the communist world, moreover, damaged the idea of world revolution. World communism offered a powerful story of global belonging, deployed in revolutionary action on every continent, but as remarkable as the force of its rise and dramatic collapse was, more stunning was how deeply it divided world politics in the 20th century.

FOUR

Postcolonial Cosmopolitanism

While Kantianism and Marxism have been predominant traditions in modern cosmopolitan thought, postcolonial cosmopolitanism has offered a distinct way of imagining global belonging in the modern global world. Intellectuals such as Rabindranath Tagore, Frantz Fanon, and W. E. B. Du Bois and postcolonial statespersons such as Kwame Nkrumah have each in their way expressed a distinct kind of narrative about global belonging and alternative global orders beyond racial divisions and hierarchies. Statespersons of the Non-Aligned Movement also developed and mobilized a serious bid for an alternative global order model with internationalist cosmopolitan features, through the New International Economic Order movement.

In this chapter, I am interested in why these alternative postcolonial cosmopolitan visions of global order have not been more realized, and why and how they were resisted and counteracted. I make the case that postcolonial cosmopolitanism advanced distinct ways of imagining global belonging and global order, rising to a pitch in the 1970s, where it encountered hierarchy legitimation conflicts and recognition struggles with developed liberal powers. Neoliberal economic globalization that emerged out of this encounter and expanded in the post–Cold War world began by undercutting and co-opting the challenge posed by the New International Economic Order movement.

Postcolonial Cosmopolitan Thought

Postcolonial cosmopolitan ways of imagining global belonging emerged out of the global experience of colonialism and decolonization. The combination of the colonial experience, anticolonial revolutions, anticolonial congresses, and the decolonization era enabled another way of imagining global belonging as a world free from domination and division.[1] Through this global experience, a distinct and more thoroughly inclusive cosmopolitan mode of global belonging became possible to imagine.

In broad terms, the tradition of postcolonial cosmopolitanism generated narratives about humankind overcoming the structural legacies of colonialism and global racial divisions through the construction of a properly free and equally inclusive political order for all humankind, beyond hierarchies of exploitation and domination.[2] Postcolonial cosmopolitanism tends to envision internationalist cosmopolitan order alternatives, to be more fully realized in the future, but whose beginnings are possible today. Adom Getachew suggests that "the normative and utopian core of a postcolonial cosmopolitanism remains the principle of nondomination at the center of anticolonial worldmaking."[3] Getachew explains further that "postcolonial cosmopolitanism that takes seriously the idea that hierarchy and unequal integration are structural features of the international order entails a more expansive account of political responsibility rather than a limited duty of assistance."[4] Beyond Kantian cosmopolitan demands for rights fulfilment in political liberties and humanitarian and possibly development assistance, postcolonial cosmopolitanism pursues a more inclusive and egalitarian global order in which such practices of assistance and aid are less necessary. The postcolonial theorist Julian Go suggests postcolonial cosmopolitanism has two main features:

> (1) Its idea of decolonization as involving a cultural revolution heralding true human relations and exchange in opposition to colonialism's bifurcations and exploitation; and (2) its emphasis upon human identity as opposed to local attachments like race or nation.[5]

The International Relations scholar Rahul Rao has also argued that postcolonial cosmopolitanism considers the communitarian-cosmopolitan distinction to be too simplistic, and limited to bourgeois, and largely Eurocentric, assumptions.[6]

The cosmopolitan thought of postcolonial thinkers such as Rabindranath Tagore, Frantz Fanon, and W. E. B. Du Bois can be considered representative of this tradition, but there is no single definitive version or expression of postcolonial cosmopolitanism; there is no obvious Kant or Marx figure, although there are candidates among thinkers in the postcolonial tradition. All cosmopolitan traditions are internally diverse, but pluralism of political, social, and moral imaginaries tends to be an under-lying assumption and constitutive principle of postcolonial cosmopolitan thought. In this way of picturing it, a plurality of cosmopolitan imaginaries is included within a broadly defined postcolonial cosmopolitan imaginary.

Tagore's fictional works, for instance, such as *The Home and the World* and political works such as *Creative Unity*, explored a subtle, complex, and philosophical postcolonial cosmopolitanism with pluralistic but also transformative qualities.[7] Fanon for his part suggested that

> in fact there must be an idea of man and of the future of humanity. . . . After the conflict there is not only the disappearance of colonialism but also the disappearance of the colonized man. This new humanity cannot do otherwise than define a new humanism both for itself and for others.[8]

Postcolonial cosmopolitan modes of imagining global belonging tend to be about the liberation of humankind not only in a negative sense of liberation from colonial dominance but also in a positive sense of the generative transformation of global political culture in the revolutionary process.

Du Bois's writing provides some of the most eloquent expressions of a postcolonial cosmopolitan outlook. A lengthy passage of Du Bois's *The World and Africa* still repays reading:

> The broader the basis of a culture, the wider and freer its conception, the better chance it has for the survival of its best elements. This is the basic hope of world democracy. No culture whose greatest effort must go to suppress some of the strongest contributions of mankind can have left in itself strength for survival. War which typifies suppression and death can never support a lasting culture. Peace and tolerance is the only path to eternal progress. Europe can never survive without Asia and Africa as free and interrelated civilizations in one world. . . .
>
> I dream of a world of infinite and invaluable variety; not in the laws of gravity or atomic weights, but in human variety in height and weight, color and skin, hair and nose and lip. But more especially and far above and beyond this, in a realm of true freedom: in thought and dream, fantasy and imagination; in gift and aptitude, and genius—all possible manner of difference, topped with free-

dom of soul to do and be, and freedom of thought to give to a world and build into it, all wealth of inborn individuality. . . . There can be no perfect democracy curtailed by color, race, or poverty. But with all we accomplish all, even Peace.[9]

Among the foremost leaders of Pan-Africanism, Du Bois envisioned a federalist United States of Africa, which in the long term he imagined would contribute to world democracy too. For Du Bois, "the Problem of the Color Line" could be counteracted through democratic decolonization and, eventually, world democracy.[10]

Postcolonial cosmopolitanism has been associated with socialism both in theory and in practice but its imaginary and up to a point its practice tended to be distinct from traditional or narrow Marxist communism. A leading Pan-Africanist author, George Padmore, sought to clarify the differences between communism and Pan-Africanism in his book *Pan-Africanism or Communism?*

> Pan-Africanism recognizes much that is true in the Marxist interpretation of history. . . . But it nevertheless refuses to accept the pretentious claims of doctrinaire Communism, that it alone has the solution to all the complex racial, tribal, and socio-economic problems facing Africa.[11]

Other revolutionary and anticolonial thinkers, such as C. L. R. James, straddle the traditions of Marxism and postcolonialism, but the traditions can be distinguished.

Postcolonial statespersons such as Kwame Nkrumah and Jawaharlal Nehru also contributed to the emerging postcolonial cosmopolitan imaginary as a global political project. Nkrumah's *Neocolonialism* articulated a key concept for defining the financial and international organizational levers through which states could continue to hem in and interfere with the domestic and foreign policies of decolonized states.[12] A postcolonial order aimed to unmake these levers of neo-imperialism present after decolonization.

In the epilogue of his history of India, *The Discovery of India*, Nehru describes some elements of a new internationalist postcolonial future:

> It was India's way in the past to welcome and absorb other cultures. That is much more necessary today, for we march to the world of

tomorrow where national cultures will be intermingled with the international culture of the human race. We shall therefore seek wisdom and knowledge and friendship and comradeship wherever we can find them, and co-operate with others in common tasks, but we are no suppliants for others' favours and patronage. Thus, we shall remain true Indians and Asiatics, and become at the same time good internationalists and world citizens.[13]

To sum up, postcolonial cosmopolitanism, in various expressions, imagined global belonging in an inclusive pluralist way, through the colonial experience, toward alternative internationalist global orders defined by nondomination.

Decolonization

In practice, postcolonial cosmopolitanism emerged in international anti-colonial congresses. These congresses were not purely aimed at gaining national sovereignty. They had broad political agendas. The Pan-African Congresses in the interwar era were among the most active, involving the participation of prominent black Atlantic intellectuals, among them W. E. B. Du Bois, Kwame Nkrumah, Julius Nyerere, George Padmore, Michael Manley, and Nnamdi Azikiwe.[14] Francophone intellectuals, notably Aimé Césaire, were also active in this era.[15]

The immediate and steepest hurdle set before postcolonial visions of international order was decolonialization itself. The League of Nations lived up to almost no one's expectations. It was disappointing not least to colonized states.[16] Self-determination was restricted to European states, while the colonial possessions of the recently defeated empires were transferred to League mandates.[17] The hierarchies of the global imperial order were maintained for victor powers. In the Americas, the majority of Latin America had already achieved independence from European powers during the Napoleonic Wars and Canada's de facto independence emerged following its military mobilization during the First World War. Colonies in Asia and Africa remained, however. The exceptions at the time, Liberia and Ethiopia, were integrated into international society, but unequally Getachew argues, being subject to oversight through the League.[18] Petitions for decolonization present in Versailles and throughout the 1920s were resisted by imperial powers and the architects of the League. The legitimation of imperial hierarchies was increasingly challenged and contested, however. Mahatma Gandhi's nonviolent independence movement, for instance, was the largest in the British Empire. Decolonization ambitions in the 1930s suffered from Italian colonial adventurism in Ethiopia. The League's failure to intervene, or even to enforce sanctions, stemmed from France's vulnerability and appeasement, while Du Bois at the time asked, "If Italy takes her pound of flesh by force, does anyone suppose that Germany will not make a similar attempt?"[19]

Into the 1940s, Roosevelt's vision of universal international order and a "great union of humanity" in world peace was highly doubtful of European empires as sources of order. Instability in British India suggested to Roosevelt that the old empires were rather sources of disorder. In the adoption of decolonization in the United Nations Charter, different interpretations of trusteeship emerged.[20] Meanwhile, the demand for self-determination in Asia and Africa in the 1940s had more popular furor behind it than even in the 1920s. Wars of decolonization emerged, in numerous conflicts.[21] Through these considerable upheavals and in United Nations processes unmaking imperial hierarches across the 1940s to the 1960s, the recognized membership in the United Nations more than doubled in number.

Nonalignment and Global Economic Order

Into the era of sovereign independence, postcolonial visions of cosmopolitan international order that were once the activity of activists became the activity of diplomats and statespersons. Histories of decolonization draw attention to the importance of the international Bandung Conference, not only for the scope of its participants, but for its anticolonial international order ambitions and legacies.[22] The conference included delegations from over two dozen independent Asian and African states and was held in in Bandung, Indonesia in 1955. It was chaired by Indonesia's president Sukarno and included prominent statespersons such as Gamal Abdel Nasser, the president of Egypt, Nehru, the prime minister of India, and Zhou Enlai, the first premier of the People's Republic of China. Martin Wight in his LSE lectures at the time suggested that from this conference emerged a "Bandung philosophy," which he categorized as an anticolonial variant of revolutionary cosmopolitan politics.[23] In their study *Meanings of Bandung*, Quỳnh N. Phạm and Robbie Shilliam suggest that "Bandung introduced anti-colonialism and anti-racism as constitutive principles of a new world order rather than as background aspirations in a bipolar rivalry of great powers."[24] Getachew also argues that states-persons at Bandung were working to not only develop nation-states, but were actively working to construct a nonhierarchical and inclusive global order beyond the nation-state.[25] In this context, this diplomatic interaction developed postcolonial cosmopolitan agendas and ambitions across a wide range of states, seeking resistance to the geostrategic agendas of Washington and Moscow.

The development of the Non-Aligned Movement, influenced by Bandung and its legacies, advanced a new vision of an alternative global order. As the Non-Aligned Movement took shape, however, it further divided world politics into three blocs, even while it offered a new alternative vision of a more inclusive global order. The advancement of demands for a New International Economic Order (NIEO) became a major international project that carried this movement forward. It also aimed to overcome and readjust global divisions and inequities in a world of increasing economic interdependence. This international movement calling for reform of the global economic order was demanded by Global South states, toward a more egalitarian economic order that would enable proper, more complete independence and freedom. The 1974 UN Declaration on the Establishment of a New International Economic Order, for instance, states, "All these changes have thrust into prominence the reality of interdependence of all the members of the world community."[26] The aim to construct a more inclusive global economic order, as a response to its contradictions and inequities as such, also included the language and idea of a world community beyond the society of states. If implemented, this project would have aimed to construct an internationalist, cosmopolitan, global order configuration.

Why was this project resisted by Western states, and how did that resistance and conflict both divide and modify international society? The first call for a new economic order in practice is said to have been made by the secretary general of UNCTAD (United Nations Conference on Trade and Development), Raul Prebisch, at the first UNCTAD conference in Geneva, in 1964.[27] Following the activities of the Group of 77, this movement became a prominent moment in the discourse of world order when the United Nations General Assembly adopted the "Declaration on the Establishment of a New International Economic Order" and the "Programme of Action on the Establishment of a New International Economic Order" in May 1974. This movement for a New International Economic

Order demanded vast redistribution of wealth through financial, trade, and monetary reforms. The Declaration called "urgently for the establishment of a new international economic order based on equity, sovereign equality, interdependence, common interest and cooperation among all States."[28] The scope of world order reform this movement demanded was substantial, and it assumed significant prominence as a set of demands, being adopted by UN General Assembly resolutions, while being debated and contested by world leaders at the highest levels of world politics.

The strategy of the NIEO movement was premised on an attempt to leverage the combined economic clout of developing countries to gain far-reaching and fundamental reform demands. The 1974 Declaration also brought attention to uneven exposure to the global economic crisis:

> The present international economic order is in direct conflict with current developments in international political and economic relations. Since 1970, the world economy has experienced a series of grave crises which have had severe repercussions, especially on the developing countries because of their general vulnerability to external economic impulses. The developing world has become a powerful factor that makes its influence felt in all fields of international activity.[29]

The ambition of these declarations and resolutions was unrealized and gradually it dispersed as a movement. A combination of setbacks from economic circumstances following the oil embargo (1973), in a context of increasing debt, constrained developing states within international financial institutions.[30] Ultimately, this strategy was ineffective, partly because the bargaining power held by Global South states was overestimated, but also because developed states advanced economic globalization as an expedient alternative.

Vijay Prashad argues that the ambitions of Global South states were stymied and abandoned, not entirely because of the overwhelming power still held by Global North states, but also from the internal problems of postcolonial states.[31] In Prashad's account, these states struggled with militarism, failures to achieve more radical state reforms, and their eventual separation of economic policies from their political aspirations. Prashad explains, "The adoption of what became globalization (or hegemony of neo-liberal economics) came not only from imperialist pressure but also from those forces within the countries that fundamentally disagreed with the strategic direction of social development *chosen* by the political parties of national liberation."[32] It was partly a story of abandonment, as such, as he explains further: "The politics of NAM [the Non-Aligned Movement] moved to symbolism. The creation of a powerful unity to change the political manipulation of the planet in the bipolar Cold War was destroyed."[33] Economic globalization was adopted at the expense of the more radical political reform and the global notions of belonging they entailed. For example, "The [Asian] Tigers' success dampened the enthusiasm for the Third World's exertions to transform the world order."[34] The opportunity to participate in economic globalization enabled this shift away from the NIEO, which was resisted by Global North states.

Reagan and Thatcher were perhaps especially unlikely to be convinced of an alternative international economic order that involved more state action, not less. They wanted to retrench the state domestically, to overcome economic malaise and turmoil.[35] Reducing taxes, eliminating expenses, free market deregulation—these were their aims. A new international economic order globally redistributing wealth through new international mechanisms was quite the opposite of what Reagan and Thatcher had in mind. Into the early 1980s, moreover, Reagan and especially Thatcher faced domestic pressure in an economic recession to improve economic conditions at home, more than doing so abroad. Joining forces, Reagan and Thatcher's leadership articulated a counterdiscourse expressed in the phrases "stratified order" and the early articulation of the "liberal international order." This neoliberal counterdiscourse and set of practices aimed to legitimate an open market economic order, as a part of stimulating growth in the advanced economies, while deflecting demands for an alternative international economic order from Global South states. The hierarchies of the advanced capitalist democracies of the United States and the United Kingdom in the international economic order needed some legitimation, after all. Moreover, the approach co-opted and divided underdeveloped states.

Neoliberalism as a political project was an economic project, but in its ascendance onto the international stage, it brought with it a politics of identity. Reagan and Thatcher also deflected postcolonial narratives of a larger sense of belonging and global economic obligations with simple neoliberal ideas about atomized identities and liberties. Their neoliberal counterwave was also a counternarrative based on identities of individual responsibility in a free global economy. Speaking at Cancun, Mexico in 1981, for example, President Ronald Reagan ventured his counternarrative, connecting domestic politics of freedom to an international economic order: "We are mutually interdependent, but, above all, we are individually responsible . . . the critical test is whether government is genuinely working to liberate individuals by creating incentives to work, save, invest, and succeed. . . . Without it, no amount of international good will and action can produce prosperity."[36] These ideas, which are all too familiar today, were in this early stage of neoliberalism's ascendance in tension with the hierarchical conflict posed by the NIEO, and deliberately deployed against them.

The historian of international political economy Quinn Slobodian conveys precisely the beginnings and tensions of this counterdiscourse in a passage discussing the rise of neoliberalism:

> While the G-77 and the global reformists envisioned a world economy of nation-states in relationships of unevenness, dependency, and deteriorating exchange produced by a history of colonialism, the GATT reformers followed Hayek to propose a vision of the world economy as a "homeostatic self-equilibrating system"—and information-processing mechanism with strata of evolved laws helping to guide price signals to direct the behavior of the world's individuals. At stake was the question of order. Against the NIEO vision of an end-state of redistributive justice, Geneva School neoliberals defined order as a perpetually shifting relationship of exposure to stimuli requiring response and adaptation in a necessarily unknowable future. More than simply a rearguard action to defend the status quo, the neoliberals proposed a framework and an ethos to defend the counterintuitive claim that "order is adjustment."[37]

The globalization of the neoliberal international order reordered international politics and carried with it the neoliberal individualistic identities and liberal entrepreneurial notions of freedom. Calls for a new international economic order disappeared as its movement declined, against the rise of neoliberal economic globalization. What is interesting here is the encounter of two oppositional narratives, postcolonial and neoliberal, around hierarchy conflicts of developed states responding to NIEO demands with neoliberal economic globalization.

New Postcolonial Cosmopolitanism?

Postcolonial cosmopolitanism continued to form a major current of political thought and practice in the post–Cold War world.[38] The historian and postcolonial theorist Paul Gilroy has previously pointed to South African antiapartheid politics as an example of a pluralistic postcolonial cosmopolitan belonging beyond race, class, and nation.[39] African cosmopolitan political thought in particular has continued to be a source of cosmopolitan imaginaries.[40] The philosopher Achille Mbembe's concept of "Afropolitanism," for instance, has articulated a cosmopolitan outlook from the perspective of Africa as a part of a global order, which is understood to be incomplete without Africa.[41] Afropolitanism, moreover, is understood to be one among many cosmopolitanisms, in a "common world," "tout-monde," with a common cosmopolitan order "project of a world in common founded on the principle of "equal shares."[42] More pluralistic multi-faith postcolonial and "post-secular" religious cosmopolitan imaginaries are also gaining new expression.[43]

Development remains a priority for many postcolonial states and populations, even while many states have made considerable advances through economic globalization. Colonization remains structurally incomplete and problematic for indigenous populations and other groups, however, placing demands to take account of continued structural injustice within and across states.[44] Internationally, postcolonial cosmopolitanism in the post–Cold War world has tended to support regional and interregional international order projects, in an emerging pluralist post-Western global order.[45] Western standards of modernity are increasingly contested, and the emergence of "civilizational states" discourses, most vocally in India, China, and also Russia, has increasingly supported calls for a post-Western order recognizing the legitimacy of non-Western civilizations.[46] Geopolitical tensions in international society moreover have seen the rise of a "neo-non-aligned" or "active non-aligned" grouping of states, resisting alignment with either Washington or Beijing.[47] These states again have increasingly demanded international order reform, including United Nations Security Council reform, as well as reform of the global trade order. In the foreign policies of multi- and active non-aligned states, it is not clear how influential internationalist postcolonial cosmopolitan thought currently is at present, however, above the upswell of nationalism.

Conclusion

Contemporary postcolonial science fiction on occasion imagines freedom found on distant worlds. The point of these worlds of future freedom, included in books and collected volumes such as Nalo Hopkinson and

Uppinder Mehan's *So Long Been Dreaming*, seems to be an exploration of how steep the hurdles to freedom on Earth have been—so steep that its realization requires a world to itself.[48] Postcolonial cosmopolitan visions of global belonging and alternative internationalist orders remain unrealized in world politics today. To explain the resistance to these visions, a realist story of preponderant capitalist hegemony and security incentives would be unsatisfying—and misleading. To the contrary, it was a conflict over the legitimacy of the hierarchies themselves, and a demand for recognition of the role that postcolonial states play in a global economy, through a more equal distributive scheme. The character of the response from developed states, and the process by which it evolved, was not a balancing of power; it was a reconfiguration of its economic relations into a new relegitimated state of affairs. Postcolonial cosmopolitanism advanced distinct ways of imagining cosmopolitan belonging and global order, rising to a pitch in the NIEO of the 1970s, where it encountered and was undercut by neoliberal globalization. In the post–Cold War world, postcolonial cosmopolitanism remained a prominent and growing current of political thought and practice, albeit in a globalized context. As international society begins to redivide in a new era of strategic competition, postcolonial cosmopolitan thought and practice remains present but still a considerable distance from achieving an alternative and properly free global order.

FIVE

Green Cosmopolitics

Green "cosmopolitan" politics imagines larger horizons of planetary belonging, including all humankind and living species in a moral sphere. Anticipations of climate catastrophe have excited this reimagination of planetary belonging and raised widespread and urgent calls for change. Yet, while green activism has been gaining steam over recent decades, it has highly limited accomplishments relative to its ambitions. Green internationalist advocates have encountered hierarchy legitimation conflicts between a range of developed and developing states, and within societies environmentalism has become embroiled in recognition struggles with forces of nationalist climate denialism, limiting climate governance to a thin and embattled green internationalism.

Why, after decades of climate activism, has so little been accomplished at a global level? The climate regime is far more limited in scope and apparent effectiveness than many consider to be necessary to manage climate change. What is interesting about this puzzling and worrisome history is how decades of climate activism for global ecological management have been met not only by ecological irresponsibility or negligence *between* states but also by persistent, divisive, and often hard to understand "climate denialism" *within* states. Climate change has strangely posed more than a "collective action" problem of North-South burden sharing or competing geopolitical policy priorities. Climate change politics has also become divisive within societies, and across them, dividing groups and classes not only with different distributive incentives but also contending and conflicting ways of life. Vertically, climate activism has encountered hierarchy legitimation conflict between the developed states that have benefitted from carbon energy but suggest limiting its use for developing states in a possible carbon-neutral economic order. Horizontally, climate activism at the same time has encountered the recognition struggles with climate denialists mobilizing conservative and exclusionary nationalist identities. These conflicts have limited climate regimes to a thin internationalism, including some sense of a shared cosmopolitan purpose, but with little authority or compliance. As a result, more radical green cosmopolitan world order models are essentially impossible, given not only the hierarchy legitimation conflicts that they pose but also the heightened political stakes that geopolitical competition is imposing.

Exploring and reflecting on these complex global politics, my argument in this chapter is that green cosmopolitan narratives and practices of planetary belonging, gaining greater expression over the past several decades, have encountered hierarchy legitimation conflicts with a range of states, while becoming embroiled in recognition struggles with forces of nationalist climate denialism, limiting climate action to a thin and embattled internationalist green cosmopolitanism.

Planetary Imaginaries

In the history of cosmopolitan imaginaries, it is helpful to recall the importance of Pythagoras. There could be no concept of the *cosmopolis* without his idea of a cosmic order, *cosmos*. A precondition of Diogenes' and Zeno's *cosmopolis* was the awe inspiring and dazzling grandeur of Pythagoras' teachings of a mathematically ordered *cosmos*. Of equal significance to Pythagoras' connections between earth and knowledge through measurement, that is, geometry, is his harmonic connection between an ordered cosmos and spiritual life. His vision carries that polymathic genius of remote antiquity, holistic thought:

> The essence and power of [Pythagoras's] vision lies in its all-embracing, unifying character; it unites religion and science, mathematics and music, medicine and cosmology, body, mind and spirit in an inspired and luminous synthesis.[1]

What Diogenes and Zeno did was make this grand cosmology political with their idea of the cosmopolis. Some millennia later, today, concepts of humankind's place in the world are changing in response to climate change, in a green strand of cosmopolitan thought reimagining international order.[2]

What is different and potentially transformative about green cosmopolitan politics is that it enlarges moral concerns and concepts of belonging from interhuman relations to include global ecological relations.[3] There is an extrahuman imperative about ecological politics, because of the idea of extrahuman security interdependence. In the changing nature of nature, the Anthropocene has been defined by humankind's impact on the Earth's history.[4] Underlying and making possible the range of responses to the global climate crisis are varieties of what we might call green or planetary imaginaries, the increasingly taken for granted assumptions and deeper but changing cognitive frameworks people hold about what and who environment stewardship involves.[5] Green cosmopolitan imaginaries grasp a larger mode of belonging.

These changing social imaginaries of humankind in nature are arguably a prerequisite to the realization of an internationalist green cosmopolitan order.[6] Their imagination at this point in history is not entirely new, and after several decades have realized some international action, but not anything like climate activists have called for. Ideas of green cosmopolitan belonging emerged in the environmental movement of the 1960s and 1970s. This included intellectuals such as Barbara Ward, Kenneth Boulding, Buckminster Fuller, and the Club of Rome members who developed the idea of "spaceship earth."[7] NASA's image of the "blue marble" also came to be seen as an iconic symbol of planetary community.[8] Carl Sagan's *Cosmos* and earlier *Cosmic Connection* also popularized a new perspective on human existence on Earth. Sagan's perspective attempted to reconnect humankind and nature, on the level and scale of a modern secularized cosmos, by drawing attention to the scientific awareness of the atomic composition of everything and everyone.[9] As early as 1970, George Kennan offered an essay, "To Prevent a World Wasteland," in *Foreign Affairs*, proposing a world environment organization managed by the superpowers.[10] In 1971, Richard Falk published the landmark text *This Endangered Planet*, an influential and among the first applications of climate concerns to international order thinking, calling for radical international order change.[11]

States first acknowledged the responsibilities of environmental stewardship in the 1970s, initially with the UN Stockholm conference in 1972. Into the 1980s and 1990s, global climate activism gained serious momentum, including new concepts and calls for environmental justice.[12] In 1992, the norm of environmental stewardship gained more general assent in international society at the Rio Earth Summit. Today, the concept of responsibilities for climate stewardship is widespread in world politics, with emergent institutionalization as a global climate regime complex.[13]

"At its core, environmental stewardship posits a fundamental responsibility of the state, and of international society, to protect the natural environment. States are expected to act as guardians of the environment not just within their own territory but also in a regional and global context."[14] Climate responsibility has become a mark of legitimacy for the "green state" in international society.[15] The global climate regime organizes mainly state-centric solidarity around the norm of environmental stewardship, although corporations increasingly take part in governance conferences and play a role in implementation and compliance.

Climate Change and Its Denial

Decades of climate activism have globalized the norm of environmental stewardship, but still with limited results relative to the risks of climate change and the expectations of climate activists. International society has been gradually "greening," but it struggles to meet its basic ecological responsibilities.[16] It would be challenging to say that there is more than the thinnest possible international ecological order today. The Paris Agreement is arguably a diplomatic achievement in setting targets and commitments to maintain global temperatures below 2 degree Celsius and to enhance the capacities of states to manage the effects of climate change.[17] Yet commitments to green governance through international society are primarily procedural, and their performance includes detractors and undercompliance.[18] The ecological order is also predominantly state-centric, seemingly contradicting the global-level nature of the crisis, although some consultation of nonstate actors is an emerging practice at climate summits. The securitization of the climate remains even more state-centric, and less internationalist, as militaries prepare for security threats that are multiplied and intensified by climate change.[19]

What explains the limited greening of international society? The emergence of an *internationalist green cosmopolitan order* that is so limited and lacking solidarity follows from the seemingly deadlocked competing interests between developed and developing states. At the global international level, the priority of climate change conflicts with competing strategic priorities of development and continued economic growth, as well as geostrategic interests in oil reserves. But these contradictions between capital, climate, and geopolitics are further complicated by the hierarchy conflicts of developed and developing states and ensuing diplomatic deadlock over burden-sharing responsibilities. Today, "international society remains divided over the degree to which environmental stewardship gives rise to a global justice agenda . . . with normative contestation focusing on questions of the historical responsibility of established industrialised countries versus new responsibilities of emerging economies."[20] The benefits of industrialization for developed states are seen as creating historical responsibilities by developing states, while the right to development conflicts with the responsibility of environmental stewardship, creating diplomatic contestation over the burdens of climate responsibilities between developed and developing states. While the state-centric international climate regime remains in deadlock, a more ambitious climate-globalism *institutional green cosmopolitan order* remains far-fetched, because nonstate actors have limited legitimation strategies in global international society based on principles of sovereignty. Nonstate actors have instead tended to work in a tandem of coordination with state direction, and in pressuring state action. Continued climate activism from "bottom up" world society actors remains a major source of urgency and pressure on states, whose best hope is forming an informal global coalition of climate states and nonstate actors to manage global responsibilities.

At the domestic level, however, further hurdles to the greening of world politics have arisen from the bizarre and aggressive politics of "climate denialism," emerging from recognition struggles with remobilized nationalist identities. This movement undermines and destabilizes climate ordering at an international level by capturing and constraining domestic and foreign policies, reneging on climate commitments. Climate denialist opposition to climate advocacy is almost as long-standing as climate activism, mobilizing in the 1980s, especially in the United Sates during the Reagan administration.[21] This movement has connections to invested industries, which are resistant to regulation, as well as to conservative think tanks. Yet to understand this movement as being driven purely by profit and power-seeking motives would be to misunderstand or miss its identity politics, conceptions of self, and underlying imaginaries of belonging.[22] Environmental skepticism and climate denialism that forcefully rejects narratives of planetary ecological belonging have emerged not from networks of corporate-funded lobbying and think tanks alone, but also from certain modern identities tied to certain modern ways of life and the surrounding international order that sustains it. In somewhat simple terms, the perception of global scarcity has generated a climate denial politics by segments of elites but also by segments of wider populations in developed economies, seeking to refuse to share burdens.[23] Hence the increasing connection between climate denialism, climate rejection, and increased border controls with tighter restrictions over perceived or imagined threats of increasing climate refugees.

Climate denialism and climate rejection politics at a national level, combined with protracted hierarchy legitimation conflicts and collective action problems at an international level, have dragged out the management of climate change for decades, producing an encroaching global climate crisis. While the US rejoined the Paris Agreement, the Trump administration's climate policy was the most high-level and fervent manifestation of climate denialism. Henry Shue has argued that it is irresponsible and immoral to expect that "something will turn up" in the near term to avoid climate catastrophe, and that leadership must stop such "climate dreaming," but climate denialists deny facts.[24] It is not entirely clear how climate recognition struggles will be resolved, because these kinds of struggles—as struggles—can resolve in numerous ways, although one at least senses that climate denialism is gradually losing ground, domestically and internationally.

The countervailing forces against climate denialism include shifting incentives toward a green energy technology transition. The steadily lowering costs of alternative energy sources away from fossil fuels increases the potential management of climate change through aggregate purchasing and investment. However, adding green technologies to energy economies only increases absolute energy consumption, and does not reduce fossil fuel consumption without heavy state intervention to subsidize green technologies and to place bans and caps on fossil fuels.[25] This creates a distributional political hurdle for all economies and aggravates the sources of climate denialism when state intervention constrains energy-intensive conservative ways of life. Ambitions of a "green new deal" are not simply an issue of sufficient climate initiative agency from governments; they are a considerable political hurdle. Dreams of eco-techno futures from breakthrough alternative energy technologies hope to dissolve these political hurdles, but technologies such as nuclear fusion and superconductors are not readily forthcoming.

Climate advocates have proposed a variety of modified global order responses to climate change, ranging from bottom-up green democracy, to green internationalism, an international "climate club," and pluralist green "cosmopolitan" globalism.[26] Because the hierarchy legitimation conflicts and recognition struggles facing an institutional green cosmopolitan order are excessively steep and intense, a thin pluralist internationalist green order interacting with "bottom-up" climate activists is the most that appears possible for the foreseeable future.[27] In a condition of world affairs that today is dividing horizontally by climate denial and vertically by North-South hierarchies plus East-West geopolitics, the integration of a green cosmopolitan future appears less than likely if not impossible. An internationalist green cosmopolitan order integrating state and nonstate actors appears to be the most feasible, with limited hierarchies and pluralist principles. While an *internationalist* green cosmopolitan order struggles to emerge, an *institutional* green cosmopolitan order is a relatively utopian prospect.

Green Utopias

The 21st century will be littered with failed and abandoned green utopias, but most will never be attempted.[28] Green globalism faces too many hurdles. A limited *internationalist green cosmopolitan order* is struggling to take shape. An *institutional green cosmopolitan order* with global-level green authorities is beyond the realm of possibility in the near to medium-term future.

Numerous green cosmopolitan utopias still populate political discourse today, however. Many of the leading public intellectuals of our times espouse them. None were more inventive and impressive than Bruno Latour's. For Latour, it is the modern distinction between human beings and nature that has made the ecological crisis possible, generating an entirely new form of "geo"-politics.[29] Unmaking this distinction, in making a "common world," is the mission.[30] In this sense, for thinkers such as Latour and Isabella Stengers, how the cosmos is understood is political. Latour's actor-network idea of "Gaia," the total planetary human and nonhuman network, is a framing device in that project.[31] For Latour, the planetary scale network of actant things is Gaia, the earth systems, incorporating everything and everyone on earth into one vast network of networks.[32] There is no human-only network.[33] From this framing of world politics, Latour proposed a "parliament of things" and other green political ordering innovations, including modified sovereignty.[34] Most spectacularly, the experiment "Make It Work," where participants simulated a parliament of things, desperately struggled to work, even in the absence of geopolitical actors, let alone climate denialists. Other thinkers have instead argued for a noninstitutional guerrilla-like "swarming" strategy of multilocal global activism, with doubtful prospects of success in a world of geostrategic competition, uneven development, and climate denialism.[35]

Daniel Deudney, among the most impressive and inventive thinkers in the field of International Relations, has argued that if planetary infrastructure were developed, then a radical green "cosmopolitan" order of sorts would also likely emerge, as a necessity, because the use of that infrastructure would have central control but planetary effects.[36] Climate-engineering proposals, for instance, striving to turn climate change into climate control, would require considerable international negotiations, as well as challenging demands to sell to publics an international climate-engineering agreement.[37] Anticipating the steep hierarchy legitimation challenges needed for such global-scale projects, Deudney has suggested, as a pragmatic normative proposal, a "terrapolitan" narrative of a planetary homeland needs to be spiritually supplemented by a "Gaia Earth religion."[38] A "terrapolitan" outlook, for Deudney, is the sense of all the Earth as a common homeland.[39] Deudney suggests that "the central basis of association in the global village must be the Earth (terra) and its requirements," and gestures toward "Earth nationality" and "Gaian Earth religion" as potentially common and unifying global identities.[40] To be clear, Deudney argues that "terrapolitanism" *should* be adopted, as a normative proposal, although it is unlikely that it *could*, especially on a global scale, due to the exceptionally steep hierarchy legitimation conflicts associated with it, ongoing climate recognition struggles, and geostrategic interests stymying any international negotiations.[41]

Awaiting an epochal green transformation of humankind is a new millenarianism, because it anticipates a future history that "must" happen, but, by all estimates and historical examples, won't. Dipesh Chakrabarty puzzles over the challenge of even imagining it:

> Climate change poses for us a question of a human collectivity, an us, pointing to a figure of the universal that escapes our capacity to experience the world. It is more like a universal that arises from a shared sense of a catastrophe. It calls for a global approach to politics without the myth of a global identity, for, unlike a Hegelian universal, it cannot subsume particularities. We may provisionally call it a "negative universal history."[42]

Sadly for green utopians, and possibly for all humankind, the future history of nature is subject to the nature of history. R. G. Collingwood grasped much of the puzzle, in his *Idea of Nature*, "that no one can understand natural science unless he understands history: and that no one can answer the question what nature is unless he knows what history is."[43]

The possible futures of the climate are not infinite, and most are bleak. There is a spectrum of possibilities, on a narrow band of from 2 to 6 degrees of global warming. While there are uncertainties about when climate "tipping points" will be reached and "runaway" climate change will accelerate warming to the higher ranges of the spectrum, the most likely climate future is a middle range 3 to 4 degrees. Action is being taken on a global scale and new technologies are being developed, but with not enough effect to realize the more ambitious climate future of 2 degrees of global warming. In a 3 to 4 degrees of global warming climate future, there will be mass migrations of hundreds of millions, with island nations, coastlines, and major cities— including London, Shanghai, and New York—slipping into the seas without major infrastructure investments, while mass global food shortages and the general intensification of insecurity will account for immense suffering and upwards of hundreds of millions of deaths. A 3 to 4 degrees global warming future is not apocalyptic in itself, but its stresses increase the risk of complete global entropy and the collapse of civilization. In this 3 to 4 degree future, global solidarities will be unforthcoming because they will have become pointless in a world too late to unmake climate change. States and the great powers will instead turn to their own interests. In this scenario, so clearly conveyed by Robert Falkner,

> humanity could find itself not in a "spaceship," with a captain ably steering its passengers to safety, but in a "lifeboat" that floats precariously on the ocean, without a leader in charge. . . . The desire to survive would not become a shared, collective, imperative for humanity, it would translate into a zero-sum logic that drives people and communities apart. . . . As the global climate crisis spirals out of control, collective management via international cooperation to reduce emissions is abandoned as nations individually seek to adapt to rising temperatures and safeguard their survival.[44]

Because states will need to adapt to survive, a climate catastrophe would be unlikely to compel demands for a green cosmopolitan order, because it will be too late.[45]

Conclusion

Modern science fiction is among other things a genre of cautionary tales. The new subgenre of climate science fiction such as the superstorms of Bruce Sterling's *Heavy Weather* tend to depict climate catastrophe as the bleak background of tales of misery and danger. It is not a nice place to be. For all its urgency, climate activism has yielded the bare minimum of its desired change. Anticipations of climate apocalypse and new imaginaries of planetary belonging have not really brought humankind together. Calls for an internationalist green cosmopolitan order tend to rely on legitimation strategies of disaster alarmism and vaguer promises of green techno-futures. But even the most accurate scientific estimates have encountered not only international buck-passing and foot-dragging, but, more oddly, climate deniers. Embroiled in recognition struggles with forces of nationalist climate denialism within states, and endless negotiations between states, only the thinnest and embattled climate regime has taken shape. In the long run, climate denialism may likely recede, as many reactionary movements do. It is not clear when is too late. The rise of geostrategic competition, however, has only further strained these tensions and the responsibilities of environmental stewardship. The greening of humankind in a dividing and disorderly world still has a long way to go.

PART III

SIX

Cosmopolitan Politics in a Disorderly World

In an era of international disorder, how is cosmopolitan belonging being reimagined and what role if any will cosmopolitan politics play? In the modern imagination, cosmopolitanism was always Derrida's "to come," yet to be, but today the future itself has become less clear in the wake of certain post–Cold War liberal cosmopolitan certainties.[1] In this era of uncertain disorder, Kant's criticism that Grotius' *civitas maxima* is "cold comfort" is as concerning as ever. States neglect restraint on the use of force and growing numbers of the vulnerable in international society have less and less recourse. Exploring these tensions between the uncertain future and disorderly present, my argument in this chapter is that cosmopolitanism today lacks the strengths and confidences it once had, and for some good reasons, but cosmopolitan politics broadly defined will remain important as an appeal to issues of injustice and minimal order in contexts crises and conflict. Neoliberal cosmopolitanism generated destabilizing inequality and liberal interventionism struggled to achieve its aims or legitimacy. People do not need or want that kind of cosmopolitan order, as states and populations have mobilized against it.[2] An increasingly disorderly world will, however, generate new injustices and crises, likely to be met by popular outcry and humanitarian concern. In such instances, it will remain possible to imagine and practice cosmopolitan politics and belonging in a deglobalizing and disorderly world, albeit in constrained ways and without the possibility of a cosmopolitan order.

To make this argument, I offer a sketch of the vertical and horizontal fault lines of the emerging international disorder and contrast them with past eras. I then explore the cosmopolitan tensions of this era and the role that cosmopolitan politics might play. Lastly, I consider the decline of the "future" itself for the relegitimation strategies and narratives of belonging available to cosmopolitan politics.

Disorder, Division, and the Illiberal Wave

An era of international disorder is increasingly defining international politics, as the "liberal" international order has become destabilized from within and is encountering new challengers from without.[3] By a world of increasing international disorder, I mean the frequency and intensity of disruptions and relative destabilizations of international relations, especially in the illegitimate use of force and political upheaval.[4] Since the revolt against globalism, world politics has become increasingly destabilized and disrupted in a combination of vertical geostrategic competition and horizontal populist unrest, manifesting war, political instability, and economic realignment. Cosmopolitan politics were attacked by populists and abandoned by the new nationalism in the process. "If you believe you are a citizen of the world, you are a citizen of nowhere," claimed UK prime minister Theresa May in 2016. The propagation of disorder in some respects has served the interests and ambitions of illiberal powers and illiberal populists. Russia's invasion of Ukraine meanwhile revived old dividing lines across international society, east, west, and south. In the aftermath of globalization and dividing international order, cosmopolitanism broadly defined has been almost completely displaced and delegitimated. Rather than becoming gradually more unified, world politics has become increasingly divisive, both between nations, and horizontally across groups and classes. Liberal cosmopolitanism, both economic and humanitarian, has been almost completely dispelled from world politics.

The new "illiberal tide" has used the open institutions of the liberal order for its advantage, in the contestation of liberal hierarchies and the demand for legitimacy recognition of illiberal politics.[5] Illiberal powers and populists have attacked and upended not only neoliberal globalization but also the possibility of liberal cosmopolitan politics more broadly. Like all political movements, the illiberal wave is varied and multifaceted. But the contested global hierarchies and assumed self-styled superiority of the liberal order have generated recognition struggles with a "merger of its discontents."[6] The cross-cutting tensions of the illiberal wave are within liberal states, and between liberal and illiberal states, albeit with variation across international society. The nuance in the analysis of liberal hierarchies and recognition struggles offered by Rebecca Adler-Nissen and Ayse Zarakol is worth quoting at length here:

> The LIO [liberal international order] promised to remove social and economic inequalities between the West and the non-West cre-

ated by previous international orders, but never quite managed to achieve equality within its own order. States in the semiperiphery blame the LIO for perpetuating the modern international system's historical hierarchies, and they resent its failed promises of equality. By contrast, in the core, discontented groups blame the LIO (and its elites) for stating aspirations of equality, which they resent for undermining or failing to protect historical hierarchies privileging Western supremacy. The semi-periphery group challenges the LIO as a Western-centric hierarchy, best replaced by a non-Western alternative. The core group wants to retain Western supremacy by dismantling the LIO itself. Nevertheless, the end result is the same: as an obstacle to the high-stature recognition they feel entitled to, the LIO is the perceived enemy of both recognition struggles.[7]

The new illiberalism has mobilized a wide range of illiberal political forces, connecting illiberal powers and actors to a wave of nationalist populist unrest.

The character of the new illiberalism is diverse in its composition, but commonly opposed to liberal internationalism and liberal cosmopolitan ideas of human rights. Like the 19th century and 20th century instantiations of illiberalism, the new illiberalism is highly anti-positivist. Its populist expression is even more feverishly against liberal democratic practices of facticity, while illiberal powers are now armed with digital subversion and information warfare capabilities.[8] On the international field, illiberal powers are recontesting the central institutions of international society and its predominant liberal norms by reviving and refurbishing old illiberal practices of sovereignty, international law, and illiberal economic order.[9] Illiberal war is also returning, in the illiberal character of Russia's war in Ukraine for instance, which has deeply contested the legitimate causes and conduct of war.[10] This contest of liberalism and illiberalism over the "rules of the game" will define the century, but its conduct is also defining the contestants. US national security advisor Jake Sullivan explains that a new era of geostrategic competition requires "laying a new foundation of American strength" and "revisiting long-held assumptions."[11] The United States and the vision of liberal internationalism is being reinvented, once more, casting off neoliberal cosmopolitan globalization for a new national economic and foreign policy.

Cosmopolitanism appears to be completely jettisoned from world politics, but this is not the first era of geostrategic competition and international disorder. The Cold War was not so long ago in the historical picture. By geostrategic competition, I mean a vertical relation of at least two great powers deploying force and levers of power in strategic interaction to gain advantage and constrain adversaries on a global scale.[12] The 18th century, for instance, experienced the competition of Britain and France, connecting Europe and their imperial periphery, followed in the 19th century by the competition of Britain and Russia, which, in the 20th century, following Germany and Japan's bids for hegemony in Europe and Asia, experienced the geostrategic competition of the US and USSR in the global Cold War. The central players in today's geostrategic competition are the US and China, plus Russia. All these eras of geostrategic competition have included a range of middle powers and geostrategically significant small powers playing a part in the strategic-diplomatic drama. These eras of geostrategic competition have also interestingly pitted a democratic or nominally democratic great power against an authoritarian great power.[13] The Cold War was more ideologically heated than other eras, as a contest over the definition of modernity and competing universal cosmopolitan visions.

The character of the political contest today is closer to a contest between alternative models of modernity, between the US-led liberal democratic global West and China plus Russia's cultural nationalist alternative, although again the crosscurrents of illiberalism cut across populism in liberal societies. Each power has its conceits. China, Russia, and other illiberal powers see themselves as carrying distinct cultural and historical missions to rebalance world politics away from the West toward a multipolar order, where the US and global West retain confidence in the merits of the liberal-democratic model. China has new confidence in its authoritarian capitalist model, while the West sees it as self-contradictory. China is not exporting revolution as the USSR did but China's leadership is confident about the contradictions of liberal capitalism and the strengths of their alternative model.[14] China's discourse of the "common destiny of mankind" is seemingly only in reference to the thinnest sense of common interests. In turn, the West retains beliefs in the resilience of market capitalism and the virtues of democracy, while China sees these as contradictory. Human rights and liberal democratic values have far less reach and appeal across the global south and in parts of the West today. The US nevertheless is seeking to *outcompete* China by leveraging the weight of its alliances and dynamism of its innovative permissive market model, while China is seeking to *outnumber* and *outlast* the West by leveraging the global south and the durability of its greater domestic stability.

Neither however has a strategy that in principle could feasibly apply to all humankind. World order politics are at an impasse and the future is being made increasingly uncertain the more intensely the great powers compete to shape it.

In this contest, the fracturing of world politics is both deeper and less rigid than many tend to appreciate.[15] The Cold War had its reliable certainties. Economic inequalities during the Cold War were less intense in the West, and political polarization was less severe. The horizontal divisions today are more unstable in the Western world, with ongoing mobilizations of domestic unrest. "Western political fragmentation and volatility have also exposed new vulnerabilities, as illiberal states have sought to capitalize on these divisions by stoking nationalism and fomenting unrest within the West."[16] On the international level, alliances and nonalignment were also more fixed during the Cold War, and offered an alternative global vision, while an array of multialigned and active nonaligned states today have no fixed positions, engaging on issue-specific agendas and shifting initiatives. New and revived vertical status "in-groups" are forming around the BRICS (Brazil, Russia, India, China, South Africa) and the Group of 7 (G7), while inclusive multilateral groupings have diminished utility under geopolitical constraints but also increased reform contestation.[17] Vertical divisions between states today remain complicated by their already globalized economies, placing limits on strategic deglobalization and economic realignments.[18] Crosscutting the vertical and the horizontal divisions furthermore are new "digital empires" being constructed by the United States, China, and the EU. Even the biggest big tech companies struggle in navigating this new geo-digital strategic competition:

> This is part of a broader challenge faced by tech companies that operate globally, navigating different demands of American, Chinese, and European regulatory models. When these models collide, they can fuel horizontal battles between governments. . . . But they also fuel vertical battles featuring tech companies on one side and governments on the other. . . . In these instances, different vertical battles intersect, thrusting tech companies into the midst of conflicting regulatory regimes and presenting them with increasingly irresolvable regulatory dilemmas.[19]

The era of digital-cosmopolitan Silicon Valley utopianism is long past. Information warfare is deliberately dividing publics against themselves with increasing sophistication, and cyber warfare capabilities have produced an era described as "unpeace," a state of constant and persistent low intensity disorder subject to uncertain thresholds of escalation.[20] The liberal cosmopolitan warriors of the 1990s and early 2000s have been replaced not only by new nationalist and mercenary forces in today's battlefields but also by multidomain "connectivity warriors" manipulating nodes in vertical and horizontal networks.[21] This ripening international disorder is dividing international society vertically and dividing societies horizontally in ways unlike past eras of geostrategic competition.

In this divisive disordering of world politics, cosmopolitanism has been completely displaced, attacked, and disoriented. In a world dividing horizontally and vertically between new "digital empires," Orwell's dystopian vision of a divided global disorder depicted in his *Nineteen Eighty-Four* more closely approximates the future than Tennyson's federation of the world. What place is there for a cosmopolitan politics in a world where geostrategic competition is redividing the world and where populations mobilizing national identities express open hostility to it?

Cosmopolitanism after Globalism

The emergence of "globalism" in the early 20th century, and its revival in the early 21st, was a response to the perception that political division in a global setting was both a source of and obstacle to addressing pressing international order problems.[22] In the 21st century collapse of globalism and the fracturing of world politics, institutional cosmopolitanism is impossible and internationalist cosmopolitanism is increasingly difficult because of deepening vertical threat perceptions between the US and China and horizontal exclusionary nationalist politics. As a body of ideas and practices about global belonging challenging divisive interests and injustices in international society, cosmopolitan politics is no longer able to reasonably take on a revolutionary transformative ambition. Instead, cosmopolitan politics will continue to play an activist role in a dividing world, where humanitarian crises and injustices emerge and neglected global challenges intensify. The form cosmopolitan politics will take is yet to be seen, but cosmopolitan politics broadly understood has numerous currents with contemporary expression, as we have seen. Local cosmopolitan responses to local injustices also continue to matter.[23] International-level issues of distributive justice, the humanitarian laws of war, nuclear arms control, and ecological stewardship remain important but increasingly neglected causes in a dividing international society. Even while more ambitious cosmopolitan order transformations are unlikely to emerge any time soon, advocating from the "bottom up" will likely matter for issues of injustice and calls for a minimal degree of order in extreme crises.

As much as the emerging international disorder differs from past eras of geostrategic competition, it is remarkable how many of the unfinished challenges and problems troubling the Cold War era feed into the New Cold War today, including not least nuclear proliferation and ecological crisis, and the Korean War itself. It is astonishing moreover how far these problems have gradually worsened over the decades. The gradual intensification of the global climate crisis is reaching critical thresholds, North Korea is now a nuclear power, and the United States faces not one peer nuclear weapons power, as in the Cuban Missile Crisis, but now faces two, in China and Russia, plus North Korea. These challenges have suggested to some the need for reviving the World Order Models Project.[24] This project was the largest and longest lasting world order study in its field, aiming to develop feasible world order models addressing common global interests as institutional cosmopolitan alternatives to contending Cold War visions.[25] In this new era of geopolitical tensions, the World Order Models Project appears to be dramatically ahead of its time, in the global diversity of its membership and in the pluralism of its world order proposals. A new WOMP-style project today can provide "a counter-narrative in globoskeptical times," as an alternative to geostrategic visions.[26] As a practical possibility, radical cosmopolitan world order alternatives are virtually utopian in present circumstances, although incremental modifications to practice are possible. The same geostrategic divisions that cosmopolitan politics aims to ameliorate intensify the obstacles and resistance to cosmopolitan alternatives into the foreseeable future.

Many see this impasse at the geopolitical level as devolving cosmopolitan responsibility and global governance to the regional level, in an emerging "multiplex" order. Through a regional path to order, in the very long term, a picture is imaginable of overlapping regional orders and security communities[27] that through a "stepping-stone" process gradually integrate regional institutions into global-level institutions, forming a globally semi-integrated and pluralistic institutional cosmopolitan order including nonstate actors alongside states.[28] The possibility for the realization of this picture as a gradual stepping-stone pathway to world order is arguably so far into the future, however, that its likelihood is not open to reasonable speculation in the present. Insofar as a "multiplex" order is emerging, its horizontal and vertical divisions manifesting war and disorder in every region remain steep hurdles to more than minimal order in world politics.

The arguments made in chapter 1 suggest that the theorized structural-security interdependence imperatives of modernity have not and cannot be reasonably expected to generate the long-term global positive social-ization processes that Wendt anticipates. In 100 years, the unanticipated should be anticipated, and the lack of any evidence of nuclear security–imperative socialization after decades of nuclear arms races and prolifera-tion suggests that the speculative theory is based on false or misguided assumptions. Wendt's argument was based on the security interdepen-dence challenges of nuclear proliferation. But what about artificial intel-ligence? Well, there is a danger of "species replacement."[29] Does this give an added but also different push behind a kind of cosmopolitan order-ing response? Unlikely, because what ghosts in machines as are being made today are growing up in an era of geostrategic competition and resurgent nationalism. Illiberal powers moreover make illiberal uses of technology. Russia uses precision missiles to target civilians in its illib-eral war in Ukraine, while liberal powers invented these weapons for their formerly opposite liberal humane warfare.[30] The AI will have a mind of its own, however, and it may be better. An AI super intelligence may be able to grasp the cosmos in ways beyond human comprehension. An AI super intelligence cosmopolitan of the future will embrace much more than humans and machines, in the great macro-techno cyber belonging. Whether humans would accept it is unclear, although they may need it. Humans would need more than Kantian or techno-utilitarian arguments to accept it. Only an artificial intelligence can truly be a Kantian.[31] For humankind and intelligent machine to embrace, the machine would have to tell a very good story that humankind could get behind, to legitimate the machine's de facto hierarchy, and to recognize human self-worth.

Back to the present, some may insist that a cosmopolitan peace is in principle possible today with the right guidance. The latest in the tradition of perpetual peace proposals is Alex Bellamy's *World Peace (And How We Can Achieve It)*. Like others in this tradition, including such celebrated and admirable thinkers as William Penn, L'Abbé de Saint-Pierre, Imman-uel Kant, and Jeremy Bentham, Bellamy's *World Peace* is eloquent, uplift-ing, and intellectually formidable. Consistent with its tradition, however, the hurdles to a cosmopolitan world peace are steeper and more treacher-ous than the presentation of its proposal would suggest. Bellamy holds three "building blocks" as necessary conditions of peace: (1) "the modern state, the bedrock of everyday peace"; (2) making war unprofitable and its irrationality more widely known, "to make war less appealing as a rational option"; and (3) "to reshape our emotional sensibilities away from nationalism and war, toward more cosmopolitan, compassionate, and peaceful inclinations."[32] On these building blocks, Bellamy proposes a peace plan, with six preliminary articles, three definitive articles, and one additional imperative article, together constituting an internationalist cosmopolitan order model, nesting a multitude of local "minor utopias." For Bellamy, the costs of a cosmopolitan world state are unnecessary and problematic in the absence of an existing cosmopolitan community. "A sense of community reaching across nations is possible only if there is peace in the first place."[33] The problem of international peace that Bellamy's studied articles aim to resolve is compliance with international law by constructing peace, rather than the enforcement of international law. World politics today is obviously far away from such a peace, but that's not the point; it is the hurdles that crop up along the way of its pursuit. The hurdles I see most clearly are hierarchy legitimation conflicts and recognition struggles, although there are more. Bellamy's first article, for example, is compliance with international law on the use of force, plus—somewhat remarkably—the collective security proviso that "no Permanent Member of the UN Security Council should use a veto to prevent collective action in response to armed aggression of the threat or commission of genocide, war crimes, and crimes against humanity."[34] The modification of the veto itself is not proposed, only the norms of its use, which in principle is possible. The issue is the hierarchy situations that this threatens—especially the five permanent members of the UN Security Council, the P5 states—in the political uncertainty of whose view will prevail on what instances will count as armed aggressions or crimes against humanity. If a resolution passes that declares that a conflict counts as such, all international society would be legally required to obey, making the hierarchy legitimation conflict considerably steep. Article 4 of Bellamy's proposal requires that "states shall establish and sustain security communities with their neighbours."[35] Again, this in principle is possible, through positive social interaction, but the hurdle of recognition struggles crops up in the process, within regions and between liberal and illiberal security communities, for instance, making the outcome of the process unclear, disorderly, and likely socially negative. I am not saying that such a peace is impossible, but that it is more difficult that we might be led to hope. The construction of peace, moreover, may take a much longer time in overcoming its hurdles than is at first even fathomed, not least because the construction of war has such a head start.[36]

In our world today, the role that cosmopolitan politics is likely to play in a context of increasing geopolitical and geostrategic competition is at best to pressure great powers to exercise responsibility and restraint, especially in contexts of severe injustice and humanitarian emergency. Cosmopolitan politics is not necessarily a source of disorder, and, quite the opposite, through norm entrepreneurship and public pressure, is a source of more just order in world politics.[37] Across the modern international experience, nonstate actors demanding rights, freedoms, and pointing out moral obligations have made not inconsiderable advances, even while their more ambitious visions are unrealized. Cosmopolitan politics will likely continue to do so in future, although major inroads and change are unlikely to arise until past the peak of this era of division and disorder, when geopolitical tensions subside again and the illiberal wave rolls back.

Cosmopolitanism in Uncertain Times

The real problem for cosmopolitans is not so much the fracturing of world politics (imagining cosmopolitan belonging never required actual connections or interdependence; these things actually made practicing liberal cosmopolitan belonging difficult in practice);[38] it is the delegitimation of cosmopolitan politics as such, vertically between the liberal West and illiberal powers, and horizontally with antiglobalist nationalist populism. There is no obvious legitimation strategy available because liberal cosmopolitanism has been so embattled and displaced.

What's more, while it is true that international politics has never been especially orderly, the stories about better-ordered futures have begun to fall away, especially in the West. The death of triumphalist liberal globalism has at once been the "death of the stories that gave us a future and proposed a means of acting in a politically efficacious manner."[39] Has history returned, or has a Western idea of the future been abandoned?[40] China's history is its own; it does not claim modernity for itself, only to have made an alternative model. Cosmopolitan imaginaries in the modern global world have almost exclusively occupied the future. Contrary to the realist tradition that believes in a timeless international politics, revolutionary cosmopolitan orders were the destination of Kantian and Marxian philosophies of history. Francis Fukuyama thought that destination had been reached in liberal capitalism, and when its spell broke, he left no obvious candidates to take its place. In his Hegelian history, however, "Fukuyama departs from the most important discovery in modern science. As understood by Charles Darwin, evolution has no destination."[41] The problem cosmopolitanism faces in these uncertain times is not overcoming a dividing world but overcoming the idea of its necessary unity in the future.[42]

Samuel Moyn instead wishes to reinvent the future, by reinventing liberalism. In his widely read *Liberalism against Itself*, Moyn suggests that Cold War liberalism's construction of ideas against Soviet utopias and totalitarian realities also—somewhat accidentally—displaced the potential for "Hegelian progress." In the wake of neoliberalism, Moyn calls for liberalism's progressive reinvention:

> The endless revival of its Cold War version has been a means of avoiding the only hope for liberalism, which is to reinvent it beyond the terms we have known. It would have to be freed from the entanglements that were invented or intensified during the early Cold War years. And it would have to reincorporate some of the nineteenth-century impulses purged and left behind in the Cold War years, in particular its commitment to the emancipation of our powers, the creation of the new as the highest life, and the acquisition of both in a story that connects our past and our future.[43]

Abandoning Cold War liberalism precisely in an era of geostrategic competition is counterintuitive, but like most utopian calls, it is deliberately out of step with practice. Moyn argues that Cold War liberalism legitimated the prosecution of the Cold War and so wishes to invent a better liberalism, to avoid legitimating a New Cold War and make another future possible. Sadly, geostrategic competition will proceed with or without intellectual justification, and it is doubtful that any reinvented liberal future will realize emancipation any more than its past attempts.

Conclusion

In the opening discussion of his "Plan for an Universal and Perpetual Peace," the 19th century utilitarian philosopher Jeremy Bentham argued, "Let it not be objected that the age is not ripe for such a proposal: the more it wants of being ripe, the sooner we should begin to do what can be done to ripen it; the more we should do to ripen it."[44] The times today are especially unripe because the belief that they can be ripened in the future is unclear. Neoliberal cosmopolitanism's end of history generated destabilizing inequality and liberal interventionism struggled to achieve its aims or legitimacy. People do not need or want that kind of cosmopolitan order, as states and populations have mobilized against it.[45] Cosmopolitan concerns and action are nevertheless likely to return, in some yet to be seen expression, where extreme crisis and injustice arise. Even while the tensions of the modern global world are insufficient to transform it (as many once anticipated), they nevertheless continue to generate popular outcry against intolerable injustices and disorders where they crop up. It will remain possible to imagine global belonging in a deglobalizing world and to practice cosmopolitan politics without the possibility of a cosmopolitan order. Dividing horizontally and vertically in multiple domains and every region, international politics is experiencing an era of intensifying disorder, rather than the once widespread anticipations of an emerging global cosmopolitan order. At what time conditions may again ripen for something different is beyond reckoning, so remote into the future. Until such times return, rather than reimagining its own future, cosmopolitan politics will do better to focus on the injustices and crises present in a disorderly world today.

Conclusion

In 1920, H. G. Wells met V. I. Lenin in Moscow, in the Kremlin, in Lenin's office. Wells's later essay on this meeting, "The Dreamer in the Kremlin," could have been better titled "The Two Dreamers in the Kremlin," since Wells himself was an even more prolific dreamer of an idyllic planetary utopia than Lenin. The two shared a dream of a global socialist union of humankind, with some differences, while they disagreed on how to realize it. Wells wrote later, in 1933:

> Our talk was threaded throughout and held together by two—what shall I call them?—*motifs*. One was from me to him: "What do you think you are making of Russia? What is the state you are trying to create?" The other was from him to me: "Why does not the social revolution begin in England? Why do you not work for the social revolution? Why are you not destroying Capitalism and establishing the Communist State?"[1]

Wells returned to Moscow in 1934. In conversation with Stalin, he suggested, "The big ship is humanity, not a class." Stalin responded, "You, Mr Wells, evidently start out with the assumption that all men are good. I, however, do not forget that there are many wicked men. I do not believe in the goodness of the bourgeoisie."[2] None of these dreamers—Wells, Lenin, Stalin—grasped the future all that clearly, because they filled it with dreams that had little to do with the political conflicts and struggles of their present realities.

Released into the modern global world, these dreams of cosmopolitan orders were overwhelmed by the very divisions and disorder they sought to overcome. The Kantian Cosmopolitan call for universal human rights continually encountered hierarchy legitimation conflicts with a range of states as well as recognition struggles with illiberal societies. The Marxian imaginary of a universal proletariat struggled with internal schisms and was met with liberal counterrevolutionary forces of unanticipated resolve and resilience, up to the dissolution of global Marxist struggle itself. Amid these upheavals, postcolonial cosmopolitanism advanced distinctive ways of imagining cosmopolitan belonging and global order alternatives, but was resisted and undercut by neoliberal globalization. Lastly, green cosmopolitan imaginaries may today be taking root, but remain puzzlingly resisted and embattled by nationalist climate denialism.

The argument of this book has been that cosmopolitan ordering discourses and practices have encountered and been overwhelmed by hierarchy legitimation conflicts and recognition struggles that have reasserted modern state power and remobilized exclusionary nationalist identities, especially when intensified in contexts of international instability and economic turmoil. Advocating cosmopolitan ordering in practice, be it through internationalist cosmopolitan obligations or as cosmopolitan institutions, implies hierarchical relations formal or informal and real or imagined, of some states or authorities over others, needing legitimation. Claims to the existence of a cosmopolitan community virtually always generate recognition struggles with identities not finding themselves included and not "fitting in" the supposedly all-embracing cosmopolitan vision. Cosmopolitan narratives of global belonging are particularly prone to recognition struggles precisely because they aim to be all-embracing. This argument does not explain the collapse of globalism, the rise of populism, and deglobalization as such, which have their own growing literatures.[3] My argument instead understands these destabilizing trends as contexts intensifying ongoing hierarchy legitimation conflicts and recognition struggles that have embroiled and repeatedly overwhelmed cosmopolitan politics in the modern world.

This argument has implications for the theory of international order and for advocates and critics of cosmopolitan order alternatives in practice. For theory, this argument clarifies the explanation and understanding of the limits of cosmopolitan ordering in the modern global world. It explains why the increasing "dynamic densities" of globalizing interdependence and interaction capacities have been insufficient to generate global solidarity and stabilize a cosmopolitan order.[4] It also offers a counterargument to realists who suggest that the return of great power politics and the collapse of globalism have vindicated their theoretical assumptions. Conventional structural realist explanations of persistent global disunity remain unconvincing and misleading.[5] I make the case that cosmopolitan and national belonging have been co-constitutive in the modern international experience, that nations are not latent or pre-existing obstacles to internationalist cosmopolitanism as realists assume but are instead reconstituted as exclusionary in processes of recognition struggle and reassertion of nation-state authority. Contrary to realist thinkers, moreover, I make the case that it is not only or simply the continued diffusion of power that matters, but also the social processes of hierarchy legitimation conflicts and recognition struggles that have reconstituted a socially and politically divided international society. Along the way, these theoretical correctives of constructivism and criticism of realist assumptions and explanations also take issue with Alexander Wendt's arguments about the structural socialization imperatives of modernity, as well as his concept of (world) state as a substantive "person" dissolving identities, rather than "nesting" overlapping identities.[6] These theoretical arguments are not good news for advocates of cosmopolitan politics, but it does clarify the hurdles to managing legitimation strategies and recognition struggles in practice.

If Tennyson's dream is ever to be made real, who is to say but perhaps one day. For how it might or might not happen, and why it has not yet, think about the long story of struggles and dreams in the modern international experience: the call for liberties and human rights, their trials and upheavals; the universal proletariat and its global revolutionary struggle; the unmaking of empires, the remaking of freedom, and battles of decolonization; and in the greening of humankind in a dividing and disorderly world.

Epilogue

Cosmopolitanism without Fanaticism?

Martin Wight's thought on international politics has been a source of help-ful reflection and inspiration in researching this book, and his category of cosmopolitan "revolutionist" international thought and practice has provided an instrumental framing device in its design. Engaging Wight's thought across this study has drawn out lingering questions about Wight's categories. Are there general impressions about this category of thought left by Wight that offer any further insight and reflection?

On the one hand, Wight devised the category simply as a pedagogical device, to organize international theory in a way suitable for teaching and learning at an introductory level.[1] On the other hand, Wight was a Cold War thinker crafting intellectual defenses against revolutionary commu-nism, as well as a British thinker grappling with the decline of the British Empire.[2] Consider how Wight describes the category of "revolutionist" international thought:

> The Revolutionists can be defined more precisely as those who believe so passionately in the moral unity of the society of states or international society, that they identify themselves with it, and therefore they both claim to speak in the name of this unity, and experience an overriding obligation to give effect to it, as the first aim of their international policies. For them, the whole of inter-national society transcends its parts; they are cosmopolitan rather than "internationalist," and their international theory and policy has "a missionary character."[3]

Wight's disciple, Hedley Bull, echoes this framing:

The Kantian or universalist tradition, at the other extreme, takes the essential nature of international politics to lie not in conflict among states, as on the Hobbesian view, but in the trans-national social bonds that link the individual human beings who are the subjects or citizens of states. The dominant theme of international relations, on the Kantian view, is only apparently the relationship among states, and is really the relationship among all men in the community of mankind—which exists potentially, even if does not exist actually, and which when it comes into being will sweep the system of states into limbo.[4]

These descriptions are not damning, but neither are they clearly sympathetic.[5] Perhaps Wight wished to avoid giving the impression that the entire category of Kantian revolutionary thought and practice was a pejorative device. But his framing of international theory favors Grotian rationalism by casting the alternatives as extremes.

A careful reading shows that Wight distinguished "hard" from "soft" revolutionists:

> *Hard Revolutionists* believe in creating the brotherhood of mankind, or *civitas maxima*, in which international politics will be assimilated to the condition of domestic politics, by violence. *Soft Revolutionists* aim at this through yearning and talk.[6]

Wight includes Lenin as a hard revolutionist, but also "Kant, William Jennings Bryan, Andrew Carnegie, Woodrow Wilson, Cordell Hull, Franklin Roosevelt, Henry Wallace, the British and French neutralists, and Nehru."[7] If not an outright counterrevolutionary, Wight sees problems in revolutionary strategy, in his concerns about the violence of *hard* revolutionism and his dismissal of *soft* revolutionism as "yearning and talk."

Wight himself was a pacifist in early life, possibly what he called an "Inverted Revolutionist."[8] For Wight, this category

> is "inverted" because it repudiates the use of power altogether; it is "Revolutionist" because it sees this repudiation as a principle of universal validity, and energetically promotes its acceptance. It has a missionary character. . . . Inverted Revolutionism has two main sources: one is Hindu philosophy and the example of Gandhi; the other is Anglo-Saxon Christianity and the example of the Quakers. However its most articulate theorist was a Russian, Tolstoy[9]

He explains:

> Inverted Revolutionism in its classic form is fed by a pessimistic estimate of human nature, not an optimistic one. This bleak view of mankind may explain why pacifists, if they descend from being above the battle to entering the fray, tend to adopt a Realist stance.[10]

Amid the intellectual fray of the Cold War, Wight often displayed classical realist characteristics, although he insisted on a Grotian understanding of Western values.[11]

Bull elsewhere suggests that, for Wight, "there was much about the Kantians—'The Political Missionaries or Fanatics', as he called them in his early drafts of his lectures—that repelled him."[12] In an early draft of his LSE lectures, however, Wight encourages the "idealism of the Kantians, without their fanaticism."[13] Another Cold War thinker, Isaiah Berlin, in his essay "A Revolutionary without Fanaticism," applauds the Russian Alexander Herzen for being this kind of political thinker whose

> attitude led not to detachment or quietism—to the tolerant conservativism of Hume or Bagehot—but was allied to an impatient, passionate, rebellious temperament, which made him the rarest of characters, *a revolutionary without fanaticism*, a man ready for violent change, never in the name of abstract principles, but only of actual misery and injustice, of concrete conditions so bad that men were morally not permitted—and knew they were not permitted—to let them exist.[14]

Not for abstract principles, but for actual miseries and injustices. Revolutionaries without fanaticism for Berlin include "Erasmus, Montaigne, Bayle and Fontenelle, Voltaire and Constant, Humbolt and the English philosophical radicals."[15] Among 20th and 21st century intellectuals, we could venture to consider a number more.

Wight suggested that revolutionism is "less a tradition than a series of waves."[16] In a divisive era after liberal cosmopolitanism's high point, perhaps a more pluralistic revolutionism without fanaticism will be the character of its next wave.

Notes

Introduction

1. Kathryn Sikkink, *The Justice Cascade: How Human Rights Prosecutions Are Changing World Politics* (New York: W.W. Norton, 2011); Michael Barnett and Kathryn Sikkink, "From International Relations to Global Society," in *The Oxford Handbook of International Relations*, ed. Christian Reus-Smit and Duncan Snidal (Oxford: Oxford University Press, 2008), 62–83; Ulrich Beck, *The Cosmopolitan Vision* (Cambridge: Polity Press, 2006); Barry Buzan, *From International to World Society? English School Theory and the Social Structure of Globalization* (Cambridge: Cambridge University Press, 2004); Mary Kaldor, "The Idea of Global Civil Society," *International Affairs* 79, no. 3 (2003): 583–93; David Held and Anthony McGrew, "The End of the Old Order? Globalization and the Prospects for World Order," *Review of International Studies* 24, no. 5 (1999): 219–45; J. G. Ruggie, *Constructing the World Polity: Essays on International Institutionalization* (London: Routledge, 1998); Jessica T. Mathews, "Power Shift," *Foreign Affairs* 76 (1997): 50–66.

2. Peter Trubowitz and Brian Burgoon, *Geopolitics and Democracy: The Western Liberal Order from Foundation to Fracture* (Oxford: Oxford University Press, 2023); Gary Gerstle, *The Rise and Fall of the Neoliberal Order: America and the World in the Free Market* (Oxford: Oxford University Press, 2022); Markus Kornprobst and T. V. Paul, "Globalization, Deglobalization and the Liberal International Order," *International Affairs* 97, no. 5 (2021): 1305–16; Pippa Norris and Ronald Inglehart, *Cultural Backlash: Trump, Brexit, and Authoritarian Populism* (Cambridge: Cambridge University Press, 2019).

3. J. G. Ruggie, "Continuity and Transformation in the World Polity: Towards a Neorealist Synthesis," *World Politics* 35, no. 2 (1983): 261–85.

4. I say conventional "realist" explanations, because realism is an internally diverse tradition, some strains of which have been argued to be compatible with "cosmopolitan" world order proposals. William E. Scheuerman, "Realism and the Kantian Tradition: A Revisionist Account," *International Relations* 26, no. 4 (2012): 453–77; Richard Beardsworth, "Cosmopolitanism and Realism: Towards a Theoretical Convergence?," *Millennium: Journal of International Studies* 37, no. 1 (2008): 69–96.

5. The theoretical correctives of constructivism and criticism of realist assumptions

and explanations I make also take issue with Alexander Wendt's arguments about the structural socialization imperatives of modernity, as well as his concept of a world state "as person" dissolving identities, rather than "nesting" overlapping identities. Alexander Wendt, "Why a World State Is Inevitable," *European Journal of International Relations* 9, no. 4 (2003): 491–542.

6. By the modern global world, I mean the emergence of modern sources of power and globalization of the modern society of states. Tim Dunne and Christian Reus-Smit, eds., *The Globalization of International Society* (Oxford: Oxford University Press, 2017); Barry Buzan and George Lawson, *The Global Transformation: History, Modernity and the Making of International Relations* (Cambridge: Cambridge University Press, 2015); Jurgen Osterhammel, *The Transformation of the World: A Global History of the Nineteenth Century* (Princeton: Princeton University Press, 2014).

7. Susan Pedersen, *The Guardians: The League of Nations and the Crisis of Empire* (Oxford: Oxford University Press, 2015); Ian Clark, *International Legitimacy and World Society* (Oxford: Oxford University Press, 2007); Margaret MacMillan, *Paris 1919: Six Months That Changed the World* (New York: Random House, 2003).

8. Tara Zahra, *Against the World: Anti-Globalism and Mass Politics between the World Wars* (New York: W.W. Norton, 2023); Mark Mazower, *Dark Continent: Europe's Twentieth Century* (London: Penguin, 1998).

9. Other notable interwar calls for world federation include W. B. Curry, *The Case for Federal Union: A New International Order* (Harmondsworth: Penguin, 1939); Oscar Newfang, *World Government* (New York: Barnes & Noble, 1942); E. B. White, *The Wild Flag* (Boston: Houghton Mifflin, 1943); Ralph Barton Perry, *One World in the Making* (New York: Current Books, 1945).

10. Among academics active at the time was the world community symposium whose attendance notably included Hans Morgenthau, Margaret Mead, Kenneth Boulding, Harold Laswell, Talcott Parsons, and Karl Polanyi. Quincy Wright, ed., *The World Community* (Chicago: University of Chicago Press, 1948).

11. Hans J. Morgenthau, *Politics among Nations: The Struggle for Power and Peace*, 1st ed. (New York: Alfred A. Knopf, 1948), 412–13; David Mitrany, *A Working Peace System: An Argument for the Functional Development of International Organization* (London: Royal Institute of International Affairs, 1943); numerous thinkers in this era called for similar world order models as problem-solving theory, such as E. B. Haas, *Beyond the Nation State: Functionalism and International Organization* (Stanford: Stanford University Press, 1964); E. H. Carr, *Nationalism and after, with a New Introduction from Michael Cox* (London: Macmillan, [1945] 2021); See William E. Scheuerman, *The Realist Case for Global Reform* (Cambridge: Polity Press, 2011); Campbell Craig, *Glimmer of a New Leviathan* (New York: Columbia University Press, 2003).

12. Thomas G. Weiss, "What Happened to the Idea of World Government?," *International Studies Quarterly* 53, no. 2 (2009): 253–71.

13. Wendell Wilkie, *One World* (New York: Simon and Schuster, 1943); Samuel Zipp, *The Idealist: Wendell Wilkie's Wartime Quest to Build One World* (Cambridge, MA: Belknap Press of Harvard University Press, 2020).

14. Franklin D. Roosevelt, "Fourth Inaugural Address," January 20, 1945. https://avalon.law.yale.edu/20th_century/froos4.asp

15. Nancy Fraser, et al., *Transnationalizing the Public Sphere* (Cambridge: Polity

Press, 2014); Nancy Fraser, *Scales of Justice: Reimagining Political Space in a Globalizing World* (New York: Columbia University Press, 2009); Nancy Fraser, "Reframing Justice in a Globalizing World," *New Left Review* 36 (2005): 69–88; Daniele Archibugi and David Held, eds., *Cosmopolitan Democracy: An Agenda for a New World Order* (Cambridge: Polity, 1995); David Held, *Democracy and the Global Order: From the Modern State to Cosmopolitan Governance* (Cambridge: Polity, 1995).

16. Ayse Zarakol, ed., *Hierarchies in World Politics* (Cambridge: Cambridge University Press, 2017). I take a broadly Weberian-influenced view of the concept of "legitimation," as the social processes of constructing beliefs in populations that relations of political authority are legitimate, contributing to its stabilization. Legitimation in this way sets parameters for tolerable and intolerable relations and actions. Legitimation as such is an exercise of social power and the mechanisms of legitimation combine ongoing processes of discursive action and performative practice, enabling a wide range of legitimation strategies. As an exercise of power, it is not coercive as such, but subject to legitimation strategies. Calls for cosmopolitan orders, in this sense, tend to seek legitimation through discursive appeals to moral authority, justice, and common interests, combined with "selfless" or "other-regarding" practices, such as international humanitarian action or institutional cosmopolitan ordering arrangements. Jens Steffek, "The Legitimation of International Governance: A Discourse Approach," *European Journal of International Relations* 9, no. 2 (2003): 271; Patrick Thaddeus Jackson, "Rethinking Weber: Towards a Non-Individualist Sociology of World Politics," *International Review of Sociology* 12, no. 3 (2002): 439–68; Ian Clark, *Legitimacy in International Society* (Oxford: Oxford University Press, 2005).

17. I do not define recognition struggles as demands for recognition of an "internal" authentic self, which is a culturally specific conception of identity. Nor do I define recognition as *thymos*, or similar ancient Greek concepts. Rebecca Adler-Nissen and Ayse Zarakol, "Struggles for Recognition: The Liberal International Order and the Merger of Its Discontents," *International Organization* 75, no. 2 (2020): 611–34; Michelle Murray, *The Struggle for Recognition in International Relations: Status, Revisionism, and Rising Powers* (Oxford: Oxford University Press, 2019); Francis Fukuyama, *Identity: The Demand for Dignity and the Politics of Resentment* (New York: Profile Books, 2018); Jens Bartelson, "Three Concepts of Recognition," *International Theory* 5, no. 1 (2013), 107–29; Hans Agné et al., "Symposium: The Politics of International Recognition," *International Theory* 5 no. 1 (2013): 94–107; Axel Honneth, "Recognition between States: On the Moral Substrate of International Relations," in *The I in We: Studies in the Theory of Recognition* (Cambridge: Polity, 2012), 137–52; Axel Honneth, *The Struggle for Recognition: The Moral Grammar of Social Conflicts* (Cambridge, MA: MIT Press, 1995); Charles Taylor, "The Politics of Recognition," in *Multiculturalism*, ed. Amy Gutman (Princeton: Princeton University Press, 1994), 25–74.

18. Craig Calhoun, *Nations Matter: Culture, History, and the Cosmopolitan Dream* (London: Routledge, 2007); James Mayall, *Nationalism and International Society* (Cambridge: Cambridge University Press, 1990); Benedict Anderson, *Imagined Communities: Reflections on the Origin and Spread of Nationalism* (London: Verso, 1983).

19. Martha C. Nussbaum, *The Cosmopolitan Tradition: A Noble but Flawed Ideal* (Cambridge, MA: Belknap Press of Harvard University Press, 2019).

20. Adam K. Webb, *Deep Cosmopolis: Rethinking World Politics and Globalization*

(London: Routledge, 2015); Robert J. Holton, *Cosmopolitanisms: New Thinking and New Directions* (London: Palgrave, 2009); Pheng Cheah and Bruce Robbins, eds., *Cosmopolitics: Thinking and Feeling beyond the Nation* (Minneapolis: University of Minnesota Press, 1998).

21. Martin Wight, *International Theory: The Three Traditions* (New York: Holmes & Meier for the Royal Institute of International Affairs, 1992).

22. Luis Cabrera, ed., *Institutional Cosmopolitanism* (Oxford: Oxford University Press, 2018).

23. For ideal types, see Patrick Thaddeus Jackson, *The Conduct of Inquiry in International Relations: The Philosophy of Science and Its Implications for the Study of World Politics* (London: Routledge, 2011), 37; Edward Keene, "International Society as an Ideal Type," in *Theorising International Society: English School Methods*, ed. Cornelia Navari (London: Palgrave, 2009), 104–24.

24. This is further clarified in chapter 1.

25. Andrew Hurrell, *On Global Order: Power, Values and the Constitution of International Society* (Oxford: Oxford University Press, 2007); G. John Ikenberry, *After Victory: Institutions, Strategic Restraint, and the Rebuilding of Order after Major Wars* (Princeton: Princeton University Press, 2001). Insofar as structural realists contend that order may emerge spontaneously between independent security-seeking balancing powers, without additional institutionalization and stabilization processes such orders are typically unstable and insufficient for the maintenance of order, being prone to insecurity spirals in overlapping deterrence fields. The balance of power, even when conducted as coactive independent security-seeking policies, is an institutional configuration, just as markets—in the prime analogy—are institutional configurations for coactive independent profit-making. Randall L. Schweller, "The Balance of Power in World Politics," *Oxford Research Encyclopedia of Politics* (2016), https://doi.org/10.1093/acrefore/97801 90228637.013.119; Morten Skumsrud Andersen and William C. Wohlforth, "Balance of Power: A Key Concept in Historical Perspective," in *Routledge Handbook of Historical International Relations*, ed. Benjamin de Carvalho, Julia Costa Lopez, and Halvard Liera (London: Routledge, 2021), 289–301; Daniel Nexon, "The Balance of Power in the Balance," *World Politics* 61, no. 2 (2009): 330–59; Martin Wight, "The Balance of Power and International Order," in *The Bases of International Order: Essays in Honour of C.A.W. Manning*, ed. Alan James (London: Oxford University Press, 1973), 85–115.

26. Andrew Phillips, *War, Religion and Empire: The Transformation of International Orders* (Cambridge: Cambridge University Press, 2011), 43.

27. William Bain, *Political Theology of International Order* (Oxford: Oxford University Press, 2020); Hendrik Spruyt, *The World Imagined: Collective Beliefs and Political Order in the Sinocentric, Islamic and Southeast Asian International Societies* (Cambridge: Cambridge University Press, 2020).

28. I take seriously the constructivist idea that international orders and modes of belonging underpinning them are subject to sources of power, and that international orders, including the idea of a cosmopolitan order, are in this sense not necessarily a purely consensual or socially contracted state of affairs. Rather, these political arrangements of relations are relatively stabilized in ongoing processes of political discursive action and practice. A cosmopolitan order could not be a transcendence of politics, only a change in politics. The point is that institutional configurations are not purely

social contracting configurations but are subject to the exercise of power. Andrew Phillips, *War, Religion and Empire: The Transformation of International Orders* (Cambridge: Cambridge University Press, 2011); Patrick Thaddeus Jackson and Daniel H. Nexon, "Relations before States: Substance, Process and the Study of World Politics," *European Journal of International Relations* 5, no. 3 (1999): 291–332.

29. Cooley and Nexon advance analysis of the aggregation of multiple orders, in a nonsingular global order. Alexander Cooley and Daniel Nexon, *Exit from Hegemony: The Unraveling of the American Global Order* (Oxford: Oxford University Press, 2020), chapter 2. Colgan advances an analysis of the "sub-orders" of international order, in the case of energy. Jeff Colgan, *Partial Hegemony: Oil Politics and International Order* (Oxford: Oxford University Press, 2021). Stroikos advances "sectoral" analysis of international orders in international society, in the case of outer space order. Dimitrios Stroikos, "Engineering World Society? Scientists, Internationalism, and the Advent of the Space Age," *International Politics* 55 (2018): 73–91.

30. Ian Clark, *The Vulnerable in International Society* (Oxford: Oxford University Press, 2013).

31. Steven Pinker's *The Better Angels of Our Nature* claims that the rate of violent death has in fact gone down markedly since Grotius's age. The issue with this argument is not so much statistical elision of uncounted deaths and undocumented miseries, although it is a problem when states deliberately manipulate statistics, including by disappearing victims. The main issue in Pinker's argument, however, is that the decline of violent death has statistically been reduced because there has not yet been a nuclear war, and that it is threats of nuclear deterrents that arguably are a major source of their nonuse, not any better angels of human nature. Steven Pinker, *The Better Angels of Our Nature: Why Violence Has Declined* (London: Viking, 2011); on the problem of violence, see Jenny Pearce, *Politics without Violence? Towards a Post-Weberian Enlightenment* (London: Palgrave, 2020).

32. Michael Ignatieff, *Blood and Belonging: Journeys into the New Nationalism* (New York: Farrar, Straus and Giroux, 1993), 10.

33. Jens Bartelson, *Visions of World Community* (Cambridge: Cambridge University Press, 2009).

34. Calhoun, *Nations Matter*; Anderson, *Imagined Communities*.

35. This is the sense of "imaginaries" developed in Charles Taylor, *Modern Social Imaginaries* (Durham: Duke University Press, 2004). Modern social imaginaries, as bundles of pervasive taken-for-granted discourse and practice, in this sense are the social background contents of the *primary constitutive* institutions of modern international society, such as sovereignty, diplomacy, and international law. Modern *cosmopolitan* imaginaries have struggled to become embedded in international society and realized as secondary organizational and regulative institutions, being restricted to limited construction of a human rights regime and humanitarian international order. Aaron McKeil, "The Modern 'International' Imaginary: Sketching Horizons and Enriching the Picture," *Social Imaginaries* 4, no. 2 (2018): 159–80; Charlotta Friedner Parrat, "On the Evolution of Primary Institutions of International Society," *International Studies Quarterly* 61 (2017): 623–30.

36. Catherine Lu, "The One and Many Faces of Cosmopolitanism," *Journal of Political Philosophy* 8, no. 2 (2000): 244.

37. Kang Youwei's *Da Tongshu* (*The Book of Great Harmony* 1935) adapted Confucius's concept of Da Tong, envisioning a modern and global great unity of humankind. But, of its times, Kang's vision involved a global eugenics program, blending and unifying some races while eliminating others. William A. Callahan, *China Dreams: 20 Visions of the Future* (Oxford: Oxford University Press, 2013), 109–14.

38. David Armitage, *Foundations of Modern International Thought* (Cambridge: Cambridge University Press, 2013).

39. R. J. Vincent, "Western Conceptions of a Universal Moral Order," *British Journal of International Studies* 4, no. 1 (1978): 20–46.

40. Ayse Zarakol, *Before the West: The Rise and Fall of Eastern World Orders* (Cambridge: Cambridge University Press, 2022); Andrew Phillips, *How the East Was Won: Barbarian Conquerors, Universal Conquest and the Making of Modern Asia* (Cambridge: Cambridge University Press, 2021).

41. S. M. Stern, *Aristotle on the World-State* (Columbia: University of South Carolina Press, 1968), 7.

42. Walter D. Mignolo, "The Many Faces of Cosmo-Polis: Border Thinking and Critical Cosmopolitanism," in *Cosmopolitanism*, ed. Carole A. Breckenridge, Sheldon Pollock, Homi K. Bhabha, and Dipesh Chakrabarty (Durham: Duke University Press, 2002), 157–88.

43. Henri Saint-Simon, *Selected Writings on Science, Industry and Social Organisation*, trans. Keith Taylor (London: Croom Helm, 1975), 136.

44. Stephen Toulmin, *Cosmopolis: The Hidden Agenda of Modernity* (Chicago: University of Chicago Press, 1990).

45. Katrin Flikschuh and Lea Ypi, *Kant and Colonialism: Historical and Critical Perspectives* (Oxford: Oxford University Press, 2014); Pauline Kleingeld, *Kant and Cosmopolitanism: The Philosophical Ideal of World Citizenship* (Cambridge: Cambridge University Press, 2013).

46. Benjamin F. Trueblood's *The Federation of the World* (1899) also displays characteristic features of a modern cosmopolitan imagination, with more detail than Tennyson. Trueblood's *Federation* starts with the question "Was Tennyson's dream of 'the parliament of man, the federation of the world,' nothing but a poetic fancy, or was it a rational prophesy of an actual condition to be realized in some future, near or far?" Living at the height of the 19th century, Trueblood also perceived processes of globalization, and pointed to an emerging "new world society" and "world mind" arising from global communication, as well as a growing international peace movement as the leading spirit of the times. To explain the "causes of disunity," he also pointed to the war system as a source of hatreds, and also to a lack of understanding between peoples. As a Christian American, he envisioned the future unification of humankind as the "United States of the world." In that federation, he explained, because the war system would be ended, "Tennyson's dream will then be more than realized; there will be no longer any battle-flags to furl." Benjamin F. Trueblood, *The Federation of the World* (Boston: Houghton, Mifflin and Company, 1899), 1, 28, 149.

47. Alfred Lord Tennyson, *Alfred Lord Tennyson: Selected Poems* (London: Penguin, 1991), 338–39.

48. Duncan Bell, *Dreamworlds of Race: Empire and the Utopian Destiny of Anglo-America* (Princeton: Princeton University Press, 2020), 184; Duncan Bell, "Founding

the World State: H. G. Wells on Empire and the English-Speaking Peoples," *International Studies Quarterly* 62 (2018): 867–79; Sarah Cole, *Inventing the Future: H. G. Wells and the Twentieth Century* (New York: Columbia University Press, 2020).

49. H. G. Wells, *The Outline of History: Being a Plain History of Life and Mankind* (New York: Garden City Publishing, 1931), 1157, 1170.

50. The highest-selling science fiction series ever, Isaac Asimov's *Foundation*, tells the tale of the fall and resurrection of a galactic empire, inspired by Gibbon's *Decline and Fall of the Roman Empire*. In this story and the others it has inspired (from *Star Wars* to *Dune*), ancient imaginaries of Rome still enable but also confine the modern Western popular imagination of the distant future. Jutta Weldes, "Globalisation Is Science Fiction," *Millennium: Journal of International Studies* 30, no. 3 (2001): 647–67.

51. Jacques Derrida, *On Cosmopolitanism and Forgiveness* (London: Routledge, 2001).

52. Monsieur de Vattel, *The Law of Nations; or Principles of the Law of Nature, applied to the Conduct and Affairs of Nations and Sovereigns* (Philadelphia: T&J.W. Johnson & Co, 1863), 139, book 2, chap. 1, §16. In the footnote to this passage, Vattel quotes Cicero in support. "Here, again, let us call in the authority of Cicero to our support. 'All mankind (say that excellent philosopher) should lay it down as their constant rule of action, that individual and general advantage should be the same: for, if each man strives to grasp every advantage for himself, all the ties of human society will be broken. And, if nature ordains that man feel interested in the welfare of his fellow man, whoever he be, and for the single reason that he is a man, —it necessarily follows, that, according to the intentions of nature, all mankind must have one common interest.'"

53. Jean-Jacques Rousseau, *The Plan for Perpetual Peace* (Lebanon, NH: University Press of New England, 2005).

54. Hidemi Suganami, *The Domestic Analogy and World Order Proposals* (Cambridge: Cambridge University Press, 1989).

55. Andrew Linklater, *Men and Citizens* (London: Palgrave, 1982); Chris Brown, *International Society, Global Polity: An Introduction to International Political Theory* (London: Sage, 2015).

56. As related by Hedley Bull, "Martin Wight and the Theory of International Relations," in Martin Wight, *International Theory: The Three Traditions* (New York: Holmes & Meier for the Royal Institute of International Affairs, 1992), xvi.

57. Hedley Bull, *The Anarchical Society: A Study of Order in World Politics*, 3rd ed. (London: Palgrave, 2002), xii.

58. Arnold J. Toynbee, as something of the Huntington-Fukuyama debate of his generation rolled into the thought of a single public intellectual, cautioned against the dangers of civilizational conflict and collapse, while also urging for the realization of a new world community. Arnold J. Toynbee, "World Sovereignty and World Culture: The Trend of International Affairs since the War," *Pacific Affairs* 4, no. 9 (1931): 753–78; Arnold J. Toynbee, *A Study of History: Abridgement of Volumes VII–X* (London: Oxford University Press, 1957); Martin Wight, influenced by Toynbee's study of ancient empires, speculated whether a world state would emerge after the Cold War. "Whichever won," he once wrote, "Russia or America, would establish upon the ruins a world state," in Martin Wight, "The Apostasy of Christendom," in the LSE Martin Wight Archives 9 (1948–1950), 10; for Wight, however, a world state would also present "a frightful con-

centration of power," in Martin Wight, "The Church, Russia and the West," *Ecumenical Review* 1, no. 1 (1948): 43; See Ian Hall, *The International Thought of Martin Wight* (London: Palgrave, 2006), 159.

59. Martin Wight, *Power Politics* (New York: Holmes & Meier for the Royal Institute of International Affairs, 1978), 81–94.

60. Eric Hobsbawm, *Age of Extremes: The Short Twentieth Century, 1914–1991* (London: Abacus, 1994).

61. Martin Wight, "The Disunity of Mankind," *Millennium: Journal of International Studies* 44, no. 1 (2015): 129; Ian Hall, "Unity in Christ? Martin Wight on the 'Disunity of Mankind,'" *Millennium: Journal of International Studies* 44, no. 1 (2015): 134–36; Jacinta O'Hagan, "Martin Wight and the Problem of Difference," *Millennium: Journal of International Studies* 44, no. 1 (2015): 137–40; Chris Brown, "On the Disunity of Mankind," *Millennium: Journal of International Studies* 44, no. 1 (2015): 141–43; Yongjin Zhang, "Early Cultural Orientations and Ancient International Thought," *Millennium: Journal of International Studies* 44, no. 1 (2015): 144–46.

62. Nicholas Rengger, "Between Transcendence and Necessity: Eric Voegelin, Martin Wight and the Crisis of Modern International Relations," *Journal of International Relations and Development* 22 (2019): 327–45; Voegelin argued that ideas of the "unity of mankind" were produced by "world empires" and were unworkable after the decline of empires. Eric Voegelin, "World-Empire and the Unity of Mankind," *International Affairs* 38, no. 2 (1962): 170–88.

63. In an unpublished study, Wight explored how historical figures such as Napoleon Bonaparte and Adolf Hitler tend to be labeled as "antichrists." Martin Wight, "Some Reflections on the Historic Antichrist," LSE Martin Wight Archives, 43; Hall, *International Thought of Martin Wight*, 36–37, 55–58, 79. The idea of the end of days has in it a kind of cosmopolitanism in humankind reaching heaven, if humankind cannot make a heaven on earth. Kant's essay "The End of All Things" (1794) is perhaps the clearest expression of these ideas: "the *antichrist* . . . would begin his certainly short regime (presumably based on fear and selfishness), because in that instance, while Christianity was indeed *determined* to be the world's universal religion, it would not be *favoured* by fate to become so. And from a moral point of view the (perverse) *end of all things* would make its entrance," Immanuel Kant, "The End of All Things," in *Perpetual Peace and Other Essays* (Indianapolis: Hackett, 1983), 103.

64. Peter Wilson, "Retrieving Cosmos: Gilbert Murray's Thought on International Relations," in *Gilbert Murray Reassessed: Hellenism, Theatre, and International Politics*, ed. Christopher Stray (Oxford: Oxford University Press, 2007), 239–60; The most expansive example of this retrotopianism is Lionel Curtis, *Civitas Dei*, in three volumes, vol. I (1934), II (1937), and III (1937).

65. Daniel H. Nexon, *The Struggle for Power in Early Modern Europe: Religious Conflict, Dynastic Empires, and International Change* (Princeton: Princeton University Press, 2009), 292.

66. Nexon, *Struggle for Power*, 3.

67. Edmund Burke, *Reflections on the French Revolution* (London: J.M. Dent & Sons, 1951), 288–99.

68. The economic globalization of the late 19th and early 20th centuries produced an early literature calling for radical integrated world orders, not only Marxian, but a

wide range. Bridgman in 1905, for instance, called for "world organization" to match an emerging "world unity," in Raymond L. Bridgman, *World Organization* (Boston: Ginn & Company, 1905), 1.

69. Martin Wight considered the League of Nations and the United Nations to be newfangled secular attempts at a Conciliar Movement (1409–49) world order model, which in its time sought to replace papal authority with a parliamentary authority for Christendom. The League and the UN, however, did not replace any authority in particular, and gave the great powers institutional authority.

70. Dag Hammarskjold, "Address to Both Houses of Parliament, 2 April, 1958," in *The Quest for Peace: The Dag Hammarskjöld Memorial Lectures* (New York: Columbia University Press, 1965), 46.

71. Paul Kennedy, *The Parliament of Man: The United Nations and the Quest for World Government* (London: Penguin, 2006); Mark Mazower, *No Enchanted Palace: The End of Empire and the Ideological Origins of the United Nations* (Princeton: Princeton University Press, 2009).

72. A sampling of this wave of literature on cosmopolitanism includes Gerard Delanty, *The Routledge Handbook of Cosmopolitanism Studies* (London: Routledge, 2012); Garrett Wallace Brown and David Held, eds., *The Cosmopolitanism Reader* (Cambridge: Polity, 2010); Gavin Kendall, Ian Woodward, and Zlatko Skrbis, eds., *The Sociology of Cosmopolitanism: Globalization, Identity, Culture and Government* (London: Palgrave, 2009); Holton, *Cosmopolitanisms*; Gerard Delanty, *The Cosmopolitan Imagination: The Renewal of Critical Social Theory* (Cambridge: Cambridge University Press, 2009); Beck, *Cosmopolitan Vision*; Steven Vertovec and Robin Cohen, eds., *Conceiving Cosmopolitanism: Theory, Context, and Practice* (Oxford: Oxford University Press, 2002); Cheah and Robbins, *Cosmopolitics*; Archibugi and Held, *Cosmopolitan Democracy*; Held, *Democracy and the Global Order*.

73. Samuel Moyn, *The Last Utopia: Human Rights in History* (Cambridge, MA: Belknap Press of Harvard University Press, 2010); R. J. Vincent, *Human Rights and International Relations* (Cambridge: Cambridge University Press, 1986).

74. Wight, *Power Politics*, 140; The source of Koestler's phrase is his *The Yogi and the Commissar* (London: Jonathan Cape, 1945).

75. Wight, *Power Politics*, 140.

76. W. E. B. Du Bois, "Worlds of Color," *Foreign Affairs* 3, no. 3 (1925): 423–44; Kwame Anthony Appiah, "Race in the Modern World: The Problem of the Color Line," *Foreign Affairs* 94, no. 2 (2015): 1–8; Alexander Anievas, Nivi Manchanda, and Robbie Shilliam, eds., *Race and Racism in International Relations: Confronting the Global Colour Line* (London: Routledge, 2015).

77. Fred Halliday, *Revolution and World Politics: The Rise and Fall of the Sixth Great Power* (London: Palgrave Macmillan, 1999), 15, 193–94.

78. I do not conceive of political ideologies as ideas "in the mind," as in the 19th century or Humean-empiricist conception of ideology. I understand ideologies as social narrative constructs, constitutive of the social relations they are applied to, which in the case of cosmopolitan narratives includes—or aspires to include—the relational social network of all humankind.

79. I resist a socialization explanation of conformity as advanced by Armstrong, sensing Parsonian elision of ongoing conflict and strained relations, even in relatively

stable contexts. David Armstrong, *Revolution and World Order: The Revolutionary State in International Society* (Oxford: Oxford University Press, 1993). I also critique Stephen Walt's *Revolution and War* that revolutions tend to precipitate war because they provoke threat perceptions and intensify security dilemmas. Departing from this realist outlook, I emphasize the social construction of threat perceptions that reconstitute divisive and antagonistic political identities, realized in the realignment of force. Stephen M. Walt, *Revolution and War* (Ithaca: Cornell University Press, 1996), 5–6.

80. Variation in sociological conditions across international society helps explain where the dividing lines fall in counterrevolutionary waves, although further social process concepts such as hierarchy legitimation conflicts and recognition struggles are needed to explain generative social changes. Charles Tilly, "The Analysis of a Counter-Revolution," *History and Theory* 3, no. 1 (1963): 30–58.

81. For the modern mode of power, see Buzan and Lawson, *Global Transformation*.

82. For the authoritative study of revolution in world politics, see George Lawson, *Anatomies of Revolution* (Cambridge: Cambridge University Press, 2019).

83. John J. Mearsheimer, *The Great Delusion: Liberal Dreams and International Realities* (New Haven: Yale University Press, 2018), 69, 87, 137, 150.

84. Calhoun, *Nations Matter*; Anderson, *Imagined Communities*.

Chapter 1

1. For ideal types, see Patrick Thaddeus Jackson, *The Conduct of Inquiry in International Relations: The Philosophy of Science and Its Implications for the Study of World Politics* (London: Routledge, 2011), 37; Keene, "International Society as an Ideal Type."

2. A "cosmopolitan" global order in this sense imagines humankind as forming a larger polity, in which all others are nested. Without an ability to act and mobilize resources to some degree, a "cosmopolitan" global order would be purely symbolic or de jure only, and unreal in some important respects. By resources, I mean not only material support, such as taxes or forces, but also political resources, in popular support. In this concept, I also include either supranational authorities or independent autonomous authorities and legitimated nonstate actors alongside states, because the concept would otherwise be hard to distinguish from an organized but not internationalist *cosmopolitan* international society. The offices of the UN Secretary-General, for example, have a degree of independence, but also no power over states, or ability to raise resources without them. My concept of an integrated cosmopolitan order here is influenced by Ferguson and Mansbach's concept of "polities." Yale H. Ferguson and Richard W. Mansbach, *A World of Polities: Essays in Global Politics* (London: Routledge, 2008), 60–61. This concept of a cosmopolitan global order is also influenced by Buzan's integrated "world society" model, but I suggest that a cosmopolitan order configuration, ideal typically speaking, is not necessarily limited to "liberal" politics, as Buzan suggested, or even Kantian cosmopolitan politics, and could in principle take on a wide range of cosmopolitan identities, discourses, and practices. Buzan, *From International to World Society?*

3. Andrew Hurrell, *On Global Order: Power, Values and the Constitution of International Society* (Oxford: Oxford University Press, 2007); Ikenberry, *After Victory*.

4. Andrew Phillips, *War, Religion and Empire*, 43.

5. Bain, *Political Theology of International Order*; Hendrik Spruyt, *The World Imagined*.

6. Because international orders and the modes of belonging underpinning them are subject to sources of power, a cosmopolitan order would not emerge as a purely consensual or socially contracted state of affairs. A cosmopolitan order could not be a transcendence of politics as such, only a change in politics. Phillips, *War, Religion and Empire*; Jackson and Nexon, "Relations before States."

7. Alexander Cooley and Daniel Nexon advance analysis of the aggregation of multiple orders in a nonsingular global order; Cooley and Nexon, *Exit from Hegemony*, chapter 2. In *Partial Hegemony*, Jeff Colgan advances analysis of the "sub-orders" of international order, in the case of energy. Dimitrios Stroikos advances a "sectoral" analysis of international orders in international society in the case of outer space order. Stroikos, "Engineering World Society?"

8. Zarakol, *Hierarchies in World Politics*. I take a broadly Weberian-influenced view of the concept of "legitimation" as the social processes of constructing beliefs in populations that relations of political authority are legitimate, contributing to its stabilization. Legitimation in this way sets parameters for tolerable and intolerable relations and actions. Legitimation as such is an exercise of social power and the mechanisms of legitimation combine ongoing processes of discursive action and performative practice, enabling a wide range of legitimation strategies. As an exercise of power, it is not coercive as such, but subject to legitimation strategies. Calls for cosmopolitan orders, in this sense, tend to seek legitimation through discursive appeals to moral authority, justice, and common interests, combined with "selfless" or "other-regarding" practices, such as international humanitarian action or institutional cosmopolitan ordering arrangements. Steffek, "Legitimation of International Governance, 271; Jackson, "Rethinking Weber"; Clark, *Legitimacy in International Society*.

9. I do not define recognition struggles as demands for recognition of an "internal" authentic self, which is a culturally specific conception of identity. Nor do I define recognition as *thymos*, or similar ancient Greek concepts. Adler-Nissen and Zarakol, "Struggles for Recognition"; Murray, *The Struggle for Recognition in International Relation*; Fukuyama, *Identity*; Bartelson, "Three Concepts of Recognition"; Hans Agné et. al., "Symposium"; Honneth, "Recognition between States"; Axel Honneth, *The Struggle for Recognition: The Moral Grammar of Social Conflicts* (Cambridge, MA: MIT Press, 1995); Taylor, "The Politics of Recognition."

10. For the concept of the modern state, I find Michael Mann's four-part concept to be well-developed: "(1). The state is a differentiated set of institutions and personnel (2). embodying centrality, in the sense that political relations radiate to and from a centre, to cover a (3). territorially demarcated area over which it exercises (4). some degree of authoritative, binding rule making, backed up by some organised physical force." Michael Mann, *The Sources of Social Power*, vol. 2, *The Rise of Classes and Nation-States, 1760–1914*, new ed. (Cambridge: Cambridge University Press, 2012), 55.

11. Ruggie, "Continuity and Transformation in the World Polity"; John Barkdull, "Waltz, Durkheim, and International Relations: The International System as an Abnormal Form," *American Political Science Review* 89, no. 3 (1995): 669–80.

12. In one passage, Durkheim suggests that "because the different nations of Europe are . . . much less independent of one another" they are "all part of the same society, still

incohesive, it is true, but one becoming increasingly conscious of itself." Émile Durkheim, *The Division of Labour in Society* (London: Macmillan, 1984), 76–77. This only gestures at a unifying process, where Ruggie does not specify thresholds of density. By solidarity, in this context, we can conceive of this as mutual commitment to support, what Durkheim called "positive" solidarity.

13. Buzan, *From International to World Society?*, 202–3, 260–61. A world society configuration other or more than a thin liberal one may have yet undefined alternative pluralistic modes of belonging. Barry Buzan, "Revisiting World Society," *International Politics* 55, no. 1 (2018): 125–40; Yannis A. Stivachtis and Aaron McKeil, "Conceptualizing World Society," *International Politics* 55, no. 1 (2018): 1–10; Aaron McKeil, "A Silhouette of Utopia: A Comparative Assessment of English School and Constructivist Conceptions of World Society," *International Politics* 55, no. 1 (2018): 41–56; Matthew S. Weinert, "Reframing the Pluralist-Solidarist Debate," *Millennium: Journal of International Studies* 40, no. 1 (2011): 21–41; John Williams, "Pluralism, Solidarism and the Emergence of World Society in English School Theory," *International Relations* 19, no. 1 (2005): 19–38.

14. Martin Shaw, *Theory of the Global State: Globality as an Unfinished Revolution* (New York: Cambridge University Press, 2000).

15. Ulrich Beck, "Redefining the Sociological Project: The Cosmopolitan Challenge," *Sociology* 46, no. 1 (2012): 7–12; Ulrich Beck, "Cosmopolitanism as Imagined Communities of Global Risk," *American Behavioral Scientist* 55, no. 10 (2011): 1346–61; Beck, *Cosmopolitan Vision*; Ulrich Beck, "The Cosmopolitan Perspective: Sociology of the Second Age of Modernity," *British Journal of Sociology* 51, no. 1 (2000): 79–105.

16. Brett Bowden, "Civil Society, the State, and the Limits to Global Civil Society," *Global Society* 20, no. 2 (2006): 155–78; Chris Brown, "Cosmopolitanism, World Citizenship and Global Civil Society," *Critical Review of International Social and Political Philosophy* 3, no. 1 (2000): 7–26; Jens Bartelson, "Making Sense of Global Civil Society," *European Journal of International Relations* 12, no. 3 (2006): 371–95; Hans-Martin Jaeger, "Global Civil Society and the Political Depoliticization of Global Governance," *International Political Sociology* 1, no. 3 (2007): 257–77; Kenneth Anderson and David Rieff, "Global Civil Society: A Sceptical View," in *Global Civil Society 2004–2005*, ed. Mary Kaldor, Helmut Anheier, and Marlies Glasius (London: Sage, 2004), 28–36; Kaldor, "Idea of Global Civil Society"; John Keane, *Global Civil Society?* (Cambridge: Cambridge University Press, 2003).

17. Hurrell, *On Global Order*, 224–28; Barnett and Sikkink, "From International Relations to Global Society," 62–83.

18. Friedrich Kratochwil, "Global Governance and the Emergence of World Society," in *The Puzzles of Politics: Inquiries into the Genesis and Transformation of International Relations* (London: Routledge, 2011), 262–80.

19. Iver B. Neumann and Ole Jacob Sending, *Governing the Global Polity: Practice, Mentality, Rationality* (Ann Arbor: University of Michigan Press, 2010), 18–44; Olaf Corry also theorizes "global polity" formation as a structural shift beyond hierarchy and anarchy arising through the discursive emergence of a "global governance object," Olaf Corry, *Constructing a Global Polity: Theory, Discourse and Governance* (London: Palgrave, 2013), 1–17. On power, see Stefano Guzzini, *Power, Realism and Constructivism*

(London: Routledge, 2013); Michael Barnett and Robert Duvall, "Power in International Relations," *International Organization* 59, no. 1 (2005): 43, 55–57.

20. Stephen Gill and Claire Cutler, eds., *New Constitutionalism and World Order* (Cambridge: Cambridge University Press, 2014).

21. Anthony F. Lang Jr. and Antje Wiener, eds., *Handbook on Global Constitutionalism*, 3rd ed. (Cheltenham, UK: Edward Elgar, 2023).

22. Antje Wiener, Tanja Borzel, and Thomas Risse, eds., *European Integration Theory*, 3rd ed. (Oxford: Oxford University Press, 2019); Thomas Diez and Nathalie Tocci, *The EU, Promoting Regional Integration, and Conflict Resolution* (London: Palgrave, 2017); Thomas Diez, "Europe as a Discursive Battleground: Discourse Analysis and European Integration Studies," *Cooperation and Conflict* 36, no. 1 (2001): 5–38; Thomas Diez, "Speaking 'Europe': The Politics of Integration," *Journal of European Public Policy* 6, no. 4 (1999): 598–613.

23. Michael Zurn, *A Theory of Global Governance: Authority, Legitimacy, and Contestation* (Oxford: Oxford University Press, 2018); Michael Zurn, "Global Governance and Legitimacy Problems," *Government and Opposition* 39, no. 2 (2004): 260–87.

24. Frank Schimmelfennig, "Regional Integration Theory," *Oxford Research Encyclopedia of Politics* (2018): https://doi.org/10.1093/acrefore/9780190228637.013.599; Liesbet Hooghe and Gary Marks, "A Postfunctionalist Theory of European Integration: From Permissive Consensus to Constraining Dissensus," *British Journal of Political Science* 39, no. 1 (2009): 1–23.

25. Bruce Cronin, *Community under Anarchy: Transnational Identity and the Evolution of Cooperation* (New York: Columbia University Press, 1999).

26. Amitai Etzioni, *Political Unification Revisited: On Building Supranational Communities* (Lanham, MD: Lexington Books, 2001), xxii.

27. Stuart Kauffman suggested that international systems are "consolidated" under largescale hegemonic orders benefiting from a coincidental confluence of centralizing forces, including when "self-help" and "economic" interests encourage expansion of units, when identities extend rather than fragment, and when "administrative capabilities" are sufficient to manage large-scale units. Stuart J. Kauffman, "The Fragmentation and Consolidation of International Systems," *International Organization* 51, no. 2 (1997): 173–208.

28. This question of whether a system of multiple units can be integrated and nested in a larger system-wide polity has intellectual significance for the possible range of international system configurations and the understanding of International Relations as social science and disciplinary field. Iver B. Neumann, "International Relations as a Social Science," *Millennium: Journal of International Studies* 43, no. 1 (2014): 330–50; Justin Rosenberg, "International Relations in the Prison of Political Science," *International Relations* 30, no. 2 (2016): 127–53.

29. Kenneth Waltz, *Theory of International Politics* (Reading: Addison Wesley, 1979), 111–12.

30. We might also recall that the Roman Empire experienced repeated civil war and rebellions. Although, to be clear, Roman *civil wars* were waged by elite groups to dominate and reunify the empire, not to deconstruct it, while *rebellions* in the empire were launched to gain independence from it.

31. Mearsheimer, *Great Delusion*, 150.

32. Joseph M. Parent, *Uniting States: Voluntary Union in World Politics* (Oxford: Oxford University Press, 2011).

33. Ronald Reagan, speaking before the United Nations General Assembly, perhaps deviating from his speech writers, also said, "I occasionally think how quickly our differences worldwide would vanish if we were facing an alien threat from outside this world." Ronald Reagan, "Address to the 42nd Session of the United Nations General Assembly," September 21, 1987. The renowned physicist Stephen Hawking suggested that the nearest historical example to an extra-planetary invasion was the invasion of the New World. In that case, the indigenous peoples did not form a grand alliance against the conquistadors, but instead were divided, some aligning with their conquerors, to gain advantage against their local enemies. The Wellsian trope of a "war of the worlds" reflects the culture of modern cosmopolitan imaginaries. Martin Wight noted, "It is significant of the state of our culture that virtually all science fiction imagines a condition of natural hostility between the invented creatures of outer-space and ourselves; this makes for more gripping drama of course but it is significant." Wight, *International Theory*, 50.

34. In principle, a universal cosmopolitan mode of belonging, with an all-embracing collective identity, does not require or necessarily constitute an "other" identity in order to have social coherence. Arash Abizadeh, "Does Collective Identity Presuppose an Other? On the Alleged Incoherence of Global Solidarity," *American Political Science Review* 99, no. 1 (2005): 45–60.

35. Wendt, "Why a World State Is Inevitable."

36. Wendt, "Why a World State Is Inevitable," 505–28.

37. Wendt, "Why a World State Is Inevitable," 494, 517.

38. Hidemi Suganami, "On Wendt's Philosophy: A Critique," *Review of International Studies* 28, no. 1 (2002): 23–37; Wendt, "The State as Person in International Theory." Furthermore, care is needed in understanding the concept of recognition, which Wendt treats somewhat hastily. The modern and largely Western belief in the recognition of an "authentic" self, for instance, was not present in the ancient world.

39. We might add that the idea of a Gadamerian "fusion of horizons" is a compelling idea but implausible given the number of horizons on a global scale, and because it is already extremely challenging on national scales. Charles Taylor, "Understanding the Other: A Gadamerian View on Conceptual Schemes," in *Dilemmas and Connections: Selected Essays* (Cambridge, MA: Harvard University Press, 2011), 24–38; Richard Shapcott, *Justice, Community and Dialogue in International Relations* (Cambridge: Cambridge University Press, 2001).

40. By near term, I mean the proximate 10–15 years. By medium term, I mean 15–30 years. By long-term, I mean the remote 50–100 years.

41. Buzan, *Making Global Society*, 39.

42. Heikki Patomaki, *World Statehood: The Future of World Politics* (Cham, Switzerland: Springer, 2023); Mathias Albert, Gorm Harste, and Knud Erik Jorgensen, "Introduction: World State Futures," *Cooperation and Conflict* 47, no. 2 (2012): 145–56; Bob Jesop, "Obstacles to a World State in the Shadow of the World Market," *Cooperation and Conflict* 47, no. 2 (2012): 200–219; Christopher Chase-Dunn and K. S. Lawrence, "The Next Three Futures, Part One: Looming Crises of Global Inequality, Ecological Degradation, and a Failed System of Global Governance," *Global Society* 25, no. 2 (2011): 137–

53; Christopher Chase-Dunn and K. S. Lawrence, "The Next Three Futures, Part Two: Possibilities of Another Round of US Hegemony, Global Collapse, or Global Democracy," *Global Society* 25, no. 3 (2011): 269–85; Raffaele Marchetti, "Global Governance or World Federalism? A Cosmopolitan Dispute on Institutional Models," *Global Society* 20, no. 3 (2006): 287–305; Christopher Chase-Dunn, "World-State Formation: Historical Processes and Emergent Necessity," *Political Geography Quarterly* 9, no. 2 (1990): 108–30.

43. William E. Scheuerman, "Deudney's Neorepublicanism: One-World or America First?," *International Politics* 47, no. 5 (2010): 523–34. World government and world state thinkers debate its necessary and possible structure, centralized or federated, for instance, managing tensions between legitimation hurdles and security management, especially regarding nuclear weapons. Campbell Craig, "Solving the Nuclear Dilemma: Is a World State Necessary?," *Journal of International Political Theory* 15, no. 3 (2018): 349–66; Daniel Deudney, "Going Critical: Toward a Modified Nuclear One Worldism," *Journal of International Political Theory* 15, no. 3 (2018): 367–85; William E. Scheuerman, "Cosmopolitanism and the World State," *Review of International Studies* 40, no. 3 (2014): 419–41; William E. Scheuerman, "The (Classical) Realist Vision of Global Reform," *International Theory* 2, no. 2 (2010): 246–82.

44. Joseph P. Baratta, *Strengthening the United Nations: A Bibliography on U.N. Reform and World Federalism* (Westport, CT: Greenwood Press, 1987), 7–9, 12.

45. Joseph P. Baratta, "The Internationalist World Federal Movement: Toward Global Governance," *Peace & Change* 24, no. 3 (1999): 345.

46. Sovaida Ma'ani Ewing, *Bridge to Global Governance: Tackling Climate Change, Energy Distribution and Nuclear Proliferation* (Washington, DC: Center for Peace and Global Governance, 2018); Guido Montani, *Supranational Political Economy: The Globalisation of the State-Market Relationship* (London: Routledge, 2019).

47. Mark Malloch-Brown, *The Unfinished Global Revolution: The Pursuit of a New International Politics* (New York: Penguin, 2011), 180–200.

48. Richard Falk and Saul Mendlovitz, eds., *Strategy of World Order*, 4 vols. (New York: World Law Fund, 1966); Ranji Kothari, *Footsteps into the Future: Diagnosis of the Present World and a Design for an Alternative* (New York: Free Press, 1974); Richard Falk, *A Study of Future Worlds* (New York: Free Press, 1975); Ali A. Mazrui, *A World Federation of Cultures: An African Perspective* (New York: Free Press, 1976); Gustavo Lagos and Horacio H. Godoy, *Revolution of Being: A Latin American View of the Future* (New York: Free Press, 1977); Johan Galtung, *The True Worlds: a Transnational Perspective* (New York: Free Press, 1980); R. B. J. Walker, *One World, Many Worlds: Struggles for a Just World Peace* (London: Zed, 1987). Hedley Bull was highly skeptical of this literature, arguing that such models could not be constructed in the absence of international order and that their adoption would necessarily be through international society actors, not "bottom up" world society actors. Bull was too critical of the role of nonstate actors, at least in his early work, and contemporary thinking suggests coalitions of like-minded state and nonstate actors are needed to generate international initiative. The argument that an order provided by states enables a cosmopolitan order or facilitates integrating states to such an extent that they form a larger state-like union has more merit (with qualifications and complications). Hedley Bull, *The Anarchical Society: A Study of Order in World Politics*, 3rd ed. (London: Palgrave, 2002); Hidemi Suganami, Madeline Carr,

and Adam Humphreys, eds., *The Anarchical Society at 40: Contemporary Challenges and Prospects* (Oxford: Oxford University Press, 2017); Aaron McKeil, "Revisiting the World Order Models Project: A Case for Renewal?," *Global Policy* 13, no. 4 (2022): 417–26; Luis Cabrera, "Advancing Global Citizenship and Cosmopolitanism in an Age of Globoskepticism: Insights from the World Order Models Project," *Globalizations* 20, no. 7 (2023): 1102–19.

49. Jawaharlal Nehru to Edward Clark, April 6, 1948. Quoted in Baratta, *Politics of World Federation*, vol. 2, 299. For Nehru's early but later abandoned interest in world federalism, see Manu Bhagavan, *India and the Quest for One World: The Peacemakers* (London: Palgrave Macmillan, 2013).

50. Wight, *International Theory*, 41.

51. Wight, *International Theory*, 45. This in a sense is the world order proposal of anarchist cosmopolitan thinkers, classically Mikhail Bakunin, Peter Kropotkin, and Pierre-Joseph Proudhon, who propose the deconstruction of hierarchical ordering authorities for a maximally decentralized but "united" global anarchical order. These proposals struggle with the same social integration challenge of necessary inclusive social processes, while adding on more practical governance challenges, by deconstructing governance structures. Proudhon described an anarchist notion of unity without structure, where he says, "the centre is everywhere, circumference nowhere. This is unity." Cited in Ruth Kinna, Alex Prichard, and Thomas Swann, "Occupy and the Constitution of Anarchy," *Global Constitutionalism* 8, no. 2 (2019): 363. It is notable, furthermore, albeit with awareness of the anachronism, that Zeno, the ancient philosopher of the *cosmopolis*, had a nonhierarchical "anarchical" conception of its order. See Isaiah Berlin, "Socialism and Socialist Theories," in *The Sense of Reality: Studies in Ideas and Their History*, ed. Henry Hardy (London: Pimlico, 1996), 78. See, also, Alex Prichard, "Introduction: Anarchism and World Politics," *Millennium: Journal of International Studies* 39, no. 2 (2010): 373–80; Richard Falk, "Anarchism without 'Anarchism': Searching for Progressive Politics," in *(Re)Imagining Humane Global Governance* (London: Routledge, 2014), 145–61.

52. Bull, *The Anarchical Society*, 244.

53. The same logic applies to a climate catastrophe, which, if severe enough, will have become impossible to unmake, undermining solidarity incentives. See chapter 5 and Robert Falkner, *Environmentalism and Global International Society* (Cambridge: Cambridge University Press, 2021), 297.

54. Eva Erman, "Does Global Democracy Require a World State?," *Philosophical Papers* 48, no. 1 (2019): 123–53; Laura Valentini, "No Global Demos, No Global Democracy? A Systemization and Critique," *Perspectives on Politics* 12, no. 4 (2014): 789–807; Mathias Koenig-Archibugi, "Is Global Democracy Possible?," *European Journal of International Relations* 17, no. 3 (2011): 519–42; Robert A. Dahl, "Can International Organizations be Democratic? A Skeptics View," in *Democracy's Edges*, ed. Ian Shapiro and Casiano Hacker-Cordon (Cambridge: Cambridge University Press, 1999), 19–36; Daniele Archibugi, "Cosmopolitan Democracy and Its Critics: A Review," *European Journal of International Relations* 10, no. 3 (2004): 437–73; Daniele Archibugi and David Held, "Cosmopolitan Democracy: Paths and Agents," *Ethics & International Affairs* 25, no. 4 (2011): 433–61.

55. Thomas Hale and Mathias Koenig-Archibugi, "Could Global Democracy Satisfy

Diverse Policy Values? An Empirical Analysis," *Journal of Politics*, 81, no. 1 (2018): 112–26; Jo Leinen and Andreas Bummel, *A World Parliament: Governance and Democracy in the 21st Century* (Berlin: Democracy Without Borders, 2018); Koenig-Archibugi, "Is Global Democracy Possible?"; Jan Aart Scholte, "Reinventing Global Democracy," *European Journal of International Relations* 20, no. 1 (2014): 3–28; Daniele Archibugi, *The Global Commonwealth of Citizens: Towards Cosmopolitan Democracy* (Princeton: Princeton University Press, 2008); Richard Falk and Andrew Strauss, *A Global Parliament: Essays and Articles* (Berlin: Committee for a Democratic U.N., 2011); Archibugi and Held, "Cosmopolitan Democracy: Paths and Agents"; John S. Dryzek, "Discursive Representation," *American Political Science Review* 102, no. 4 (2008): 481–93.

56. Margaret R. Somers, "The Narrative Constitution of Identity: A Relational and Network Approach," *Theory and Society* 23, no. 5 (1994): 605–49; Jackson and Nexon, "Relations before States," 305; David M. McCourt, "Practice Theory and Relationalism as the New Constructivism," *International Studies Quarterly* 60, no. 3 (2016): 475–85.

57. By discourse, I mean a system of meanings for the formation of statements, which hang together with practices as socially recognized forms of activity. Discourse and practice, together, form a concept of culture. See Iver B. Neumann, "Returning Practice to the Linguistic Turn: The Case of Diplomacy," *Millennium: Journal of International Studies* 31, no. 3 (2002): 630–31.

58. Margaret R. Somers and Gloria D. Gibson, "Reclaiming the Epistemological 'Other': Narrative and the Social Constitution of Identity," in *Social Theory and the Politics of Identity*, ed. Craig Calhoun (Oxford: Blackwell, 1994), 49.

59. Charles Tilly, "Ties That Bind . . . and Bound," in *Identities, Boundaries, and Social Ties* (Boulder: Paradigm, 2005), 3–12; Harrison C. White, *Identity and Control: How Social Formations Emerge* (Princeton: Princeton University Press, 2008).

60. Nexon, *Struggle for Power in Early Modern Europe*, 114.

61. Bull, *The Anarchical Society*, 244.

62. James A. Yunker, *The Idea of World Government: From Ancient Times to the Twenty-First Century* (London: Routledge, 2011).

63. Martin Wight, *Systems of States* (Leicester: Leicester University Press, 1977); Adam Watson, *The Evolution of International Society: A Comparative Historical Analysis* (London: Routledge, 1992); Barry Buzan and Richard Little, *International Systems in World History: Remaking the Study of International Relations* (Oxford: Oxford University Press, 2000); Victoria Tin-bor Hui, *War and State Formation in Ancient China and Early Modern Europe* (Cambridge: Cambridge University Press, 2005); Stuart J. Kaufman, Richard Little, and William C. Wohlforth, eds., *The Balance of Power in World History* (Basingstoke: Palgrave, 2007). My basic definition of an international system is a relational network of strategic and diplomatic interaction of multiple polities. Andrew Phillips, "International Systems," in *The Globalization of International Society*, ed. Tim Dunne and Christian Reus-Smit (Oxford: Oxford University Press, 2017), 43–62.

64. In this literature, Toynbee's pioneering *A Study of History* (and up to a point for Wight's work as well) implied that modernity had taken a dangerous path toward fragmentation and disunity, unlike many ancient and medieval orders that he studied in his survey of world history. For Toynbee, sovereignty had problematically divided humankind in a modern and global context, and the search for a new universalism and common spiritual reawakening constituted a challenge for modern civilization. Toyn-

bee also suggested that there was a role for "world" religions in stabilizing these ancient universal orders. Toynbee's concept of "civilization" was somewhat fuzzy and struggled to sustain coherence. Toynbee later abandoned the concept of civilization for world religion, although not entirely with more success. Arnold J. Toynbee. *Change and Habit: The Challenge of Our Time* (Oxford: Oxford University Press, [1966] 1992), 195; Arnold J. Toynbee, *A Study of History: Abridgement of Volumes VII–X* (London: Oxford University Press, 1957). Toynbee later led an anti-imperial campaign, which he understood as a political and spiritual corrective response needed by Western civilization. See Ian Hall, "'The Toynbee Convector': The Rise and Fall of Arnold J. Toynbee's Anti-Imperial Mission to the West," *European Legacy* 17, no. 4 (2012): 455–69.

65. Reinhold Niebuhr, "The Illusion of World Government," *Foreign Affairs* 27, no. 3 (1949): 379–88; Frederick L. Shuman, *The Commonwealth of Man: An Inquiry into Power Politics and World Government* (London: Robert Hale, 1954); Craig, *Glimmer of a New Leviathan*; Scheuerman, *Realist Case for Global Reform*. Daniel Deudney has also drawn inspiration from the Roman Republic, to devise an alternative "negarchical" world government model; see Daniel Deudney, *Bounding Power: Republican Security Theory from the Polis to the Global Village* (Princeton: Princeton University Press, 2006).

66. Zarakol, *Before the West*; Phillips, *How the East Was Won*; Spruyt, *The World Imagined*; David C. Kang, "International Order in Historical East Asia: Tribute and Hierarchy beyond Sinocentrism and Eurocentrism," *International Organization* 74, no. 1 (2020): 65–93; David C. Kang, *East Asia before the West: Five Centuries of Trade and Tribute* (New York: Columbia University Press, 2010); Manjeet S. Pardesi, "Mughal Hegemony and the Emergence of South Asia as a 'Region' for Regional Order-Building," *European Journal of International Relations* 25, no. 1 (2019): 276–301; Manjeet S. Pardesi, "Region, System, and Order: The Mughal Empire in Islamic Asia," *Security Studies* 26, no. 2 (2017): 249–78; Erik Ringmar, "Performing International Systems: Two East-Asian Alternatives to the Westphalian Order," *International Organization* 66, no. 1 (2012): 1–25.

67. Quoted in Edward Keene, "World-City, Empire and Natural Law," in *International Political Thought: A Historical Introduction* (Cambridge: Polity Press, 2005), 46.

68. Clifford Ando, *Roman Social Imaginaries: Language and Thought in the Context of Empire* (Toronto: University of Toronto Press, 2015), 7–28.

69. Daniel S. Richter, *Cosmopolis: Imagining the Community in Late Classical Athens and the Early Roman Empire* (Oxford: Oxford University Press, 2011), 1–14.

70. Catharine Edwards and Greg Woolf, "Cosmopolis: Rome as World City," in *Rome the Cosmopolis*, ed. Catharine Edwards and Greg Woolf (Cambridge: Cambridge University Press, 2003), 1–20.

71. Quoted in Judith Perkins, *Roman Imperial Identities in the Early Christian Era* (London: Routledge, 2009), 18.

72. Ando, *Roman Social Imaginaries*, 88.

73. Ando, *Roman Social Imaginaries*, 92.

74. Josiah Osgood, *Rome and the Making of a World State: 150 BCE–20 CE* (Cambridge: Cambridge University Press, 2018).

75. Daniel Deudney, "A Republic for Expansion: The Roman Constitution and Empire and Balance-of-Power Theory," in *The Balance of Power in World History*, ed.

Stuart Kaufman, Richard Little, and William C. Wohlforth (Basingstoke: Palgrave, 2007), 158.

76. Katja Maria Vogt, *Law, Reason, and the Cosmic City: Political Philosophy in the Early Stoa* (Oxford: Oxford University Press, 2008). W.W. Tarn argued that Alexander had a cosmopolitan ambition, following Zeno, but this is refuted by contemporary scholarship. The Stoic narrative was not used by the Hellenistic monarchies and the Macedonian kingdoms practically had and in principle recognized no superior among them. Hellenistic monarchies widely practiced legitimation based on the right of "spear-won" conquest and the military authority and excellence of the Macedonian kings.

77. Cicero, *On Duties* (Cambridge: Cambridge University Press, 1991), 23 [Book 1.53].

78. Marcus Aurelius, *Meditations* (Oxford: Oxford University Press, 2013), 21 [Book 4.4].

79. Clifford Ando, *Imperial Rome, A.D. 193–284: The Critical Century* (Edinburgh: Edinburgh University Press, 2012), 78–79.

80. Clifford Ando, *Imperial Ideology and Provincial Loyalty in the Roman Empire* (Berkeley: University of California Press, 2000), 8.

81. Richard Hingley, *Globalizing Roman Culture: Unity, Diversity, and Empire* (London: Routledge, 2005), 49–59.

82. Greg Woolf, *Becoming Roman: The Origins of Provincial Civilization in Gaul* (Cambridge: Cambridge University Press, 1998); Perkins, *Roman Imperial Identities in the Early Christian Era*, 26–27.

83. Jane Burbank and Frederick Cooper, *Empires in World History: Power and the Politics of Difference* (Princeton: Princeton University Press, 2011), 29, 444.

84. Louise Revell, *Roman Imperialism and Local Identities* (Cambridge: Cambridge University Press, 2009); Richter, *Cosmopolis*, 5–9.

85. Clifford Ando, *A Matter of the Gods: Religion and the Roman Empire* (Berkeley: University of California Press, 2008).

86. D. J. Mattingly, *Imperialism, Power, and Identity: Experiencing the Roman Empire* (Princeton: Princeton University Press, 2011), 206.

87. Ando, *A Matter of the Gods*, 102.

88. Quoted in Chester G. Starr, *The Roman Empire, 27 B.C.–A.D. 476* (Oxford: Oxford University Press, 1982), 99.

89. Yu Ying-Shih, "Han Foreign Relations," in *The Cambridge History of China*, vol. 1, *The Ch'in and Han Empires, 221 B.C.–A.D. 220*, ed. Denis Twitchett and John K. Fairbank (Cambridge: Cambridge University Press, 1986), 377.

90. Mark Edward Lewis, *The Early Chinese Empires: Qin and Han* (Cambridge, MA: Harvard University Press, 2007), 11.

91. Victoria Tin-bor Hui, "The Triumph of Domination in the Ancient Chinese System," in *The Balance of Power in World History*, ed. Stuart Kaufman, Richard Little, and William C. Wohlforth (London: Palgrave, 2007), 123.

92. Lewis, *Early Chinese Empires*, 186.

93. Hui, *War and State Formation in Ancient China and Early Modern Europe*, 123–25.

94. Michael Loewe, *The Men Who Governed Han China* (Leiden: Brill, 2004), 9.

95. Ying-Shih Yu, *Chinese History and Culture*, vol. 1, *Sixth Century B.C.E. to Seventeenth Century* (New York: Columbia University Press, 2016), chapter 2.

96. Michael Nylan, *The Five "Confucian" Classics* (Oxford: Oxford University Press, 2001), 3; Lewis, *Early Chinese Empires*, 206–7.

97. Chun-shu Chang, *The Rise of the Chinese Empire*, vol. 1, *Nation, State, and Imperialism in Early China, ca. 1600 B.C.–A.D. 8* (Ann Arbor: University of Michigan Press, 2007); Chun-shu Chang, *The Rise of the Chinese Empire*, vol. 2, *Frontier, Immigration and Empire in Han China, 130 B.C.–A.D. 157* (Ann Arbor: University of Michigan Press, 2007).

98. Robert P. Kramers, "The Development of the Confucian Schools," in *The Cambridge History of China*, vol. 1, *The Ch'in and Han Empires, 221 B.C.–A.D. 220*, ed. Denis Twitchett and John K. Fairbank (Cambridge: Cambridge University Press, 1986), 754.

99. Kramers, "Development of the Confucian Schools," 747–48.

100. The first emperor of the Qin dynasty favored the Legalist tradition, and in 213 BC he ordered the burning of books associated with different political traditions and later also notoriously ordered the burying alive of 460 *ju* scholars (said to include mainly Confucians). The Han dynasty emperor Wu-ti (141–87 BC) is said to be the first to officially favor Confucianism, and adopted Confucianism as official state ideology in 136 BC. The emperor is said to have been impressed by Tung Chung-shu, who introduced Confucianism to the imperial court. Wu-ti, with Tung Chung-shu, appointed imperial scholars and founded an official Confucian academy, T'ai-hsueh, with an official Confucian curriculum to train students. Kramers, "The Development of the Confucian Schools," 751–52.

101. Kramers, "Development of the Confucian Schools," 756; Hans Bielenstein, "The Institutions of Later Han," in *The Cambridge History of China*, vol. 1, *The Ch'in and Han Empires, 221 B.C.–A.D. 220*, ed. Denis Twitchett and John K. Fairbank (Cambridge: Cambridge University Press, 1986), 517.

102. Nylan, *The Five "Confucian" Classics*, 36.

103. Hans Bielenstein, "The Institutions of Later Han," in *The Cambridge History of China*, vol. 1, *The Ch'in and Han Empires, 221 B.C.–A.D. 220*, ed. Denis Twitchett and John K. Fairbank (Cambridge: Cambridge University Press, 1986), 516; Nylan, *The Five "Confucian" Classics*, 1; Robert P. Kramers, "Development of the Confucian Schools," 751–52.

104. Michael Loewe, *The Men Who Governed Han China* (Leiden: Brill, 2004); Hans Bielenstein, *The Bureaucracy of Han Times* (Cambridge: Cambridge University Press, 1980).

105. Michael Loewe, *Divination, Mythology and Monarchy in Han China* (Cambridge: Cambridge University Press, 1994), 253.

106. Michael Loewe, "The Structure and Practice of Government," in *The Cambridge History of China*, vol. 1, *The Ch'in and Han Empires, 221 B.C.–A.D. 220*, ed. Denis Twitchett and John K. Fairbank (Cambridge: Cambridge University Press, 1986), 508.

107. Lewis, *Early Chinese Empires*, 232–33, 234; A. F. P. Hulsewe, "Ch'in and Han Law," in *The Cambridge History of China*, vol. 1, *The Ch'in and Han Empires, 221 B.C.–A.D. 220*, ed. Denis Twitchett and John K. Fairbank (Cambridge: Cambridge University Press, 1986), 523.

108. Michael Loewe, "The Structure and Practice of Government," in *The Cambridge*

History of China, vol. 1, *The Ch'in and Han Empires, 221 B.C.–A.D. 220*, ed. Denis Twitchett and John K. Fairbank (Cambridge: Cambridge University Press, 1986), 485.

109. A. F. P. Hulsewe, "Ch'in and Han Law," in *The Cambridge History of China*, vol. 1, *The Ch'in and Han Empires, 221 B.C.–A.D. 220*, ed. Denis Twitchett and John K. Fairbank (Cambridge: Cambridge University Press, 1986), 524.

110. Michael Nylan, "Confucian Piety and Individualism in Han China," *Journal of the American Oriental Society* 116, no. 1 (1996): 1.

111. B. J. Mansvelt Beck, "The Fall of Han," in *The Cambridge History of China*, vol. 1, *The Ch'in and Han Empires, 221 B.C.–A.D. 220*, ed. Denis Twitchett and John K. Fairbank (Cambridge: Cambridge University Press, 1986), 317–57.

112. Hitchner, "Globalization Avant la Lettre," 1–14.

113. Ryan D. Griffiths, "The Waltzian Ordering Principle and International Change: A Two-Dimensional Model," *European Journal of International Relations* 24, no. 1 (2018): 130–52; Charles R. Butcher and Ryan D. Griffiths, "Between Eurocentrism and Babel: A Framework for the Analysis of States, State Systems, and International Orders," *International Studies Quarterly* 61, no. 2 (2017): 328.

114. Cooley and Nexon, *Exit from Hegemony*. For structures of empire, see Daniel H. Nexon and Thomas Wright, "What's at Stake in the American Empire Debate?," *American Political Science Review* 101, no. 2 (2007): 253–71; Jane Burbank and Frederick Cooper, *Empires in World History: Power and the Politics of Difference* (Princeton: Princeton University Press, 2011); Michael W. Doyle, *Empires* (Ithaca: Cornell University Press, 1986).

115. Buzan, *Making Global Society*. While the globalization of a common global institutional architecture has integrated global international society, cultural diversity in ways has increased with the number of possible cultural combinations, in expanded hybrid cultural complexes, but also decreased, in the decline of local cultures. Ulf Hannerz, *Cultural Complexity: Studies in the Social Organization of Meaning* (New York: Columbia University Press, 1991).

116. Michael N. Barnett, *The International Humanitarian Order* (London: Routledge, 2010).

117. Technological transformations are increasingly disruptive but are extending the power of states, not producing new political unit types replacing the nation-state, and the diffusion of new technological capabilities is even enough that a radical disruption in the balance of power is also unlikely, all things being even. James Der Derian and Alexander Wendt, "Quantizing International Relations: The Case for Quantum Approaches to International Theory and Security Practice," *Security Dialogue* 51, no. 5 (2020): 399–413; Daniel Drezner, "Technological Change and International Relations," *International Relations* 33, no. 2 (2019): 286–303.

Chapter 2

1. Nussbaum, *The Cosmopolitan Tradition*.

2. Flikschuh and Ypi, *Kant and Colonialism*; Kleingeld, *Kant and Cosmopolitanism*.

3. Andrew Hurrell, "Kant and the Kantian Paradigm in International Relations," *Review of International Studies* 16, no. 3 (1990): 183–205; Richard Beardsworth, *Cosmopolitanism and International Relations Theory* (Cambridge: Polity, 2011).

4. Kant, *Perpetual Peace and Other Essays*, 118.

5. Michael W. Doyle, "Kant, Liberal Legacies, and Foreign Affairs," *Philosophy & Public Affairs* 12, no. 3 (1983): 205–35; Michael W. Doyle, "Kant, Liberal Legacies, and Foreign Affairs, Part 2," *Philosophy & Public Affairs* 12, no. 4 (1983): 323–53; Kenneth N. Waltz, "Kant, Liberalism, and War," *American Political Science Review* 56, no. 2 (1962): 331–40.

6. Wight, *International Theory*.

7. Michael Donelan, "A Community of Mankind," in *The Community of States: A Study in International Political Theory*, ed. James Mayall (London: George Allen & Unwin, 1982), 140–57.

8. Janet Polasky, *Revolutions without Borders: The Call to Liberty in the Atlantic World* (New Haven: Yale University Press, 2015).

9. Aryeh Neier, *The International Human Rights Movement: A History* (Princeton: Princeton University Press, 2020); Clark, *International Legitimacy and World Society*.

10. Polasky, *Revolutions without Borders*, 5.

11. Edward Bellamy's *Looking Backward* (1888) also told a story where the protagonist awoke from an accidental 100-year sleep to discover a global socialist utopia. In Bellamy's story, capitalism's ever-greater concentration of wealth, it is revealed, produced a total monopoly that was subsequently appropriated by the state, establishing the "Great Trust," which provided everything for all, in a unified postscarcity world. Bellamy's *Looking Backward* had already sold half a million copies by 1891 and has never been out of print. Bellamy's story in this way reflected the heightened financial globalization of the late 19th century, whereas Louis-Sébastien Mercier's reflected the cry to liberty in the 18th century. Both Mercier's and Bellamy's futures depicted utopias, while H. G. Wells's *The Sleeper Awakes* (1898) instead offered a dystopian counternarrative. In Wells's story, the protagonist awakens to a capitalist future, rather than a socialist future, where workers have no labor rights.

12. A. B. Evans, "Revisiting Mercier's 'L'An 2440,'" *Science Fiction Studies* 30, no. 1 (2003): 130–32.

13. Thinker of the French Revolution, Anacharsis Cloots went further than his contemporaries, arguing that liberty and democratic sovereignty implied universal sovereignty and therefore required an integrated *institutional* cosmopolitan order, while most of his revolutionary contemporaries argued for an *internationalist* cosmopolitan order. Alexander Bevilacqua, "Conceiving the Republic of Mankind: The Political Thought of Anacharsis Cloots," *History of European Ideas* 38, no. 4 (2012): 550–69.

14. Glenda Sluga, *The Invention of International Order: Remaking Europe after Napoleon* (Princeton: Princeton University Press, 2021); Henry Kissinger, *A World Restored: The Politics of Conservativism in a Revolutionary Era* (Boston: Houghton Mifflin, 1957); Charles Webster, *The Congress of Vienna: 1814–1815* (London: G. Bell & Sons, 1950).

15. Dominic Lieven, *Russia against Napoleon: The True Story of the Campaigns of War and Peace* (New York: Penguin, 2009).

16. Wolfram Siemann, *Metternich: Strategist and Visionary* (Cambridge, MA: Belknap Press of Harvard University Press, 2019).

17. John Bew, *Castlereagh: Enlightenment, War and Tyranny* (London: Quercus, 2011).

18. Paul W. Schroeder, *The Transformation of European Politics, 1763–1848* (Oxford: Oxford University Press, 1994).

19. Percy Bysshe Shelley, "The Mask of Anarchy," in *Shelley: Poetical Works* (Oxford: Oxford University Press, 1971), 338–344.

20. Christopher Clark, *Revolutionary Spring: Fighting for a New World, 1848–1849* (London: Allen Lane, 2023).

21. Pedersen, *The Guardians*; Clark, *International Legitimacy and World Society*; MacMillan, *Paris 1919*.

22. Patrick O. Cohrs, *The New Atlantic Order: The Transformation of International Politics, 1860–1933* (Cambridge: Cambridge University Press, 2022).

23. Mazower, *Dark Continent*.

24. Daniel Levy and Natan Sznaider, "The Institutionalization of Cosmopolitan Morality: The Holocaust and Human Rights," *Journal of Human Rights* 3, no. 2 (2004): 143–57; Natan Sznaider, *Jewish Memory and the Cosmopolitan Order* (Cambridge: Polity, 2011).

25. Johannes Morsink, *The Universal Declaration of Human Rights: Origins, Drafting, and Intent* (Philadelphia: University of Pennsylvania Press, 1999).

26. "The Universal Declaration of Human Rights," United Nations, https://www.un.org/en/universal-declaration-human-rights/

27. Feminist cosmopolitan thinkers and advocates for the human rights of women have remained skeptical of "universalism" in general and its uses as pretense for hierarchies and domination. Niamh Reilly, "Cosmopolitan Feminism and Human Rights," *Hypatia* 22, no. 4 (2007): 180–98; Kimberly Hutchings, "Feminist Politics and Cosmopolitan Citizenship," in *Cosmopolitan Citizenship*, ed. Kimberly Hutchings and Roland Dannreuther (London: Macmillan, 1999), 120–42.

28. Gerry Simpson, *Law, War, and Crime: War Crimes Trials and the Reinvention of International Law* (Cambridge: Polity, 2007).

29. Jason Ralph, *Defending the Society of States: Why America Opposes the International Criminal Court and Its Vision of World Society* (Oxford: Oxford University Press, 2007).

30. Franklin D. Roosevelt, "Fourth Inaugural Address," Saturday, January 20, 1945. https://avalon.law.yale.edu/20th_century/froos4.asp

31. S. M. Plokhy, *Yalta: The Price of Peace* (London: Viking, 2010); Lloyd C. Gardner, *Spheres of Influence: The Partition of Europe, from Munich to Yalta* (London: John Murray, 1993).

32. Vincent, *Human Rights and International Relations*.

33. Moyn, *The Last Utopia*, 213.

34. Richard Falk, *Achieving Human Rights* (New York: Routledge, 2009), 4.

35. Jeff Bridoux and Milja Kurki, *Democracy Promotion: A Critical Introduction* (London: Routledge, 2014); Beate Jahn, "Rethinking Democracy Promotion," *Review of International Studies* 38, no. 4 (2012): 685–705; Michael Cox, G. John Ikenberry, and Takashi Inoguchi, eds., *American Democracy Promotion: Impulses, Strategies, and Impacts* (Oxford: Oxford University Press, 2000); Tony Smith, *America's Mission: The United States and the Worldwide Struggle for Democracy in the Twentieth Century* (Princeton: Princeton University Press, 1994).

36. Toni Erskine, *Embedded Cosmopolitanism: Duties to Strangers and Enemies in a World of "Dislocated Communities"* (Oxford: Oxford University Press, 2018); Matthew Weinert, *Making Human World Order and the Governance of Human Dignity* (Ann Arbor: University of Michigan Press, 2015); Nicholas Wheeler, *Saving Strangers: Humanitarian Intervention in International Society* (Oxford: Oxford University Press, 2000).

37. Philip Cunliffe, *Cosmopolitan Dystopia: International Intervention and the Failure of the West* (Manchester: Manchester University Press, 2020); Catherine Lu, *Just and Unjust Interventions in World Politics: Public and Private* (London: Palgrave, 2006).

38. Steven C. Roach, *Governance, Order, and the International Criminal Court: Between Realpolitik and a Cosmopolitan Court* (Oxford: Oxford University Press, 2009).

39. Alec Stone Sweet, *A Cosmopolitan Legal Order: Kant, Constitutional Justice, and the European Convention on Human Rights* (Oxford: Oxford University Press, 2018).

40. Kathryn Sikkink, *Evidence for Hope: Making Human Rights Work in the 21st Century* (Princeton: Princeton University Press, 2017); Sikkink, *Justice Cascade*; Michael Ignatieff, *The Rights Revolution* (Toronto: Anansi Press, 2007).

41. Martha Nussbaum, *For Love of Country?* (Boston: Beacon Press, 1996), 133.

42. Nussbaum, *For Love of Country?*, 138.

43. Nussbaum, *Cosmopolitan Tradition*; Martha Nussbaum, *Frontiers of Justice: Disability, Nationality, Species Membership* (Cambridge: Belknap Press of Harvard University Press, 2006).

44. Jurgen Habermas and Jacques Derrida, "What Binds Europeans Together: A Plea for a Common Foreign Policy, Beginning in the Core of Europe," *Constellations* 10, no. 3 (2003): 297; Jurgen Habermas, "A Political Constitution for the Pluralist World Society?," *Anales de la Catedra Francisco Suarez* 39 (2005): 121–32. In international theory, Andrew Linklater's movement brought Habermasian thought more directly to the problem of international order, calling for a cosmopolitan transformation of international society through an Habermasian discourse, in widening circles of open dialogical community leading up to a post-Westphalian cosmopolitan order. His realist critics argued that states under anarchy cannot participate in this Habermasian discourse proper, because they have incentives to hide information and distort it for security imperatives. This realist critique is not quite right, because it rules out groupings of security communities, which may overlap or conflict, and misses the issue that conflict and struggle can become clearer in franker discursive actions. The main limitation of a Habermasian legitimation strategy is that it aims to work out what the more widely acceptable moral and political order is along the way, and assumes that hierarchy legitimation conflicts and recognition struggles in this process can be overcome, and that power has no part to play in resolving them, even in an ideal discursive situation. Andrew Linklater, *The Transformation of Political Community: Ethical Foundations of the Post-Westphalian Era* (Cambridge: Polity Press, 1998); Randall L. Schweller, "Fantasy Theory," *Review of International Studies* 25, no. 1 (1999): 147–50; Andrew Linklater, "Transforming Political Community: A Response to the Critics," *Review of International Studies* 25, no. 1 (1999): 165–75.

45. Seyla Benhabib, *Another Cosmopolitanism* (Oxford: Oxford University Press, 2006), 36.

46. Garrett Wallace Brown, *Grounding Cosmopolitanism: From Kant to the Idea of a Cosmopolitan Constitution* (Edinburgh: Edinburgh University Press, 2009), 17.

47. Thomas Carothers, "The Backlash against Democracy Promotion," *Foreign Affairs* 85, no, 2 (2006): 55–68.

48. Ayca Cubukcu, *For the Love of Humanity: The World Tribunal on Iraq* (Philadelphia: University of Pennsylvania Press, 2018); Ayca Cubukcu, "Thinking against Humanity," *London Review of International Law* 5, no. 2 (2017): 251–67.

49. Stephen Hopgood, *The Endtimes of Human Rights* (New York: Cornell University Press, 2013), x.

50. Jack Donnelly, *Universal Human Rights in Theory and Practice* (Ithaca: Cornell University Press, 1989); Charles Beitz, "Human Dignity in the Theory of Human Rights: Nothing but a Phrase?," *Philosophy & Public Affairs* 41, no. 3 (2013): 259–90.

51. Joe Hoover, *Reconstructing Human Rights: A Pragmatist and Pluralist Inquiry into Global Ethics* (London: Routledge, 2016); Charles R. Beitz, *The Idea of Human Rights* (Oxford: Oxford University Press, 2005).

52. Mayall, *World Politics*.

53. Gerstle, *Rise and Fall of the Neoliberal Order*, 13.

54. Beitz, *Idea of Human Rights*; Thomas Pogge, *Realizing Rawls* (Ithaca: Columbia University Press, 1989); Thomas Pogge, "Cosmopolitanism and Sovereignty," *Ethics* 103, no. 1 (1992): 48–75; Huw Lloyd Williams, *On Rawls, Development and Global Justice* (London: Palgrave, 2011).

55. Martha C. Nussbaum, *Creating Capabilities: The Human Development Approach* (Cambridge: Belknap Press of Harvard University Press, 2011); Amartya Sen, *The Idea of Justice* (Cambridge, MA: Belknap Press of Harvard University Press, 2009); Michael Sandel, *The Tyranny of Merit: What's Become of the Common Good?* (New York: Penguin, 2020); Lea Ypi, *Global Justice and Avant-Garde Political Agency* (Oxford: Oxford University Press, 2012).

56. Quinn Slobodian, *Globalists: The End of Empire and the Birth of Neoliberalism* (Cambridge, MA: Harvard University Press, 2018).

57. Adler-Nissen and Zarakol, "Struggles for Recognition," 611–34.

58. Gerstle, *Rise and Fall of the Neoliberal Order*, 5, 9, 13–14.

59. Trubowitz and Burgoon, *Geopolitics and Democracy*, 18.

60. Norris and Inglehart, *Cultural Backlash*.

61. Ian Bremmer, *Us vs. Them: The Failure of Globalism* (London: Penguin, 2018): 12.

62. John Gray, *False Dawn: The Delusions of Global Capitalism* (New York: New Press, 1998), 234.

63. Trubowitz and Burgoon, *Geopolitics and Democracy*, 19.

64. John Gray, *The New Leviathans: Thoughts after Liberalism* (London: Allen Lane, 2023).

65. Nussbaum, *Cosmopolitan Tradition*, 211, 209.

66. Craig Calhoun, "Belonging in the Cosmopolitan Imaginary," *Ethnicities* 3, no. 4 (2003): 532.

67. Chris Brown, "Universal Human Rights: A Critique," in *Practical Judgement in International Political Theory: Selected Essays* (London: Routledge, 2010), 53–71.

68. Katrina Forrester, *In the Shadow of Justice: Postwar Liberalism and the Remaking of Political Philosophy* (Princeton: Princeton University Press, 2019), 8.

69. Onora O'Neill, *Bounds of Justice* (Cambridge: Cambridge University Press, 2004), 2.

70. John Rawls, *The Law of Peoples: With the Idea of Public Reason Revisited* (Cambridge, MA: Harvard University Press, 1999); Chris Brown, "The Construction of a 'Realistic Utopia': John Rawls and International Political Theory," in *Practical Judgement in International Political Theory: Selected Essays* (London: Routledge, 2010), 105–21.

71. Forrester, *In the Shadow of Justice*; John Rawls, *A Theory of Justice* (London: Belknap Press of Harvard University Press, 1971); Brian Barry, *The Liberal Theory of Justice* (Oxford: Clarendon Press, 1973); Charles Beitz, *Political Theory and International Relations*, 2nd ed. (Princeton: Princeton University Press, 1999); Pogge, *Realizing Rawls*; Pogge, "Cosmopolitanism and Sovereignty," 48–75; Williams, *On Rawls, Development and Global Justice*. Numerous other ethical arguments have been made for the existence of unseen webs of cosmopolitan obligations and duties in a globalized world, beyond Rawlsian frameworks. Mathias Risse, *On Global Justice* (Princeton: Princeton University Press, 2012); Luis Cabrera, *Political Theory of Global Justice: A Cosmopolitan Case for the World State* (London: Routledge, 2004); Peter Singer, *One World: The Ethics of Globalization* (New Haven: Yale University Press, 2002).

72. Beitz, *Political Theory and International Relations*, 8.

73. Pogge, *Realizing Rawls*, 276.

74. Chris Brown, *Sovereignty, Rights, and Justice: International Political Theory Today* (Cambridge: Polity, 2002); Charles Taylor, "The Plurality of Goods," in *The Legacy of Isaiah Berlin*, ed. Mark Lilla, Ronald Dworkin, and Robert B. Silvers (New York: New York Review of Books, 2001), 113–20.

75. Simon Caney, *Justice beyond Borders: A Global Political Theory* (Oxford: Oxford University Press, 2005); Jeremy Waldron, "What Is Cosmopolitan?," *Journal of Political Philosophy* 8, no. 2 (2000): 230; Brown, *Grounding Cosmopolitanism*.

76. Gillian Brock, *Global Justice: A Cosmopolitan Account* (Oxford: Oxford University Press, 2009), 8.

77. Brown, *Grounding Cosmopolitanism*, 123–43.

78. Charles Taylor, *A Secular Age* (Cambridge, MA: Belknap Press of Harvard University Press, 2007), 180, 554, 580, 589.

79. Martin Wight also viewed Kantian cosmopolitanism as a secularized worldview, contingent on and characterized by prior religious beliefs. For Wight, "At the heart of Kantianism . . . is a religious element: the desire to convert the world, to save mankind from the wrath to come. But the supreme test of religious emotion is how it responds to a situation where it is clear that a large proportion of mankind is obstinately uninterested in being converted," Wight *International Theory*, 205.

80. Andrew Hurrell, "Cultural Diversity within Global International Society," in *Culture and Order in World Politics*, ed. Andrew Phillips and Christian Reus-Smit (Cambridge: Cambridge University Press, 2020), 115–36.

81. William E. Connolly, "Speed, Concentric Cultures, and Cosmopolitanism," *Political Theory* 28, no. 5 (2000): 602.

82. Nussbaum, *Cosmopolitan Tradition*, 3–4.

83. Kwame Anthony Appiah, *Cosmopolitanism: Ethics in a World of Strangers* (New York: W.W. Norton, 2006).

84. Nussbaum, *For Love of Country?*, 138.

85. Nussbaum, *Cosmopolitan Tradition*, 247–48.

86. Charles Taylor, "Conditions of an Unforced Consensus on Human Rights," in *Dilemmas and Connections: Selected Essays* (Cambridge, MA: Belknap Press of Harvard University Press, 2011), 105–23.

87. Richard Rorty, *What Can We Hope For? Essays on Politics* (Princeton: Princeton University Press, 2022); Richard Rorty, *Contingency, Irony, and Solidarity* (Cambridge: Cambridge University Press, 1989); Richard Rorty, "Justice as a Larger Loyalty," *Ethical Perspectives* 4, no. 2 (1997): 139–51; Richard Rorty, "Who Are We? Moral Universalism and Economic Triage," *Diogenes* 173, no. 44/1 (1996): 5–15.

88. Richard Rorty, "Cosmopolitanism without Emancipation: A Response to Jean-Francois Lyotard," in *Objectivity, Relativism, and Truth: Philosophical Papers* (Cambridge: Cambridge University Press, 1991), 211–22.

89. Luis Cabrera, *The Humble Cosmopolitan: Rights, Diversity, and Trans-State Democracy* (Oxford: Oxford University Press, 2020), 8.

90. This phrase is Martin Wight's, in his review of Kantian historical wagers in F. H. Hinsley, *Power and the Pursuit of Peace: Theory and Practice in the History of Relations between States* (Cambridge: Cambridge University Press, 1963); Martin Wight, "Does Peace Take Care of Itself?," in *Foreign Policy and Security Strategy*, ed. David S. Yost (Oxford: Oxford University Press, 2023), 79–85.

91. Derrida, *On Cosmopolitanism and Forgiveness*, 3.

Chapter 3

1. Harold Laski, *Communism* (London: Frank Cass & Co., 1968), 22.

2. Karl Marx and Friedrich Engels, *The Communist Manifesto*, trans. Samuel Moore (London: Penguin, 2015), 7.

3. In the wake of Marxism, Hegelian history enjoyed a revival of sorts, but his political thought still did not fit an era of globalization, which Marx worked so hard to theorize. Hegel found no need for larger forms of community and seems to suggest that they would stifle the freedom of local communities. For Hegel, the freedom or *Giest* of the community would be constrained by larger political orders. He did not seem to acknowledge the vulnerability of national communities in a globalizing world to security interdependence or economic turmoil. Why Hegel was opposed to an *institutional* cosmopolitan order seems clear, for the sake of freedom, but about an *internationalist* cosmopolitanism, Hegel's thought curiously still seems unable to embrace it. Chris Brown, "Hegel and International Ethics," in *Practical Judgement in International Political Theory: Selected Essays* (London: Routledge, 2010), 133–43.

4. Marx and Engels, *The Communist Manifesto*, 52.

5. The international thought of Rosa Luxemburg, for instance, has been described as "essentially an identification with humanity as such, since the universal class ultimately liberates all." Kimberly Hutchings, "Luxemburg's Socialist International Theory," in *Women's International Thought: A New History*, ed. Patricia Owens and Katharina Rietzler (Cambridge: Cambridge University Press, 2021), 64.

6. Leon Trotsky, *The History of the Russian Revolution* (London: Pluto Press, 1977), 1026.

7. Quoted in Jonathan Haslam, *The Spectre of War: International Communism and the Origins of World War II* (Princeton: Princeton University Press, 2021), 18.

8. Arthur Herman, *1917: Lenin, Wilson, and the Birth of the New World Disorder* (New York: Harper Perennial, 2017).

9. MacMillan, *Paris 1919*, 63–82.

10. Western statespersons were initially divided on how best to respond to the civil war in Russia, whether to intervene directly, to withdraw support for the Whites, or to muddle through.

11. Archie Brown, *The Rise and Fall of Communism* (London: Vintage Books, 2009), 117; Franz Borkenau, *World Communism: A History of the Communist International* (Ann Arbor: University of Michigan Press, 1962), 421.

12. Peter Lamb, *Harold Laski: Problems of Democracy, the Sovereign State, and International Society* (London: Palgrave, 2004); Harold J. Laski, *Reflections on the Revolution of Our Time* (Frank Cass & Co., 1968).

13. E. H. Carr, *A History of Soviet Russia*, in 14 vols.; Sydney Webb and Beatrice Webb, *Soviet Communism: A New Civilization*, 3rd ed. (London: Longmans, Green, 1944); W. E. B. Du Bois, "The Riddle of Russia," in Du Bois, *Color and Democracy: Colonies and Peace* (Oxford: Oxford University Press, 2007), 312–17.

14. Gabriel Gorodetsky, ed., *The Maisky Dairies: Red Ambassador to the Court of St. James's, 1932–1943* (New Haven: Yale University Press, 2015).

15. Michael Burleigh, *The Third Reich: A New History* (London: Farrar, Straus and Giroux, 2001).

16. Mark Mazower, *Hitler's Empire: How the Nazis Ruled Europe* (New York: Penguin, 2008). "Fascist internationalism" of the era, across and between fascist powers, should not be confused with "cosmopolitan internationalism," because fascist internationalism is premised on constructing cooperation of exclusionary nationalisms, not wider cosmopolitan modes of belonging. Jen Steffek, "Fascist Internationalism," *Millennium: Journal of International Studies* 44, no. 1, (2015): 3–22.

17. Federico Romero, "Cold War Anti-Communism and the Impact of Communism on the West," in *The Cambridge History of Communism*, vol. 2, *The Socialist Camp and World Power, 1941–1960s*, ed. Norman Naimark, Silvio Pons, and Sophie Quinn-Judge (Cambridge: Cambridge University Press, 2017), 291; Haslam, *Spectre of War*.

18. Romero, "Cold War Anti-Communism and the Impact of Communism on the West," 294–97.

19. Stalin, quoted in George F. Kennan, "Telegram from Moscow to the US Secretary of State ("Long Telegram"), February 22, 1946, 2: https://www.trumanlibrary.gov/libr ary/research-files/telegram-george-kennan-james-byrnes-long-telegram?documentid= NA&pagenumber=2

20. Elizabeth Edwards Spalding, *The First Cold Warrior: Harry Truman, Containment, and the Remaking of Liberal Internationalism* (Lexington: University Press of Kentucky, 2006); Melvyn P. Leffler, *A Preponderance of Power: National Security, the Truman Administration, and the Cold War* (Stanford: Stanford University Press, 1992).

21. Romero, "Cold War Anti-Communism and the Impact of Communism on the West," 292; Arne Westad, *The Global Cold War: Third World Interventions and the Making of Our Times* (Cambridge: Cambridge University Press, 2005).

22. Andrei Zhdanov, "New Aspects of the World Conflict: The International Situ-

ation" (1947), https://soviethistory.msu.edu/1947-2/cold-war/cold-war-texts/zhdanov-on-the-international-situation/; see also Yoram Gorlizki and Oleg V. Khlevniuk, *Cold Peace: Stalin and the Soviet Ruling Circle, 1945–1953* (Oxford: Oxford University Press, 2004).

23. Arthur Koestler, *Darkness at Noon* (London: Penguin, 1946), 57.

24. Arthur Koestler, *The Invisible Writing: An Autobiography, 1931–1953* (London: Collins with Hamish Hamilton, 1954), 15.

25. Richard Bradford, *Orwell: A Man of Our Time* (London: Bloomsbury, 2020), 210.

26. George Orwell, quoted in Thomas Pynchon's "Introduction" to *Nineteen Eighty-Four* (London: Penguin, 2003), xii.

27. Arthur M. Schlesinger Jr., *The Vital Center: The Politics of Freedom* (New York: Routledge, 1998).

28. Karl Popper, *The Open Society and its Enemies*, Vol. 1, *The Spell of Plato* (London: George Routledge & Sons, 1945), 152.

29. Isaiah Berlin, "Political Ideas in the Twentieth Century," *Foreign Affairs* 28, no. 3 (1950): 351–85.

30. Isaiah Berlin, *Four Essays on Liberty* (Oxford: Oxford University Press, 1969); John Gray, *Isaiah Berlin: An Interpretation of His Thought* (Princeton: Princeton University Press, 1996).

31. Martin Wight, "Western Values in International Relations," in *Diplomatic Investigations: Essays in the Theory of International Politics*, ed. Herbert Butterfield and Martin Wight (Oxford: Oxford University Press, 2019), 171–97; William Bain, "Rival Traditions of Natural Law: Martin Wight and the Theory of International Society," *International History Review* 36, no. 5 (2014): 943–60; Ian Hall, "Martin Wight, Western Values, and the Whig Tradition of International Thought," *International History Review* 36, no. 5 (2014): 961–81.

32. Wight, "Western Values," 153.

33. R. J. Vincent later extended Wight's influential study to Western values beyond international society, noting a tension between the via media as an approach to international order and moral concerns in world society beyond it, in "Western Conceptions of a Universal Moral Order," 20–46.

34. Patrick Thaddeus Jackson, *Civilizing the Enemy: German Reconstruction and the Invention of the West* (Ann Arbor: University of Michigan Press, 2006); Patrick Thaddeus Jackson, "Defending the West: Occidentalism and the Formation of NATO," *Journal of Political Philosophy* 11, no. 3 (2003): 223–52.

35. Jackson, *Civilizing the Enemy*, 113.

36. Robert Jervis, "Identity and the Cold War," in *The Cambridge History of the Cold War*, vol. 1, *Crises and Détente*, ed. Melvyn P. Leffler and Odd Arne Westad (Cambridge: Cambridge University Press, 2010), 25.

37. Jervis, "Identity and the Cold War," 26.

38. George Orwell, *Notes on Nationalism* (London: Penguin, 1984), 7.

39. Wight, *International Theory*, 205.

40. Halliday, *Revolution and World Politics*, 5.

41. R. N. Berki, "On Marxian Thought and the Problem of International Relations," *World Politics* 24, no. 1 (1971): 80–105. Martin Wight suggested that rival doctrines and intracommunist clashes were theoretically scandalous for world communism, whose

"only solution would be the formation of a Communist world-state" because that was "the logical goal of Marxist-Leninist theory" while, however, "the practical difficulties in the way of its achievement are too great to be ignored." Martin Wight, "The Communist Theory of International Relations," in *International Relations and Political Philosophy*, ed. David S. Yost (Oxford: Oxford University Press, 2022), 140.

42. Sergey Radchenko, "The Sino-Soviet Split," in *The Cambridge History of the Cold War*, ed. Melvyn P. Leffler and Odd Arne Westad (Cambridge: Cambridge University Press), 349.

43. Stephen Gill, *Gramsci, Historical Materialism and International Relations* (Cambridge: Cambridge University Press, 1993).

44. Antonio Gramsci, *Selections from the Prison Notebooks of Antonio Gramsci* (New York: International Publishers, 1971).

45. Stanislaw Lem, *Memoirs Found in a Bathtub*, trans. Michael Kandel and Christine Rose (San Diego: Harcourt Brace, 1973), 10.

46. The White House, "Second Expanded Bilateral Session," 1989.

47. Michael Cox, *The Post–Cold War World: Turbulence and Change in World Politics since the Fall* (London: Routledge, 2019); Kristina Spohr, *Post Wall, Post Square: Rebuilding the World after 1989* (London: William Collins, 2019).

48. Jacques Derrida, *Specters of Marx: The State of Debt, the Work of Mourning and the New International* (New York: Routledge, 1994).

49. Giorgio Agamben, *The Coming Community* (Minneapolis: University of Minnesota Press, 1993); Sergei Prozorov, "Generic Universalism in World Politics: Beyond International Anarchy and the World State," *International Theory* 1, no. 2 (2009): 215–47; Jean Luc Nancy, "The Confronted Community," *Post-Colonial Studies* 6, no. 1 (2003): 23–36; Jean Luc Nancy, *Being Singular Plural* (Stanford: Stanford University Press, 2000).

50. Stephen Gill, *Power and Resistance in the New World Order*, 2nd ed. (London: Palgrave, 2008); Stephen Gill, ed., *Critical Perspectives on the Crisis of Global Governance: Reimagining the Future* (London: Palgrave, 2015); Gill and Cutler, *New Constitutionalism and World Order*.

51. Michael Hardt and Antonio Negri, *Empire* (Cambridge, MA: Harvard University Press, 2000); Michael Hardt and Antonio Negri, *Multitude: War and Democracy in the Age of Empire* (New York: Penguin, 2004); Hardt and Negri themselves were partly inspired by Agamben's *The Coming Community*.

52. Michael Hardt and Antonio Negri, *Commonwealth* (Cambridge, MA: Harvard University Press, 2009); Michael Hardt and Antonio Negri, "Empire, Twenty Years On," *New Left Review* 120 (2019): 67–92.

53. Jodi Dean, *The Communist Horizon* (London: Verso, 2012).

54. Jodi Dean, *Comrade: An Essay on Political Belonging* (New York: Penguin, 2019).

55. George Eaton, "Francis Fukuyama Interview: Socialism Ought to Come Back," *New Statesman*, October 17, 2018, https://www.newstatesman.com/politics/2018/10/francis-fukuyama-interview-socialism-ought-come-back

56. Thomas Piketty, *Capital and Ideology* (Cambridge, MA: Harvard University Press, 2020); Thomas Piketty, *Capital in the Twenty-First Century* (Cambridge, MA: Harvard University Press, 2014).

57. Rousseau, *The Plan for Perpetual Peace*, 49.

58. George Orwell, "Wells, Hitler and the World State," in *Critical Essays* (London: Secker and Warburg, 1946), https://orwell.ru/library/reviews/wells/english/e_whws

59. Elisabeth Weber, *Living Together: Jacques Derrida's Communities of Violence and Peace* (New York: Fordham University Press, 2013).

60. Martin Wight, "The Communist Theory of International Relations," in *International Relations and Political Philosophy*, ed. David S. Yost (Oxford: Oxford University Press, 2022), 131.

Chapter 4

1. Julian Go, "Fanon's Postcolonial Cosmopolitanism," *European Journal of Social Theory* 16, no. 2 (2013): 209; Nico Slate, *Colored Cosmopolitanism: The Shared Struggle for Freedom in the United States and India* (Cambridge: Harvard University Press, 2012).

2. Adom Getachew, *Worldmaking after Empire: The Rise and Fall of Self-Determination* (Princeton: Princeton University Press, 2019); Siba N. Grovogui, *Beyond Eurocentrism and Anarchy: Memories of International Order and Institutions* (London: Palgrave, 2006).

3. Getachew, *Worldmaking after Empire*, 33.

4. Getachew, *Worldmaking after Empire*, 35.

5. Go, "Fanon's Postcolonial Cosmopolitanism," 215.

6. Rahul Rao, "Postcolonial Cosmopolitanism: Making Place for Nationalism," in *The Democratic Predicament: Cultural Diversity in Europe and India*, ed. Jyotirmaya Tripathy and Sudarsan Padmanabhan (New Delhi: Routledge, 2012), 165–87.

7. Liane Hartnett, "Love Is Worldmaking: Reading Rabindranath Tagore's Gora as International Theory," *International Studies Quarterly* 66, no. 3 (2023): https://doi.org/10.1093/isq/sqac037; Saranindranath Tagore, "Tagore's Conception of Cosmopolitanism: A Reconstruction," *University of Toronto Quarterly* 77, no. 4 (2008): 1070–84.

8. Quoted in Go, "Fanon's Postcolonial Cosmopolitanism," 216–17.

9. W. E. B. Du Bois, *The World and Africa and Color and Democracy* (Oxford: Oxford University Press, 2007), 164–65.

10. Du Bois, "Worlds of Color," 444.

11. George Padmore, *Pan-Africanism or Communism? The Coming Struggle for Africa* (New York: Roy Publishers, 1956), 18–19.

12. Kwame Nkrumah, *Neo-Colonialism: The Last Stage of Imperialism* (New York: International Publishers, 1965).

13. Jawaharlal Nehru, *The Discovery of India* (New Delhi: Oxford University Press, 1985), 565.

14. Getachew, *Worldmaking after Empire*, 5.

15. Aimé Césaire, *Discourse on Colonialism*, trans. Joan Pinkham (New York: Monthly Review Press, 1972).

16. Urs Matthias Zachmann, ed., *Asia after Versailles: Asian Perspectives on the Paris Peace Conference and the Interwar Order, 1919–33* (Edinburgh: Edinburgh University Press, 2017).

17. Pedersen, *The Guardians*.

18. Getachew, *Worldmaking after Empire*, 55.

19. W. E. B. Du Bois, "Inter-Racial Implications of the Ethiopian Crisis: A Negro View," *Foreign Affairs* 14, no. 1 (1935): 86.

20. William Bain, *Between Anarchy and Society: Trusteeship and the Obligations of Power* (Oxford: Oxford University Press, 2003), 108–9, 111, 114.

21. Thijs Brocades Zaalberg and Bart Luttikhuis, eds., *Empire's Violent End: Comparing Dutch, British, and French Wars of Decolonization, 1945–1962* (Ithaca: Cornell University Press, 2022).

22. Amitav Acharya, *Constructing Global Order: Agency and Change in World Politics* (Cambridge: Cambridge University Press, 2018); Quỳnh N. Phạm and Robbie Shilliam, eds., *Meanings of Bandung: Postcolonial Orders and Decolonial Visions* (London: Rowman & Littlefield, 2016); Robert Vitalis, "The Midnight Ride of Kwame Nkrumah and Other Fables of Bandung (Ban-doong)," *Humanity: An International Journal of Human Rights, Humanitarianism, and Development* 4, no. 2 (2013): 261–88.

23. Wight, *International Theory*, 87.

24. Pham and Shilliam, "Reviving Bandung," in *The Meanings of Bandung: Postcolonial Orders and Decolonial Visions* (London: Rowman & Littlefield, 2016), 11.

25. Getachew, *Worldmaking after Empire*, 1–36.

26. United Nations, "Declaration on the Establishment of a New International Economic Order," *General Assembly, Sixth Special Session* (1974), 3.

27. Andre Gunder Frank, "Rhetoric and Reality of the New International Economic Order," in *Transforming the World-Economy? Nine Critical Essays on the New International Economic Order*, ed. Herb Addo (Kent: Hodder & Sons and the United Nations, 1984), 165–66.

28. United Nations, "Declaration on the Establishment of a New International Economic Order," *General Assembly, Sixth Special Session* (1974), 3.

29. United Nations, "Declaration on the Establishment of a New International Economic Order," *General Assembly, Sixth Special Session* (1974), 3.

30. Adom Getachew, *Worldmaking after Empire*, 171.

31. Vijay Prashad, *The Darker Nations: A People's History of the Third World* (New York: New Press, 2007).

32. Prashad, *The Darker Nations*, 215.

33. Prashad, *The Darker Nations*, 220.

34. Prashad, *The Darker Nations*, 246.

35. Andrew Adonis and Tim Hames, eds., *A Conservative Revolution? The Reagan-Thatcher Decade in Perspective* (Manchester: Manchester University Press, 1994).

36. Ronald Reagan, "Statement at the First Plenary Session of the International Meeting on Cooperation and Development in Cancun, Mexico," October 22, 1981, Reagan Library, https://www.reaganlibrary.gov/archives/speech/statement-first-plenary-session-international-meeting-cooperation-and-development

37. Slobodian, *Globalists*, 223.

38. Adam K. Webb, "Can the Global South Take Over the Baton? What Cosmopolitanism in 'Unlikely' Places Means for Future World Order," *Third World Quarterly* 37, no. 6 (2016): 1016–34; Holton, *Cosmopolitanisms*; Pnina Werbner, *Anthropology and the New Cosmopolitanism* (Oxford: Berg, 2008); Stuart Hall, "Political Belonging in a World of Multiple Identities," in *Conceiving Cosmopolitanism: Theory, Context, and Practice*, ed., Steven Vertovec and Robin Cohen (Oxford: Oxford University Press, 2002), 25–31;

Mica Nava, "Cosmopolitan Modernity: Everyday Imaginaries and the Register of Difference," *Theory, Culture & Society* 19, nos. 1–2 (2002): 81–99. Contemporary postcolonial science fiction tends to imagine freedom beyond domination found on distant worlds. The point seems to be an exploration of how steep the hurdles to freedom on earth have been; its realization requires a world to itself. Nalo Hopkinson and Uppinder Mehan, *So Long Been Dreaming: Postcolonial Science Fiction & Fantasy* (Vancouver: Arsenal Pulp Press, 2004).

39. Paul Gilroy, "A New Cosmopolitanism," *Interventions* 7, no. 3 (2005): 287–92.

40. Stephen Chan, *African Political Thought: An Intellectual Quest for the History of Freedom* (London: Hurst, 2021).

41. Sarah Balakrishnan, "Pan-African Legacies, Afropolitan Futures: A Conversation with Achille Mbembe," *Transition* 120 (2016): 28–37; Achille Mbembe, *On the Postcolony* (London: University of California Press, 2001).

42. Achille Mbembe, *Critique of Black Reason* (Durham: Duke University Press, 2017), 176–77.

43. Étienne Balibar, *Secularism and Cosmopolitanism: Critical Hypotheses on Religion and Politics* (New York: Columbia University Press, 2018); Giorgio Shani, *Religion, Identity and Human Security* (London: Routledge, 2014).

44. Catherine Lu, *Justice and Reconciliation in World Politics* (Cambridge: Cambridge University Press, 2017), 276–77.

45. Stephen Chan, *Plural International Relations in a Divided World* (Cambridge: Polity, 2017).

46. Kira Huju, "The Cosmopolitan Standard of Civilization: A Reflexive Sociology of Elite Belonging among Indian Diplomats," *European Journal of International Relations* 29, no. 3 (2023): 698–722; Christopher Coker, *The Rise of the Civilizational State* (Cambridge: Polity, 2019); Fred Dallmayr, M. Akif Kayapinar, and Ismail Yaylaci, eds., *Civilizations and World Order: Geopolitics and Cultural Difference* (Lanham, MD: Lexington Books, 2014); Peter J. Katzenstein, ed., *Civilizations in World Politics: Plural and Pluralist Perspectives* (London: Routledge, 2010); Dimitrios Stroikos, "Introduction: Rethinking the Standard(s) of Civilisation(s) in International Relations," *Millennium: Journal of International Studies* 42, no. 3 (2014): 546–56; Martin Hall and Patrick Thaddeus Jackson, eds., *Civilizational Identity: The Production and Reproduction of "Civilizations" in International Relations* (London: Palgrave, 2007); Gerrit Gong, *The Standard of 'Civilization' in International Society* (Oxford: Oxford University Press, 1984).

47. Tim Murithi, "Order of Oppression: Africa's Quest for a New International System," *Foreign Affairs*, April 18, 2023, https://www.foreignaffairs.com/africa/global-south-un-order-oppression; Leslie Vinjamuri, "Why Multilateralism Still Matters: The Right Way to Win Over the Global South," *Foreign Affairs*, October 2, 2023, https://www.foreignaffairs.com/world/why-multilateralism-still-matters

48. Hopkinson and Mehan, *So Long Been Dreaming*.

Chapter 5

1. Arthur Koestler, *The Sleepwalkers: A History of Man's Changing Vision of the Universe* (London: Macmillan, 1959), 27.

2. Bartelson, *Visions of World Community*, 181–82.

3. Falkner, *Environmentalism and Global International Society*, 33; Robyn Eckersley, *Environmentalism and Political Theory: Toward an Ecocentric Approach* (London: UCL Press, 1992).

4. Paul Wapner, "The Changing Nature of Nature: Environmental Politics in the Anthropocene," *Global Environmental Politics* 14, no. 4 (2014): 36–54.

5. Dipesh Chakrabarty, "Planetary Crises and the Difficulty of Being Modern," *Millennium: Journal of International Studies* 46, no. 3 (2018): 259–82; Paul Gilroy, "Planetarity and Cosmopolitics," *British Journal of Sociology* 61, no. 3 (2010): 620–26; Heikki Patomaki and Manfred B. Steger, "Social Imaginaries and Big History: Towards a New Planetary Consciousness?," *Futures* 42, no. 10 (2010): 1056–63; Patrick Hayden, "Globalization, Reflexive Utopianism, and the Cosmopolitan Social Imaginary," in *Globalization and Utopia: Critical Essays*, ed. Patrick Hayden and Chamsy el-Ojeili (London: Palgrave, 2009), 51–67.

6. Planetary imaginaries form the background and notion assumptions of emergent primary institutions, deeply and pervasively held, enabling and constraining secondary organizational and regulative institutions. Robert Falkner and Barry Buzan, "The Emergence of Environmental Stewardship as a Primary Institution of Global International Society," *European Journal of International Relations* 25, no. 1 (2019): 131–55.

7. Barbara Ward, *Space Ship Earth* (New York: Columbia University Press, 1966); Kenneth Boulding, "Cowboys on Spaceship Earth," *Monthly Labor Review* 97 (1974): 33.

8. Barbara Ward and Rene Jules Dubos, *Only One Earth: The Care and Maintenance of a Small Planet: An Unofficial Report Commissioned by the Secretary-General of the United Nations Conference on the Human Environment* (New York: Penguin, 1972); Benjamin B. Ferencz and Ken Keyes Jr., *Planethood: The Key to Your Survival and Prosperity* (Coos Bay, OR: Vision Books, 1988).

9. Carl Sagan, *Cosmos* (London: Macdonald & Co, 1981); Carl Sagan, *The Cosmic Connection: An Extraterrestrial Perspective* (New York: Dell, 1973).

10. George F. Kennan, "To Prevent a World Wasteland: A Proposal," *Foreign Affairs* 48, no. 3 (1970): 401–13.

11. Richard Falk, *This Endangered Planet: Prospects and Proposals for Human Survival* (New York: Random House, 1971).

12. Clare Heyward and Dominic Roser, *Climate Justice in a Non-Ideal World* (Oxford: Oxford University Press, 2016); Patrick Hayden, "The Environment, Global Justice and World Environmental Justice," in *The Cosmopolitanism Reader*, ed. Garrett Wallace Brown and David Held (Cambridge: Polity Press, 2010), 351–72.

13. Robert O. Keohane and David G. Victor, "The Regime Complex for Climate Change," *Perspectives on Politics* 9, no. 1 (2011): 7–23.

14. Falkner, *Environmentalism and Global International Society*, 76.

15. Falkner and Buzan, "Emergence of Environmental Stewardship."

16. Robert Falkner, "Global Environmentalism and the Greening of International Society," *International Affairs* 88, no. 3 (2012): 503–22; Robyn Eckersley, *The Green State: Rethinking Democracy and Sovereignty* (Cambridge, MA: MIT Press, 2004).

17. Robert Falkner, "The Paris Agreement and the New Logic of International Climate Politics," *International Affairs* 92, no. 5 (2016): 1107–25.

18. Johannes Urpelainen and Thijs Van de Graaf, "United States Non-Cooperation and the Paris Agreement," *Climate Policy* 18, no. 7 (2018): 839–51.

19. Anthony Burke, "Security Cosmopolitanism," *Critical Studies on Security* 1, no. 1 (2013): 13–28.

20. Falkner, *Environmentalism and Global International Society*, 193.

21. Riley E. Dunlap and Aaron M. McWright, "Organized Climate Change Denial," in *The Oxford Handbook of Climate Change and Society*, ed. John S. Dryzek, Richard B. Norgaard, and David Schlosberg (Oxford: Oxford University Press, 2011), 144–60.

22. Peter J. Jacques, *Environmental Skepticism: Ecology, Power, and Public Life* (London: Routledge, 2016); Peter J. Jacques, "Regard of Modernity: Environmental Skepticism as a Struggle of Citizenship," *Global Environmental Politics* 6, no. 1 (2006): 76–101.

23. Bruno Latour, *Down to Earth: Politics in the New Climatic Regime* (Cambridge: Polity, 2018).

24. Henry Shue, "Climate Dreaming: Negative Emissions, Risk Transfer, and Irreversibility," *Journal of Human Rights and the Environment* 8, no. 2 (2017): 203–16.

25. Colgan, *Partial Hegemony*, 218.

26. Robyn Eckersley, "Geopolitan Democracy in the Anthropocene," *Political Studies* 65, no. 4 (2017): 983–99; Anthony Burke et al., "Planet Politics: A Manifesto from the End of IR," *Millennium: Journal of International Studies* 44, no. 3 (2016): 499–523; Anthony Burke, "The Good State, from a Cosmic Point of View," *International Politics* 50, no. 1 (2013): 57–76; Vandana Shiva, *Earth Democracy: Justice, Sustainability, and Peace* (Berkeley, CA: North Atlantic Books, 2005); Frank Biermann and Steffen Bauer, eds., *A World Environment Organization: Solution or Threat for Effective International Environmental Governance?* (London: Ashgate, 2005).

27. Robert Falkner and Barry Buzan, eds., *Great Powers, Climate Change, and Global Environmental Responsibilities* (Oxford: Oxford University Press, 2022); Falkner, *Environmentalism and Global International Society*; Robert Falkner, "The Anarchical Society and Climate Change," in *The Anarchical Society at 40: Contemporary Challenges and Prospects*, ed. Hidemi Suganami, Madeline Carr, and Adam Humphreys (Oxford: Oxford University Press, 2017), 198–215; Terry MacDonald and Kate MacDonald, "Towards a 'Pluralist' World Order: Creative Agency and Legitimacy in Global Institutions," *European Journal of International Relations* 26, no. 2 (2020): 518–44.

28. By utopia, I mean an imagined ideal order that under no conditions or circumstances can be realized. Utopias tend to be imagined as hidden or protected from real world circumstances and conditions. Dystopias tend to be imagined as ideal orders corrupted by real world conditions or circumstances. Wells's *Modern Utopia* (1905) went so far as to imagine a planetary utopia on another world, because the modern world, he argued, had become so interconnected that it had become impossible to reasonably imagine utopia anywhere on Earth.

29. Bruno Latour, "Whose Cosmos, Which Cosmopolitics?," *Common Knowledge* 10, no. 3 (2004): 450–62; Bruno Latour, "Agency at the Time of the Anthropocene," *New Literary History* 45, no. 1 (2014): 16; Bruno Latour, "From Realpolitik to Dingpolitik: Or How to Make Things Public," in *Making Things Public: Atmospheres of Democracy* (Cambridge, MA: MIT Press, 2005), 4–31; Bruno Latour, "Onus Orbis Terrarum: About a Possible Shift in the Definition of Sovereignty," *Millennium: Journal of International*

Studies 44, no. 3 (2016): 305–20; Anna M. Agathangelou, "Bruno Latour and Ecology Politics: Poetics of Failure and Denial in IR," *Millennium: Journal of International Studies* 44, no. 3 (2016): 321–47; Marie-Eve Morin, "The Spacing of Time and the Place of Hospitality: Living Together according to Bruno Latour and Jacques Derrida," *Parallax* 2, no. 1 (2015): 26–41.

30. Bruno Latour, *Facing Gaia: Eight Lectures on the New Climatic Regime* (Cambridge, MA: Polity Press, 2017); Bruno Latour, *Reset Modernity!* (Cambridge, MA: MIT Press, 2016).

31. By Gaia, Latour does not mean James Lovelock's hypothesis of Gaia as an organism, but, like Lovelock, he does see its macro earth systems that tend toward a stable climatic equilibrium conducive to life, consistently over millions of years, as a product of a dynamic process, not a fixed design. James Lovelock, *The Revenge of Gaia: Why the Earth Is Fighting Back—and How We Can Still Save Humanity* (New York: Penguin, 2006); Latour, *Facing Gaia*.

32. Underlying Latour's intellectual movement is a Whiteheadian process cosmology, a picture of the cosmos as a web or network of interrelated processes. Gone is Isaac Newton's clockwork cosmos of fixed regularity. This worldview may appear to be a return to Heraclitus; the cosmos of flux of fire, although Latour's Whiteheadian assumptions convey more of a return to Pythagoras. It was Pythagoras who overturned the cosmological debate of the ancients from the question of the primary elemental constituents of things, to the question of the movement and transformation of things, to know things not by their constituents, but by their actions and changes, which he showed can be measured, mathematically, and analyzed to reveal the hidden harmonic patterns of the cosmos. Drop a lump of coal, a fish head, or walnut into the water, and they all produce a marvelous series of rings, Pythagoras showed. What Latour and Isabella Stengers have done with a Whiteheadian outlook is put to Pythagoras's ordered cosmos on wheels of diachronic process, giving the cosmopolitical question a diachronic perspective. It is a moving *cosmopolis*. Bruno Latour, *We Have Never Been Modern* (Cambridge, MA: Harvard University Press, 1993); Isabella Stengers, "The Cosmopolitical Proposal," in *Making Things Public*, ed. Bruno Latour and Peter Weibel (Cambridge, MA: MIT Press, 2005), 994–1003; Latour, "Whose Cosmos, Whose Cosmopolitics?"; Matthew C. Watson, "Derrida, Stengers, Latour, and Subalternist Cosmopolitics," *Theory, Culture & Society* 31, no. 1 (2014): 75–98.

33. Qualifying his movement, in crucial respects, is Latour's "modes of existence" project, answering the question of what we have been, if not modern. His answer focuses on the different modes of network connection modes including legal, political, religious, and so forth, each with a different value-based logic of connections that set their own conditions of validity. Bruno Latour, *An Inquiry into Modes of Existence: An Anthropology of the Moderns* (Cambridge, MA: Harvard University Press, 2013).

34. Bruno Latour, *The Nature of Politics: How to Bring the Sciences into Democracy* (Cambridge, MA: Harvard University Press, 2004); Mark B. Salter and William Walters, "Bruno Latour Encounters International Relations: An Interview," *Millennium: Journal of International Studies* 44, no. 3 (2016): 1–23; Bruno Latour, *Reassembling the Social: An Introduction to Actor-Network-Theory* (Oxford: Oxford University Press, 2012); Bruno Latour, "The Whole Is Always Smaller Than Its Parts: A Digital Test of Gabriel Tardes' Monads," *British Journal of Sociology* 63, no. 4 (2012): 590–615.

35. William E. Connolly, *Facing the Planetary: Entangled Humanism and the Politics of Swarming* (Durham: Duke University Press, 2017).

36. Daniel Deudney, *Dark Skies: Space Expansionism, Planetary Geopolitics, and the Ends of Humanity* (Oxford: Oxford University Press, 2020), 315.

37. Clive Hamilton, *Earthmasters: The Dawn of the Age of Climate Engineering* (New Haven: Yale University Press, 2013).

38. Daniel Deudney, "Global Village Sovereignty: Intergenerational Sovereign Publics, Federal-Republican Earth Constitutions, and Planetary Identities," in *The Greening of Sovereignty in World Politics*, ed., Karen T. Litfin (Cambridge, MA: MIT Press, 1998)," 317.

39. Deudney, "Global Village Sovereignty."

40. Deudney, "Global Village Sovereignty," 303.

41. If we can be tempted to briefly indulge in consideration of long-term futures, too, Deudney has also suggested that a solar-scale international system, with permanent polities established on Mars, Earth, moons, and asteroids, would find calls for a solar-scale astro-politan order, as the prospects for interplanetary war took shape, with asteroid projectiles and other weapons between increasingly genetically differentiated populations. What to make of this is hard to say, reaching also beyond speculation, but the thrust of the argument that an astro-politanism of the future is another utopian false dawn is persuasive. Deudney, *Dark Skies*.

42. Dipesh Chakrabarty, "The Climate of History: Four Theses," *Critical Inquiry* 35, no. 2 (2009): 222.

43. R. G. Collingwood, *The Idea of Nature* (Oxford: Clarendon Press, 1945), 177.

44. Falkner, *Environmentalism and Global International Society*, 297.

45. Robert Falkner, "The Anarchical Society and Climate Change," in *The Anarchical Society at 40: Contemporary Challenges and Prospects*, ed. Hidemi Suganami, Madeline Carr, and Adam Humphreys (Oxford: Oxford University Press, 2017), 198–215.

Chapter 6

1. Jacques Derrida, quoted in Anthony Burke, "Interspecies Cosmopolitanism: Non-Human Power and the Ground of World Order in the Anthropocene," *Review of International Studies* 49, no. 2 (2023): 207.

2. Mark Mazower, "Review Essay: Keeping the World at Bay: Does Globalism Subvert Democracy—or Strengthen It?," *Foreign Affairs*, April 18, 2023, https://www.foreig naffairs.com/reviews/democracy-globalization-keeping-world-bay

3. Aaron McKeil, "Order without Victory: International Order Theory before and after Liberal Hegemony," *International Studies Quarterly* 67, no. 1 (2023); Trubowitz and Burgoon, *Geopolitics and Democracy: The Western Liberal Order from Foundation to Fracture* (Oxford: Oxford University Press, 2023); Patrick Porter, *The False Promise of Liberal Order: Nostalgia, Delusion and the Rise of Trump* (Cambridge: Polity, 2020); G. John Ikenberry, *A World Safe for Democracy: Liberal Internationalism and the Crisis of Global Order* (New Haven: Yale University Press, 2020); Mearsheimer, *Great Delusion*; Robert L. Jervis et al., *Chaos in the Liberal Order: The Trump Presidency and International Politics in the Twenty-First Century* (New York: Columbia University Press, 2018).

4. Aaron McKeil, "On the Concept of International Disorder," *International Relations* 35, no. 2 (2021): 197–215; Aaron McKeil, "Global Disorder: A Blind Spot or Distinct Concept of the International Society Approach?," *Global Studies Quarterly* 2, no. 4 (2022).

5. Alexander Cooley and Daniel H. Nexon, "The Real Crisis of Global Order: Illiberalism on the Rise," *Foreign Affairs* 101, no. 1 (January–February 2022): 103–18.

6. Adler-Nissen and Zarakol, "Struggles for Recognition."

7. Adler-Nissen and Zarakol, "Struggles for Recognition," 613.

8. Andreas Krieg, *Subversion: The Strategic Weaponization of Narratives* (Washington, DC: Georgetown University Press, 2023).

9. Nikhil Kalyanpur, "An Illiberal Economic Order: Commitment Mechanisms Become Tools of Authoritarian Coercion," *Review of International Political Economy* 30, no. 4 (2023): 1238–54; Roland Paris, "The Right to Dominate: How Old Ideas about Sovereignty Pose New Challenges for World Order," *International Organization* 74, no. 3 (2020): 453–89.

10. Lawrence Freedman, "Humanitarian Challenges of Great Power Conflict: Signs from Ukraine," *Daedalus* 152, no. 2 (2023): 40–51; Lawrence Freedman, *Ukraine and the Art of Strategy* (Oxford: Oxford University Press, 2019); Christopher Coker, *War and the Illiberal Conscience* (London: Routledge, 1998).

11. Jake Sullivan, "The Sources of American Power: Foreign Policy for a Changed World," *Foreign Affairs*, October 24, 2023, https://www.foreignaffairs.com/united-states/sources-american-power-biden-jake-sullivan

12. Aly Wyne, *America's Great Power Opportunity: Revitalizing U.S. Foreign Policy to Meet the Challenges of Strategic Competition* (Cambridge: Polity, 2022); Cooley and Nexon, *Exit from Hegemony*; Kyle M. Lascurettes, *Orders of Exclusion: Great Powers and the Strategic Sources of Foundational Rules in International Relations* (Oxford: Oxford University Press, 2020); Stacie E. Goddard, *When Right Makes Might: Rising Powers and World Order* (Ithaca: Cornell University Press, 2018); Evelyn Goh, *The Struggle for Order: Hegemony, Hierarchy, and Transition in Post–Cold War East Asia* (Oxford: Oxford University Press, 2013).

13. It is interesting, but perhaps unsurprising, that each of these struggles have had an ideological dimension, between versions of democracy and autocracy, not necessarily because different political government types are implacable or inherent political enemies, but because ideologies are useful for mobilizing forces in political struggles, and at the macro-world level of inter-great-power politics, the question of the political organization of all humankind is at stake, whether the order will favor a political plurality, or whether an aspirational hegemonic power would threaten the political autonomy of states. This is a certain framing of history, however. Wight suggested that the modern world could easily also be portrayed as a series of revolutionary and counterrevolutionary struggles, crosscutting vertical geostrategic hegemonic competition with horizontal upheavals. Aaron McKeil, "Hegemonic Orders and the Idea of History," *International Politics* (2023): 1–14, https://doi.org/10.1057/s41311-023-00514-z; Ian Clark, *Hegemony in International Society* (Oxford: Oxford University Press, 2011); Adam Watson, *Hegemony & History* (London: Routledge, 2007).

14. Mark Leonard, "China Is Ready for a World of Disorder: America Is Not," *Foreign Affairs*, June 20, 2023, https://www.foreignaffairs.com/united-states/china-ready-world-disorder

15. John J. Mearsheimer's neo–Cold War picture of emerging "bounded orders," for instance, is mostly misleading, because states are more resourceful in negotiating multiple overlapping relations, resistant to constraints on foreign policy, and have no fixed positions, unlike the Cold War. "Bound to Fail: The Rise and Fall of the Liberal International Order," *International Security* 43, no. 4 (2019): 7–50; Aaron McKeil, "The Limits of Realism after Liberal Hegemony," *Journal of Global Security Studies* 7, no. 1 (2022).

16. Trubowitz and Burgoon, *Geopolitics and Democracy*, 119.

17. Rohan Mukherjee, *Ascending Order: Rising Powers and the Politics of Status in International Relations* (Cambridge: Cambridge University Press, 2022); Tristen Naylor, *Social Closure and International Society: Status Groups from the Family of Civilised Nations to the G20* (London: Routledge, 2018).

18. Paul Tucker, *Global Discord: Values and Power in a Fractured World Order* (Princeton: Princeton University Press, 2022).

19. Anu Bradford, *Digital Empires: The Global Battle to Regulate Technology* (Oxford: Oxford University Press, 2023), 150.

20. Mark Leonard, *The Age of Unpeace: How Connectivity Causes Conflict* (London: Penguin, 2021); Lucas Kello, *The Virtual Weapon and International Order* (New Haven: Yale University Press, 2017).

21. Leonard, *Age of Unpeace*, 139–41.

22. Or Rosenboim, *The Emergence of Globalism: Visions of World Order in Britain and the United States, 1939–1950* (Princeton: Princeton University Press, 2017).

23. Luis Cabrera, *The Practice of Global Citizenship* (Cambridge: Cambridge University Press, 2010).

24. Luis Cabrera, "Advancing Global Citizenship and Cosmopolitanism in an Age of Globoskepticism: Insights from the World Order Models Project," *Globalizations* 20, no. 7 (2023): 1102–19; Aaron McKeil, "Revisiting the World Order Models Project: A Case for Renewal?," *Global Policy* 13, no. 4 (2022): 417–26.

25. Walker, *One World, Many Worlds*; Saul Mendlovitz, "A Perspective on the Cutting Edge of World Order Inquiry: The Past, Present and Future of WOMP," *International Interactions* 8, no. 1 (1981): 151–60; Johan Galtung, *The True Worlds: a Transnational Perspective* (New York: Free Press, 1980); Gustavo Lagos and Horacio H. Godoy, *Revolution of Being: A Latin American View of the Future* (New York: Free Press, 1977); Mazrui, *World Federation of Cultures*; Saul Mendlovitz, *On the Creation of a Just World Order: Preferred Worlds for the 1990s* (New York: Institute for World Order, 1975); Richard Falk, *A Study of Future Worlds* (New York: Free Press, 1975); Ranji Kothari, *Footsteps into the Future: Diagnosis of the Present World and a Design for an Alternative* (New York: Free Press, 1974); Richard Falk and Saul Mendlovitz, eds., *Strategy of World Order*, 4 vols. (New York: World Law Fund, 1966).

26. Luis Cabrera, "Advancing Global Citizenship and Cosmopolitanism in an Age of Globoskepticism: Insights from the World Order Models Project," *Globalizations* 20, no. 7 (2023): 1102–19.

27. Diana Panke and Soren Stapel, "Exploring Overlapping Regionalism," *Journal of International Relations and Development* 21 (2018): 635–62; Emanuel Adler and Patricia Greve, "When Security Community Meets Balance of Power: Overlapping Regional Mechanisms of Security Governance," *Review of International Studies* 35 (2009): 59–84; Emanuel Adler, "The Spread of Security Communities: Communities of Practice, Self-Restraint, and NATO's Post–Cold War Transformation," *European Journal of Interna-*

tional Relations 14, no. 2 (2008): 195–230; Charles Tilly, "International Communities, Secure or Otherwise," in *Security Communities*, ed. Emanuel Adler and Michael Barnett (Cambridge: Cambridge University Press, 1992), 397–412.

28. Terry MacDonald and Kate MacDonald, "Towards a 'Pluralist' World Order: Creative Agency and Legitimacy in Global Institutions," *European Journal of International Relations* 26, no. 2 (2020): 518–44; Terry MacDonald, *Global Stakeholder Democracy: Power and Representation beyond Liberal States* (Oxford: Oxford University Press, 2008); Onuma Yasuaki, *A Transcivilizational Perspective on International Law: Questioning Prevalent Cognitive Frameworks in the Emerging Multi-Polar and Multi-Civilizational World of the Twenty-First Century* (Boston: Martinus Nijhoff, 2010).

29. Buzan, *Making Global Society*, 39.

30. Freedman, "Humanitarian Challenges of Great Power Conflict"; Samuel Moyn, *Humane: How the United States Abandoned Peace and Reinvented War* (London: Verso, 2022); Stephanie Carvin and Michael J. Williams, *Law, Science, Liberalism and the American Way of Warfare: The Quest for Humanity in Conflict* (Cambridge: Cambridge University Press, 2015); Christopher Coker, *Humane Warfare* (London: Routledge, 2001).

31. Christopher Coker, *Future War* (Cambridge: Polity, 2015), 124–25.

32. Alex J. Bellamy, *World Peace: And How We Can Achieve It* (Oxford: Oxford University Press, 2019), 177–78.

33. Bellamy, *World Peace*, 169.

34. Bellamy, *World Peace*, 175.

35. Bellamy, *World Peace*, 175.

36. Christopher Coker, *Can War Be Eliminated?* (Cambridge: Polity, 2014).

37. Roland Blieker, "Order and Disorder in World Politics," in *International Society and Its Critics*, ed. Alex J. Bellamy (Oxford: Oxford University Press, 2005), 179–92; Aaron McKeil, "The Sources of International Disorder," *Oxford Research Encyclopedia of International Studies* (2023), https://doi.org/10.1093/acrefore/9780190846626.013.695

38. Connolly, "Speed, Concentric Cultures, and Cosmopolitanism"; Craig Calhoun, "The Class Consciousness of Frequent Travelers: Toward a Critique of Actually Existing Cosmopolitanism," *South Atlantic Quarterly* 101, no. 4 (2003): 869–97.

39. Christopher Clark, "Uncertain Times," in *Prisoners of Time: Prussians, Germans and Other Humans* (London: Allan Lane, 2021), 236.

40. Jennifer Welsh, *The Return of History: Conflict, Migration, and Geopolitics in the Twenty-First Century* (Toronto: Anansi Press, 2016); R. G. Collingwood, *The Idea of History*, rev. ed. (Oxford: Oxford University Press, 1994).

41. Gray, *New Leviathans*, 20.

42. The grand cosmological backgrounds of modernity are evolving but with continuities configuring shifting imaginaries, while ongoing processes of mobilization continue to grapple with modernity's evolving contradictions. R. B. J. Walker, *After the Globe, before the World* (London: Routledge, 2010); Bentley B. Allan, *Scientific Cosmology and International Orders* (Cambridge: Cambridge University Press, 2018); Milja Kurki, *International Relations in a Relational Universe* (Oxford: Oxford University Press, 2020); Chris Brown, "Big Pictures—IR's Cosmological Turn," *Millennium: Journal of International Studies* 50, no. 2 (2022): 591–98.

43. Samuel Moyn, *Liberalism against Itself: Cold War Intellectuals and the Making of Our Times* (New Haven: Yale University Press, 2023), 176.

44. Jeremy Bentham, "A Plan for an Universal and Perpetual Peace," in *The Works of Jeremy Bentham: Vol. II* (Edinburgh: Simkin, Marshall, & Co., 1843), 546.

45. Mazower, "Review Essay: Keeping the World at Bay."

Conclusion

1. H. G. Wells, "The Dreamer in the Kremlin," in *The Open Conspiracy and Other Writings* (London: Walterlow & Sons, 1933), 261.

2. *Stalin-Wells Talks*, the Verbatim Record and a Discussion (London: New Statesman and Nation, 1934), 11, quoted in Wight, *International Theory*, 46.

3. Trubowitz and Burgoon, *Geopolitics and Democracy*; Gerstle, *Rise and Fall of the Neoliberal Order*; Kornprobst and Paul, "Globalization, Deglobalization and the Liberal International Order"; Norris and Inglehart, *Cultural Backlash*.

4. Ruggie, *Constructing the World Polity*.

5. I say conventional "realist" explanations, because realism is an internally diverse tradition, some strains of which have been argued to be compatible with "cosmopolitan" world order proposals. Scheuerman, "Realism and the Kantian Tradition"; Beardsworth, "Cosmopolitanism and Realism."

6. Wendt, "Why a World State Is Inevitable."

Epilogue

1. Hall, *International Thought of Martin Wight*, 133–34.

2. Ian Hall, *Dilemmas of Decline: British Intellectuals and World Politics, 1945–1975* (Berkeley: University of California Press, 2012).

3. Wight, *International Theory*, 8.

4. Bull, *Anarchical Society*, 25.

5. These descriptions of revolutionism are also echoed in James Der Derian, "Hedley Bull and the Case for a Post-Classical Approach," in *Critical Practices of International Relations: Selected Essays* (London: Routledge, 2009), 300.

6. Wight, *International Theory*, 47.

7. Wight, *International Theory*, 46–47.

8. Hall, *International Thought of Martin Wight*, 34–35; Michael Howard, "Ethics and Power in International Policy: The Third Martin Wight Memorial Lecture," *International Affairs* 53, no. 3 (1977): 364–76; E. Kedourie, "Religion in Politics: Arnold Toynbee and Martin Wight," *British Journal of International Studies* 5, no. 1 (1979): 6–14; Michael Nicholson, "The Enigma of Martin Wight," *Review of International Studies* 7, no. 1 (1981): 15–22; Robert H. Jackson, "Martin Wight, International Theory and the Good Life," *Millennium: Journal of International Studies* 19, no. 2 (1990): 261–72; Scott M. Thomas, "Faith, History and Martin Wight: The Role of Religion in the Historical Sociology of the English School of International Relations," *International Affairs* 77, no. 4 (2001): 905–29.

9. Wight, *International Theory*, 108.

10. Wight, *International Theory*, 110.

11. Martin Wight, "Western Values in International Relations," in *Diplomatic Investigations: Essays in the Theory of International Politics*, ed. Herbert Butterfield and Martin Wight (Oxford: Oxford University Press, 2019), 171–97.

12. Bull, "Martin Wight and the Theory of International Relations," xvi.

13. Bull, "Martin Wight and the Theory of International Relations," xvi; see also Hall, *International Thought of Martin Wight*, 65, 137.

14. Isaiah Berlin, "A Revolutionary without Fanaticism," in *The Power of Ideas*, ed. Henry Hardy (London: Pimlico, 2001), 100, italics added.

15. Berlin, "A Revolutionary without Fanaticism," 97.

16. Wight, *International Theory*, 12.

Bibliography

Abizadeh, Arash. "Does Collective Identity Presuppose an Other? On the Alleged Incoherence of Global Solidarity." *American Political Science Review* 99, no. 1 (2005): 45–60.

Adler, Emanuel. "The Spread of Security Communities: Communities of Practice, Self-Restraint, and NATO's Post–Cold War Transformation." *European Journal of International Relations* 14, no. 2 (2008): 195–230.

Adler, Emanuel, and Patricia Greve. "When Security Community Meets Balance of Power: Overlapping Regional Mechanisms of Security Governance." *Review of International Studies* 35 (2009): 59–84.

Adler-Nissen, Rebecca, and Ayse Zarakol. "Struggles for Recognition: The Liberal International Order and the Merger of Its Discontents." *International Organization* 75, no. 2 (2020): 611–34.

Adonis, Andrew, and Tim Hames, eds. *A Conservative Revolution? The Reagan-Thatcher Decade in Perspective.* Manchester: Manchester University Press, 1994.

Agamben, Giorgio. *The Coming Community.* Minneapolis: University of Minnesota Press, 1993.

Agathangelou, Anna M. "Bruno Latour and Ecology Politics: Poetics of Failure and Denial in IR." *Millennium: Journal of International Studies* 44, no. 3 (2016): 321–47.

Agné, Hans, et al. "Symposium: The Politics of International Recognition." *International Theory* 5, no. 1 (2013): 94–107.

Albert, Mathias, Gorm Harste, and Knud Erik Jorgensen. "Introduction: World State Futures." *Cooperation and Conflict* 47, no. 2 (2012): 145–56.

Alighieri, Dante. *Monarchy.* Cambridge: Cambridge University Press, 1996.

Allan, Bentley B. *Scientific Cosmology and International Orders.* Cambridge: Cambridge University Press, 2018.

Andersen, Morten Skumsrud, and William C. Wohlforth. "Balance of Power: A Key Concept in Historical Perspective." In *Routledge Handbook of Historical International Relations,* edited by Benjamin de Carvalho, Julia Costa Lopez, and Halvard Liera, 289–301. London: Routledge, 2021.

Anderson, Benedict. *Imagined Communities: Reflections on the Origin and Spread of Nationalism.* London: Verso, 1983.

Ando, Clifford. *Imperial Ideology and Provincial Loyalty in the Roman Empire.* Berkeley: University of California Press, 2000.

Ando, Clifford. *Imperial Rome, A.D. 193–284: The Critical Century*. Edinburgh: Edinburgh University Press, 2012.

Ando, Clifford. *A Matter of the Gods: Religion and the Roman Empire*. Berkeley: University of California Press, 2008.

Ando, Clifford. *Roman Social Imaginaries: Language and Thought in the Context of Empire*. Toronto: University of Toronto Press, 2015.

Anievas, Alexander, Nivi Manchanda, and Robbie Shilliam. *Race and Racism in International Relations: Confronting the Global Colour Line*. London: Routledge, 2015.

Appiah, Kwame Anthony. *Cosmopolitanism: Ethics in a World of Strangers*. New York: W.W. Norton, 2006.

Appiah, Kwame Anthony. "Race in the Modern World: The Problem of the Color Line." *Foreign Affairs* 94, no. 2 (2015): 1–8.

Archibugi, Daniele. "Cosmopolitan Democracy and Its Critics: A Review." *European Journal of International Relations* 10, no. 3 (2004): 437–73.

Archibugi, Daniele. *The Global Commonwealth of Citizens: Towards Cosmopolitan Democracy*. Princeton: Princeton University Press, 2008.

Archibugi, Daniele, and David Held, eds. *Cosmopolitan Democracy: An Agenda for a New World Order*. Cambridge: Polity, 1995.

Archibugi, Daniele, and David Held. "Cosmopolitan Democracy: Paths and Agents." *Ethics & International Affairs* 25, no. 4 (2011): 433–61.

Archibugi, Daniele, Mathias Koenig-Archibugi, and Raffaele Marchetti, eds. *Global Democracy: Normative and Empirical Perspectives*. Cambridge: Cambridge University Press, 2012.

Armitage, David. *Foundations of Modern International Thought*. Cambridge: Cambridge University Press, 2013.

Armstrong, David, *Revolution and World Order: The Revolutionary State in International Society*. Oxford: Oxford University Press, 1993.

Aurelius, Marcus. *Meditations*. Oxford: Oxford University Press, 2013.

Bain, William. *Between Anarchy and Society: Trusteeship and the Obligations of Power*. Oxford: Oxford University Press, 2003.

Bain, William. *Political Theology of International Order*. Oxford: Oxford University Press, 2020.

Bain, William. "Rival Traditions of Natural Law: Martin Wight and the Theory of International Society." *International History Review* 36, no. 5 (2014): 943–60.

Balakrishnan, Sarah. "Pan-African Legacies, Afropolitan Futures: A Conversation with Achille Mbembe." *Transition* 120 (2016): 28–37.

Balibar, Étienne. *Secularism and Cosmopolitanism: Critical Hypotheses on Religion and Politics*. New York: Columbia University Press, 2018.

Banks, Iaian M. *Consider Phlebas*. London: Orbit, 1987.

Baratta, Joseph P. "The Internationalist World Federal Movement: Toward Global Governance." *Peace & Change* 24, no. 3 (1999): 340–63.

Baratta, Joseph P. *The Politics of World Federation*. Vol. 1, *The United Nations, U.N. Reform, Atomic Control*; vol. 2, *From World Federalism to Global Governance*. Westport, CT: Praeger, 2004.

Baratta, Joseph P. *Strengthening the United Nations: A Bibliography on U.N. Reform and World Federalism*. Westport, CT: Greenwood Press, 1987.

Barnett, Michael, and Kathryn Sikkink. "From International Relations to Global Society." In *The Oxford Handbook of International Relations*, edited by Christian Reus-Smit and Duncan Snidal, 62–83. Oxford: Oxford University Press, 2008.

Barry, Brian. *The Liberal Theory of Justice*. Oxford: Clarendon Press, 1973.

Bartelson, Jens. "Making Sense of Global Civil Society." *European Journal of International Relations* 12, no. 3 (2006): 371–95.

Bartelson, Jens. "Three Concepts of Recognition." *International Theory* 5, no. 1 (2013): 107–29.

Bartelson, Jens. *Visions of World Community*. Cambridge: Cambridge University Press, 2009.

Barton Perry, Ralph. *One World in the Making*. New York: Current Books, 1945.

Beardsworth, Richard. *Cosmopolitanism and International Relations Theory*. Cambridge: Polity, 2011.

Beardsworth, Richard, "Cosmopolitanism and Realism: Towards a Theoretical Convergence?" *Millennium: Journal of International Studies* 37, no. 1 (2008): 69–96.

Beck, Ulrich. "Cosmopolitanism as Imagined Communities of Global Risk." *American Behavioral Scientist* 55, no. 10 (2011): 1346–61.

Beck, Ulrich. "The Cosmopolitan Perspective: Sociology of the Second Age of Modernity." *British Journal of Sociology* 51, no. 1 (2000): 79–105.

Beck, Ulrich. *The Cosmopolitan Vision*. Cambridge: Polity Press, 2006.

Beck, Ulrich. "Redefining the Sociological Project: The Cosmopolitan Challenge." *Sociology* 46, no. 1 (2012): 7–12.

Beetham, David. *The Legitimation of Power*. London: Palgrave, 1991.

Beitz, Charles. "Human Dignity in the Theory of Human Rights: Nothing but a Phrase?" *Philosophy & Public Affairs* 41, no. 3 (2013): 259–90.

Beitz, Charles. *The Idea of Human Rights*. Oxford: Oxford University Press, 2009.

Beitz, Charles. *Political Theory and International Relations*. 2nd ed. Princeton: Princeton University Press, 1999.

Bell, Duncan. *Dreamworlds of Race: Empire and the Utopian Destiny of Anglo-America*. Princeton: Princeton University Press, 2020.

Bell, Duncan, "Founding the World State: H. G. Wells on Empire and the English-Speaking Peoples." *International Studies Quarterly* 62 (2018): 867–79.

Bellamy, Alex J. *World Peace (And How We Can Achieve It)*. Oxford: Oxford University Press, 2019.

Benhabib, Seyla. *Another Cosmopolitanism*. Oxford: Oxford University Press, 2006.

Bentham, Jeremy. "A Plan for an Universal and Perpetual Peace." In *The Works of Jeremy Bentham: Vol. II*, 546–60. Edinburgh: Simkin, Marshall, & Co., 1843.

Berki, R. N. "On Marxian Thought and the Problem of International Relations." *World Politics* 24, no. 1 (1971): 80–105.

Berlin, Isaiah. *Four Essays on Liberty*. Oxford: Oxford University Press, 1969.

Berlin, Isaiah. "A Revolutionary without Fanaticism." In *The Power of Ideas*, edited by Henry Hardy, 88–102. London: Pimlico, 2001.

Berlin, Isaiah. *The Sense of Reality: Studies in Ideas and Their History*. London: Pimlico, 1996.

Bevilacqua, Alexander. "Conceiving the Republic of Mankind: The Political Thought of Anacharsis Cloots." *History of European Ideas* 38, no. 4 (2012): 550–69.

Bew, John. *Castlereagh: Enlightenment, War and Tyranny*. London: Quercus, 2011.

Bhagavan, Manu. *India and the Quest for One World: The Peacemakers*. London: Palgrave Macmillan, 2013.

Blieker, Roland. "Order and Disorder in World Politics." In *International Society and Its Critics*, edited by Alex J. Bellamy, 179–92. Oxford: Oxford University Press, 2005.

Borkenau, Franz. *World Communism: A History of the Communist International*. Ann Arbor: University of Michigan Press, 1962.

Boulding, Kenneth. "Cowboys on Spaceship Earth." *Monthly Labor Review* 97 (1974).

Bowden, Brett. "Civil Society, the State, and the Limits to Global Civil Society." *Global Society* 20, no. 2 (2006): 155–78.

Bradford, Anu. *Digital Empires: The Global Battle to Regulate Technology*. Oxford: Oxford University Press, 2023.

Bradford, Richard. *Orwell: A Man of Our Time*. London: Bloomsbury, 2020.

Bremmer, Ian. *Us vs. Them: The Failure of Globalism*. New York: Penguin, 2018.

Brock, Gillian. *Global Justice: A Cosmopolitan Account*. Oxford: Oxford University Press, 2009.

Brown, Archie. *The Rise and Fall of Communism*. London: Vintage Books, 2009.

Brown, Chris. "Big Pictures—IR's Cosmological Turn." *Millennium: Journal of International Studies* 50, no. 2 (2022): 591–98.

Brown, Chris. "Cosmopolitanism, World Citizenship and Global Civil Society." *Critical Review of International Social and Political Philosophy* 3, no. 1 (2000): 7–26.

Brown, Chris. "Hegel and International Ethics." In *Practical Judgement in International Political Theory: Selected Essays*, 133–43. London: Routledge, 2010.

Brown, Chris. *International Society, Global Polity: An Introduction to International Political Theory*. London: Sage, 2015.

Brown, Chris. "On the Disunity of Mankind." *Millennium: Journal of International Studies* 44, no. 1 (2015): 141–43.

Brown, Chris. *Sovereignty, Rights, and Justice: International Political Theory Today*. Cambridge: Polity, 2002.

Brown, Chris. "Universal Human Rights: A Critique." In *Practical Judgement in International Political Theory: Selected Essays*, 53–71. London: Routledge, 2010.

Brown, Garrett Wallace. *Grounding Cosmopolitanism: From Kant to the Idea of a Cosmopolitan Constitution*. Edinburgh: Edinburgh University Press, 2009.

Bull, Hedley. *The Anarchical Society: A Study of Order in World Politics*. 3rd ed. London: Palgrave, 2002.

Bull, Hedley. "Martin Wight and the Theory of International Relations." In Martin Wight, *International Theory: The Three Traditions*, x–xxiii. New York: Holmes & Meier for the Royal Institute of International Affairs, 1992.

Burke, Anthony. "The Good State, from a Cosmic Point of View." *International Politics* 50, no. 1 (2013): 57–76.

Burke, Anthony. "Interspecies Cosmopolitanism: Non-Human Power and the Ground of World Order in the Anthropocene." *Review of International Studies* 49, no. 2 (2023): 201–22.

Burke, Anthony. "Security Cosmopolitanism." *Critical Studies on Security* 1, no. 1 (2013): 13–28.

Burke, Anthony, et al. "Planet Politics: A Manifesto from the End of IR." *Millennium: Journal of International Studies* 44, no. 3 (2016): 499–523.

Burke, Edmund. *Reflections on the French Revolution*. London: J.M. Dent & Sons, 1951.

Burleigh, Michael. *The Third Reich: A New History*. London: Farrar, Straus and Giroux, 2001.

Butterfield, Herbert, and Martin Wight, eds. *Diplomatic Investigations: Essays in the Theory of International Politics*. Oxford: Oxford University Press, 2019.

Buzan, Barry. *From International to World Society? English School Theory and the Social Structure of Globalization*. Cambridge: Cambridge University Press, 2004.

Buzan, Barry. *Making Global Society: A Study of Humankind across Three Eras*. Cambridge: Cambridge University Press, 2023.

Buzan, Barry. "Revisiting World Society." *International Politics* 55, no. 1 (2018): 125–40.

Buzan, Barry, and George Lawson. *The Global Transformation: History, Modernity and the Making of International Relations*. Cambridge: Cambridge University Press, 2015.

Buzan, Barry, and Richard Little. *International Systems in World History: Remaking the Study of International Relations*. Oxford: Oxford University Press, 2000.

Cabrera, Luis. *The Humble Cosmopolitan: Rights, Diversity, and Trans-State Democracy*. Oxford: Oxford University Press, 2020.

Cabrera, Luis, ed. *Institutional Cosmopolitanism*. Oxford: Oxford University Press, 2018.

Cabrera, Luis. *Political Theory of Global Justice: A Cosmopolitan Case for the World State*. London: Routledge, 2004.

Cabrera, Luis. *The Practice of Global Citizenship*. Cambridge: Cambridge University Press, 2010.

Cabrera, Luis. "Review Article: World Government: Renewed Debate, Persistent Challenges." *European Journal of International Relations* 16, no. 3 (2010): 511–30.

Calhoun, Craig. "Belonging in the Cosmopolitan Imaginary." *Ethnicities* 3, no. 4 (2003): 531–53.

Calhoun, Craig. "The Class Consciousness of Frequent Travelers: Toward a Critique of Actually Existing Cosmopolitanism." *South Atlantic Quarterly* 101, no. 4 (2003): 869–97.

Calhoun, Craig. "Cosmopolitanism in the Modern Social Imaginary." *Daedalus* 137, no. 3 (2008): 105–14.

Calhoun, Craig. *Nations Matter: Culture, History, and the Cosmopolitan Dream*. London: Routledge, 2007.

Caney, Simon. *Justice beyond Borders: A Global Political Theory*. Oxford: Oxford University Press, 2005.

Carothers, Thomas. "The Backlash against Democracy Promotion." *Foreign Affairs* 85, no. 2 (2006): 55–68.

Carr, E. H. *Nationalism and After, with a New Introduction from Michael Cox*. London: Macmillan, (1945) 2021.

Carvin, Stephanie, and Michael J. Williams. *Law, Science, Liberalism and the American Way of Warfare: The Quest for Humanity in Conflict*. Cambridge: Cambridge University Press, 2015.

Césaire, Aimé. *Discourse on Colonialism*. Translated by Joan Pinkham. New York: Monthly Review Press, 1972.

Chakrabarty, Dipesh. "The Climate of History: Four Theses." *Critical Inquiry* 35, no. 2 (2009): 197–222.

Chakrabarty, Dipesh. "Planetary Crises and the Difficulty of Being Modern." *Millennium: Journal of International Studies* 46, no. 3 (2018): 259–82.

Chang, Chun-shu. *The Rise of the Chinese Empire*, Vol. 1, *Nation, State, and Imperialism in Early China, ca. 1600 B.C.–A.D. 8*. Ann Arbor: University of Michigan Press, 2007.

Chang, Chun-shu. *The Rise of the Chinese Empire*, Vol. 2, *Frontier, Immigration and Empire in Han China, 130 B.C.–A.D. 157*. Ann Arbor: University of Michigan Press, 2007.

Cheah, Pheng, and Bruce Robbins, eds. *Cosmopolitics: Thinking and Feeling beyond the Nation*. Minneapolis: University of Minnesota Press, 1998.

Clark, Christopher. *Revolutionary Spring: Fighting for a New World, 1848–1849*. London: Allen Lane, 2023.

Clark, Christopher. 'Uncertain Times." In *Prisoners of Time: Prussians, Germans and Other Humans*, 224–38. London: Allan Lane, 2021.

Clark, Ian. *Hegemony in International Society*. Oxford: Oxford University Press, 2011.

Clark, Ian. *International Legitimacy and World Society*. Oxford: Oxford University Press, 2007.

Clark, Ian. *Legitimacy in International Society*. Oxford: Oxford University Press, 2005.

Clark, Ian. *The Vulnerable in International Society*. Oxford: Oxford University Press, 2013.

Cohrs, Patrick O. *The New Atlantic Order: The Transformation of International Politics, 1860–1933*. Cambridge: Cambridge University Press, 2022.

Coker, Christopher. *Can War Be Eliminated?* Cambridge: Polity, 2014.

Coker, Christopher. *Future War*. Cambridge: Polity, 2015.

Coker, Christopher. *The Rise of the Civilizational State*. Cambridge: Polity, 2019.

Cole, Sarah. *Inventing the Future: H. G. Wells and the Twentieth Century*. New York: Columbia University Press, 2020.

Colgan, Jeff. *Partial Hegemony: Oil Politics and International Order*. Oxford: Oxford University Press, 2021.

Collingwood, R. G. *The Idea of History*. Rev. ed. Oxford: Oxford University Press, 1994.

Collingwood, R. G. *The Idea of Nature*. Oxford: Clarendon Press, 1945.

Connolly, William E. *Facing the Planetary: Entangled Humanism and the Politics of Swarming*. Durham: Duke University Press, 2017.

Connolly, William E. "Speed, Concentric Cultures, and Cosmopolitanism." *Political Theory* 28, no. 5 (2000): 596–618.

Cooley, Alexander, and Daniel Nexon. *Exit from Hegemony: The Unraveling of the American Global Order*. Oxford: Oxford University Press, 2020.

Corry, Olaf. *Constructing a Global Polity: Theory, Discourse and Governance*. London: Palgrave, 2013.

Cox, Michael. *The Post–Cold War World: Turbulence and Change in World Politics since the Fall*. London: Routledge, 2019.

Craig, Campbell. *Glimmer of a New Leviathan*. New York: Columbia University Press, 2003.

Craig, Campbell. "Solving the Nuclear Dilemma: Is a World State Necessary?" *Journal of International Political Theory* 15, no. 3 (2018): 349–66.

Craig, Campbell. "When the Whip Comes Down: Marxism, the Soviet Experience, and the Nuclear Revolution." *European Journal of International Security* 2, no. 2 (2017): 223–39.

Cronin, Bruce. *Community under Anarchy: Transnational Identity and the Evolution of Cooperation*. New York: Columbia University Press, 1999.

Cubukcu, Ayca. *For the Love of Humanity: The World Tribunal on Iraq*. Philadelphia: University of Pennsylvania Press, 2018.

Cubukcu, Ayca. "Thinking against Humanity." *London Review of International Law* 5, no. 2 (2017): 251–67.

Cunliffe, Philip. *Cosmopolitan Dystopia: International Intervention and the Failure of the West*. Manchester: Manchester University Press, 2020.

Curry, W. B. *The Case for Federal Union: A New International Order*. Harmondsworth: Penguin, 1939.

Dahl, Robert A. "Can International Organizations Be Democratic? A Skeptics View." In *Democracy's Edges*, ed. Ian Shapiro and Casiano Hacker-Cordon, 19–36. Cambridge: Cambridge University Press, 1999.

Dallmayr, Fred, M. Afik Kayapinar, and Ismail Yaylaci, eds. *Civilizations and World Order: Geopolitics and Cultural Difference*. Lanham, MD: Lexington Books, 2014.

Dean, Jodi. *The Communist Horizon*. London: Verso, 2012.

Dean, Jodi. *Comrade: An Essay on Political Belonging*. New York: Penguin, 2019.

Delanty, Gerard. *The Cosmopolitan Imagination: The Renewal of Critical Social Theory*. Cambridge: Cambridge University Press, 2009.

Delanty, Gerard, ed. *The Routledge Handbook of Cosmopolitanism Studies*. London: Routledge, 2012.

Derrida, Jacques. *On Cosmopolitanism and Forgiveness*. London: Routledge, 2001.

Derrida, Jacques. "'On Cosmopolitanism' in *The Cosmopolitanism Reader*." Edited by Garrett Wallace Brown and David Held, 413–22. Cambridge: Polity, 2010.

Derrida, Jacques. *Specters of Marx: The State of Debt, the Work of Mourning and the New International*. London: Routledge, 1994.

Deudney, Daniel. *Bounding Power: Republican Security Theory from the Polis to the Global Village*. Princeton: Princeton University Press, 2006.

Deudney, Daniel. *Dark Skies: Space Expansionism, Planetary Geopolitics, and the Ends of Humanity*. Oxford: Oxford University Press, 2020.

Deudney, Daniel. "Global Village Sovereignty: Intergenerational Sovereign Publics, Federal-Republican Earth Constitutions, and Planetary Identities." In *The Greening of Sovereignty in World Politics*, edited by Karen T. Litfin, 299–325. Cambridge, MA: MIT Press, 1998.

Deudney, Daniel. "Going Critical: Toward a Modified Nuclear One Worldism." *Journal of International Political Theory* 15, no. 3 (2018): 367–85.

Deudney, Daniel. "The Great Descent: Global Governance in Historical and Theoretical Perspective." In *Why Govern? Rethinking Demand and Progress in Global Governance*, edited by Amitav Acharya, 31–54. Cambridge: Cambridge University Press, 2016.

Diez, Thomas. "Europe as a Discursive Battleground: Discourse Analysis and European Integration Studies." *Cooperation and Conflict* 36, no. 1 (2001): 5–38.

Diez, Thomas. "Speaking 'Europe': The Politics of Integration." *Journal of European Public Policy* 6, no. 4 (1999): 598–613.

Diez, Thomas, and Nathalie Tocci. *The EU, Promoting Regional Integration, and Conflict Resolution*. London: Palgrave, 2017.

Donelan, Michael. "A Community of Mankind." In *The Community of States: A Study in International Political Theory*, edited by James Mayall, 140–57. London: George Allen & Unwin, 1982.

Donnelly, Jack. *Universal Human Rights in Theory and Practice*. Ithaca: Cornell University Press, 1989.

Doyle, Michael W. *Empires*. Ithaca: Cornell University Press, 1986.

Doyle, Michael W. "Kant, Liberal Legacies, and Foreign Affairs." *Philosophy & Public Affairs* 12, no. 3 (1983): 205–35.

Doyle, Michael W. "Kant, Liberal Legacies, and Foreign Affairs, Part 2." *Philosophy & Public Affairs* 12, no. 4 (1983): 323–53.

Drezner, Daniel. "Technological Change and International Relations." *International Relations* 33, no. 2 (2019): 286–303.

Du Bois, W. E. B. "Inter-Racial Implications of the Ethiopian Crisis: A Negro View." *Foreign Affairs* 14, no. 1 (1935): 82–92.

Du Bois, W. E. B. *The World and Africa and Color and Democracy*. Oxford: Oxford University Press, 2007.

Du Bois, W. E. B. "Worlds of Color." *Foreign Affairs* 3, no. 3 (1925): 423–44.

Dunlap, Riley E., and Aaron M. McWright. "Organized Climate Change Denial." In *The Oxford Handbook of Climate Change and Society*, edited by John S. Dryzek, Richard B. Norgaard, and David Schlosberg, 144–60. Oxford: Oxford University Press, 2011.

Dunne, Tim, and Christian Reus-Smit, eds. *The Globalization of International Society*. Oxford: Oxford University Press, 2017.

Durkheim, Émile. *The Division of Labour in Society*. London: Macmillan, 1984.

Eaton, George. "Francis Fukuyama Interview: Socialism Ought to Come Back." *New Statesman*, October 17, 2018.

Eckersley, Robyn. *Environmentalism and Political Theory: Toward an Ecocentric Approach*. London: UCL Press, 1992.

Eckersley, Robyn. "Geopolitan Democracy in the Anthropocene." *Political Studies* 65, no. 4 (2017): 983–99.

Eckersley, Robyn. *The Green State: Rethinking Democracy and Sovereignty*. Cambridge, MA: MIT Press, 2004.

Edwards, Catherine, and Greg Woolf. "Cosmopolis: Rome as World City." In *Rome the Cosmopolis*, edited by Catherine Edwards and Greg Woolf, 1–20. Cambridge: Cambridge University Press, 2003.

Elliott, Mark. "Hushuo: The Northern Other and the Naming of the Han Chinese." In *Critical Han Studies: The History, Representation, and Identity of China's Majority*, edited by Thomas S. Mullaney, James Leibold, Stephane Gros, and Eric Vanden Bussche, 173–90. Berkeley: University of California Press, 2012.

Erman, Eva. "Does Global Democracy Require a World State?" *Philosophical Papers* 48, no. 1 (2019): 123–53.

Erskine, Toni. *Embedded Cosmopolitanism: Duties to Strangers and Enemies in a World of "Dislocated Communities."* Oxford: Oxford University Press, 2018.

Etzioni, Amitai. *Political Unification Revisited: On Building Supranational Communities*. Lanham, MD: Lexington Books, 2001.

Evans, A. B. "Revisiting Mercier's 'L'An 2440.'" *Science Fiction Studies* 30, no. 1 (2003): 130–32.

Ewing, Sovaida Ma'ani. *Bridge to Global Governance: Tackling Climate Change, Energy Distribution, and Nuclear Proliferation.* Washington: Center for Peace and Global Governance, 2018.

Falk, Richard. *Achieving Human Rights.* New York: Routledge, 2009.

Falk, Richard. *(Re)imagining Humane Global Governance.* London: Routledge, 2014.

Falk, Richard. *A Study of Future Worlds.* New York: Free Press, 1975.

Falk, Richard. *This Endangered Planet: Prospects and Proposals for Human Survival.* New York: Random House, 1971.

Falk, Richard. "The World Order Models Project and Its Critics: A Reply." *International Organization* 32, no. 2 (1978): 531–45.

Falk, Richard, and Saul Mendlovitz, eds. *Strategy of World Order.* 4 vols. New York: World Law Fund, 1966.

Falk, Richard, and Andrew Strauss, eds. *A Global Parliament: Essays and Articles.* Berlin: Committee for a Democratic U.N., 2011.

Falkner, Robert. *Environmentalism and Global International Society.* Cambridge: Cambridge University Press, 2021.

Falkner, Robert. "Global Environmentalism and the Greening of International Society." *International Affairs* 88, no. 3 (2012): 503–22.

Falkner, Robert. "The Paris Agreement and the New Logic of International Climate Politics." *International Affairs* 92, no. 5 (2016): 1107–25.

Falkner, Robert, and Barry Buzan. "The Emergence of Environmental Stewardship as a Primary Institution of International Society." *European Journal of International Relations* 25, no. 1 (2019): 131–55.

Fanon, Franz, *The Wretched of the Earth.* London: Penguin, 2001.

Ferencz, Benjamin B., and Ken Keyes Jr. *Planethood: The Key to Your Survival and Prosperity.* Cross Bay, OR: Vision Books, 1988.

Ferguson, Yale H., and Richard W. Mansbach. *A World of Polities: Essays in Global Politics.* London: Routledge, 2008.

Flikschuh, Katrin, and Lea Ypi. *Kant and Colonialism: Historical and Critical Perspectives.* Oxford: Oxford University Press, 2014.

Forrester, Katrina. *In the Shadow of Justice: Postwar Liberalism and the Remaking of Political Philosophy.* Princeton: Princeton University Press, 2019.

Fraser, Nancy. "Reframing Justice in a Globalizing World." *New Left Review* 36 (2005): 69–88.

Fraser, Nancy. *Scales of Justice: Reimagining Political Space in a Globalizing World.* New York: Columbia University Press, 2009.

Fraser, Nancy, et al. *Transnationalizing the Public Sphere.* Cambridge: Polity Press, 2014.

Freedman, Lawrence. "Humanitarian Challenges of Great Power Conflict: Signs from Ukraine." *Daedalus* 152, no. 2 (2023): 40–51.

Fukuyama, Francis. *Identity: The Demand for Dignity and the Politics of Resentment.* New York: Profile Books, 2018.

Gardner, Lloyd C. *Spheres of Influence: The Partition of Europe, from Munich to Yalta.* London: John Murray, 1993.

Gerstle, Gary. *The Rise and Fall of the Neoliberal Order: America and the World in the Free Market*. Oxford: Oxford University Press, 2022.

Getachew, Adom. *Worldmaking after Empire: The Rise and Fall of Self-Determination*. Princeton: Princeton University Press, 2019.

Gill, Stephen. *Critical Perspectives on the Crisis of Global Governance: Reimagining the Future*. London: Palgrave, 2015.

Gill, Stephen. *Gramsci, Historical Materialism and International Relations*. Cambridge: Cambridge University Press, 1993.

Gill, Stephen. *Power and Resistance in the New World Order*. 2nd ed. London: Palgrave, 2008.

Gill, Stephen, and Claire Cutler. *New Constitutionalism and World Order*. Cambridge: Cambridge University Press, 2014.

Gilroy, Paul. "A New Cosmopolitanism." *Interventions* 7, no. 3 (2005): 287–92.

Gilroy, Paul. "Planetarity and Cosmopolitics." *British Journal of Sociology* 61, no. 3 (2010): 620–26.

Go, Julian. "Fanon's Postcolonial Cosmopolitanism." *European Journal of Social Theory* 16, no. 2 (2013): 208–25.

Goddard, Stacie E. *When Right Makes Might: Rising Powers and World Order*. Ithaca: Cornell University Press, 2018.

Goh, Evelyn. *The Struggle for Order: Hegemony, Hierarchy, and Transition in Post–Cold War East Asia*. Oxford: Oxford University Press, 2013.

Gong, Gerrit C. *The Standard of 'Civilization' in International Society*. Oxford: Oxford University Press, 1984.

Gorlizki, Yoram, and Oleg V. Khlevniuk. *Cold Peace: Stalin and the Soviet Ruling Circle, 1945–1953*. Oxford: Oxford University Press, 2004.

Gorodetsky, Gabriel, ed. *The Maisky Dairies: Red Ambassador to the Court of St. James's, 1932–1943*. New Haven: Yale University Press, 2015.

Gramsci, Antonio. *Selections from the Prison Notebooks of Antonio Gramsci*. New York: International Publishers, 1971.

Gray, John. *False Dawn: The Delusions of Global Capitalism*. New York: New Press, 1998.

Gray, John. *Isaiah Berlin: An Interpretation of His Thought*. Princeton: Princeton University Press, 1996.

Gray, John. *The New Leviathans: Thoughts after Liberalism*. London: Allen Lane, 2023.

Griffiths, Ryan D. "The Waltzian Ordering Principle and International Change: A Two-Dimensional Model." *European Journal of International Relations* 24, no. 1 (2018): 130–52.

Grovogui, Siba N. *Beyond Eurocentrism and Anarchy: Memories of International Order and Institutions*. London: Palgrave, 2006.

Guzzini, Stefano. *Power, Realism and Constructivism*. London: Routledge, 2013.

Haas, E. B. *Beyond the Nation State: Functionalism and International Organization*. Stanford: Stanford University Press, 1964.

Habermas, Jurgen. "A Political Constitution for the Pluralist World Society?" *Anales de la Catedra Francisco Suarez* 39 (2005): 121–32.

Habermas, Jurgen, and Jacques Derrida. "What Binds Europeans Together: A Plea for a Common Foreign Policy, Beginning in the Core of Europe." *Constellations* 10, no. 3 (2003): 291–97.

Hale, Thomas, and Mathias Koenig-Archibugi. "Could Global Democracy Satisfy Diverse Policy Values? An Empirical Analysis." *Journal of Politics* 81, no. 1 (2018): 112–26.

Hall, Ian. *Dilemmas of Decline: British Intellectuals and World Politics, 1945–1975.* Berkeley: University of California Press, 2012.

Hall, Ian. *The International Thought of Martin Wight.* London: Palgrave, 2006.

Hall, Ian. "Martin Wight, Western Values, and the Whig Tradition of International Thought." *International History Review* 36, no. 5 (2014): 961–81.

Hall, Ian. "'The Toynbee Convector': The Rise and Fall of Arnold J. Toynbee's Anti-Imperial Mission to the West." *European Legacy* 17, no. 4 (2012): 455–69.

Hall, Ian. "Unity in Christ? Martin Wight on the Disunity of Mankind." *Millennium: Journal of International Studies* 44, no. 1 (2015): 134–36.

Hall, Stuart. "Political Belonging in a World of Multiple Identities." In *Conceiving Cosmopolitanism: Theory, Context, and Practice*, edited by Steven Vertovec and Robin Cohen, 25–31. Oxford: Oxford University Press, 2002.

Halliday, Fred. *Revolution and World Politics: The Rise and Fall of the Sixth Great Power.* London: Palgrave Macmillan, 1999.

Hamilton, Clive. *Earthmasters: The Dawn of the Age of Climate Engineering.* New Haven: Yale University Press, 2013.

Hammarskjold, Dag. "Address to Both Houses of Parliament, 2 April 1958." in *The Quest for Peace: The Dag Hammarskjöld Memorial Lectures.* New York: Columbia University Press, 1965.

Hannerz, Ulf. *Cultural Complexity: Studies in the Social Organization of Meaning.* New York: Columbia University Press, 1991.

Hardt, Michael, and Antonio Negri. *Commonwealth.* Cambridge, MA: Harvard University Press, 2009.

Hardt, Michael, and Antonio Negri. *Empire.* Cambridge: Harvard University Press, 2000.

Hardt, Michael, and Antonio Negri. "Empire, Twenty Years On." *New Left Review* 120 (2019): 67–92.

Hardt, Michael, and Antonio Negri. *Multitude: War and Democracy in the Age of Empire.* New York: Penguin, 2004.

Haslam, Jonathan. *The Spectre of War: International Communism and the Origins of World War II.* Princeton: Princeton University Press, 2021.

Hartnett, Liane. "Love Is Worldmaking: Reading Rabindranath Tagore's Gora as International Theory." *International Studies Quarterly* 66, no. 3 (2023): https://doi.org/10.1093/isq/sqac037

Hayden, Patrick. "The Environment, Global Justice and World Environmental Justice." In *The Cosmopolitanism Reader*, edited by Garrett Wallace Brown and David Held, 351–72. Cambridge: Polity Press, 2010.

Hayden, Patrick. "Globalization, Reflexive Utopianism, and the Cosmopolitan Social Imaginary." In *Globalization and Utopia: Critical Essays*, edited by Patrick Hayden and Chamsy el-Ojeili, 51–67. London: Palgrave, 2009.

Heater, Derek. *World Citizenship and World Government: Cosmopolitan Ideas in the History of Western Political Thought.* London: Palgrave, 1996.

Held, David. *Cosmopolitanism: Ideals and Realities.* Cambridge: Polity Press, 2010.

Held, David. *Democracy and the Global Order: From the Modern State to Cosmopolitan Governance*. Cambridge: Polity Press, 1995.

Held, David. *Global Covenant: The Social Democratic Alternative to the Washington Consensus*. Cambridge: Polity Press, 2004.

Held, David, and Anthony McGrew. "The End of the Old Order? Globalization and the Prospects for World Order." *Review of International Studies* 24, no. 5 (1998): 219–45.

Herman, Arthur. *1917: Lenin, Wilson, and the Birth of the New World Disorder*. New York: Harper Perennial, 2017.

Heyward, Clare, and Dominic Roser. *Climate Justice in a Non-Ideal World*. Oxford: Oxford University Press, 2016.

Hinsley, F. H. *Power and the Pursuit of Peace: Theory and Practice in the History of Relations between States*. Cambridge: Cambridge University Press, 1963.

Hitchner, R. Bruce. "Globalization Avant la Lettre: Globalization and the History of the Roman Empire." *New Global Studies* 2, no. 2 (2008): 1–14.

Hobsbawm, Eric. *Age of Extremes: The Short Twentieth Century, 1914–1991*. London: Abacus, 1994.

Holton, Robert J. *Cosmopolitanisms: New Thinking and New Directions*. London: Palgrave, 2009.

Honneth, Axel. "Recognition between States: On the Moral Substrate of International Relations." In *The I in We: Studies in the Theory of Recognition*, 137–52. Cambridge: Polity, 2012.

Honneth, Axel. *The Struggle for Recognition: The Moral Grammar of Social Conflicts*. Cambridge, MA: MIT Press, 1995.

Hooghe, Liesbet, and Gary Marks. "A Postfunctionalist Theory of European Integration: From Permissive Consensus to Constraining Dissensus." *British Journal of Political Science* 39, no. 1 (2009): 1–23.

Hoover, Joe. *Reconstructing Human Rights: A Pragmatist and Pluralist Inquiry into Global Ethics*. London: Routledge, 2016.

Hopgood, Stephen. *The Endtimes of Human Rights*. Ithaca: Cornell University Press, 2013.

Hopkinson, Nalo, and Uppinder Mehan. *So Long Been Dreaming: Postcolonial Science Fiction & Fantasy*. Vancouver: Arsenal Pulp Press, 2004.

Hui, Victoria Tin-bor. *War and State Formation in Ancient China and Early Modern Europe*. Cambridge: Cambridge University Press, 2005.

Huju, Kira. "The Cosmopolitan Standard of Civilization: A Reflexive Sociology of Elite Belonging among Indian Diplomats." *European Journal of International Relations* 29, no. 3 (2023): 698–722.

Hurrell, Andrew. "Cultural Diversity within Global International Society." In *Culture and Order in World Politics*, edited by Andrew Phillips and Christian Reus-Smit, 115–36. Cambridge: Cambridge University Press, 2020.

Hurrell, Andrew. "Kant and the Kantian Paradigm in International Relations." *Review of International Studies* 16, no. 3 (1990): 183–205.

Hurrell, Andrew. *On Global Order: Power, Values and the Constitution of International Society*. Oxford: Oxford University Press, 2007.

Hutchings, Kimberly. "Feminist Politics and Cosmopolitan Citizenship." In *Cosmopolitan Citizenship*, edited by Kimberly Hutchings and Roland Dannreuther, 120–42. London: Macmillan, 1999.

Hutchings, Kimberly. "Luxemburg's Socialist International Theory." In *Women's International Thought: A New History*, edited by Patricia Owens and Katharina Rietzler, 52–71. Cambridge: Cambridge University Press, 2021.

Ignatieff, Michael. *Blood and Belonging: Journeys into the New Nationalism*. New York: Farrar, Straus and Giroux, 1993.

Ignatieff, Michael. *The Rights Revolution*. Toronto: Anansi Press, 2007.

Ikenberry, G. John. *After Victory: Institutions, Strategic Restraint, and the Rebuilding of Order after Major Wars*. Princeton: Princeton University Press, 2001.

Ikenberry, G. John. *A World Safe for Democracy: Liberal Internationalism and the Crisis of Global Order*. New Haven: Yale University Press, 2020.

Jackson, Patrick Thaddeus. *Civilizing the Enemy: German Reconstruction and the Invention of the West*. Ann Arbor: University of Michigan Press, 2006.

Jackson, Patrick Thaddeus. "Defending the West: Occidentalism and the Formation of NATO." *Journal of Political Philosophy* 11, no. 3 (2003): 223–52.

Jackson, Patrick Thaddeus. "Rethinking Weber: Toward a Non-Individualist Sociology of World Politics." *International Review of Sociology* 12, no. 3 (2002): 439–68.

Jackson, Patrick Thaddeus, and Daniel Nexon. "Relations before States: Substance, Process and the Study of World Politics." *European Journal of International Relations* 5, no. 3 (1999): 291–332.

Jacques, Peter J. *Environmental Skepticism: Ecology, Power, and Public Life*. London: Routledge, 2016.

Jacques, Peter J. "Regard of Modernity: Environmental Skepticism as a Struggle of Citizenship." *Global Environmental Politics* 6, no. 1 (2006): 76–101.

Jaeger, Hans-Martin. "Global Civil Society and the Political Depoliticization of Global Governance." *International Political Sociology* 1, no. 3 (2007): 257–77.

Jahn, Beate. "Rethinking Democracy Promotion." *Review of International Studies* 38, no. 4 (2012): 685–705.

Jervis, Robert L. "Identity and the Cold War." In *The Cambridge History of the Cold War*, Vol. 2, *Crises and Détente*, edited by Melvyn P. Leffler and Odd Arne Westad, 22–43. Cambridge: Cambridge University Press, 2010.

Jervis, Robert L., et al. *Chaos in the Liberal Order: The Trump Presidency and International Politics in the Twenty-First Century*. New York: Columbia University Press, 2018.

Jesop, Bob. "Obstacles to a World State in the Shadow of the World Market." *Cooperation and Conflict* 47, no. 2 (2012): 200–219.

Kaldor, Mary. "The Idea of Global Civil Society." *International Affairs* 79, no. 3 (2003): 583–93.

Kaldor, Mary, Helmut Anheier, and Marlies Glasius. *Global Civil Society 2004–2005*. London: Sage, 2004.

Kalyanpur, Nikhil. "An Illiberal Economic Order: Commitment Mechanisms Become Tools of Authoritarian Coercion." *Review of International Political Economy* 30, no. 4 (2023): 1238–54.

Kang, David C. *East Asia before the West: Five Centuries of Trade and Tribute*. New York: Columbia University Press, 2010.

Kang, David C. "International Order in Historical East Asia: Tribute and Hierarchy beyond Sinocentrism and Eurocentrism." *International Organization* 74, no. 1 (2020): 65–93.

Kant, Immanuel. *Perpetual Peace and Other Essays*. Indianapolis: Hackett, 1983.

Katzenstein, Peter J., ed. *Civilizations in World Politics: Plural and Pluralist Perspectives*. London: Routledge, 2010.

Kaufman, Stuart J. "The Fragmentation and Consolidation of International Systems." *International Organization* 51, no. 2 (1997): 173–208.

Kaufman, Stuart J., Richard Little, and William C. Wohlforth, eds. *The Balance of Power in World History*. Basingstoke: Palgrave, 2007.

Keane, John. *Global Civil Society?* Cambridge: Cambridge University Press, 2003.

Keene, Edward. *International Political Thought: A Historical Introduction*. Cambridge: Polity Press, 2005.

Keene, Edward. "International Society as an Ideal Type." In *Theorising International Society: English School Methods*, edited by Cornelia Navari, 104–24. London: Palgrave, 2009.

Kello, Lucas. *The Virtual Weapon and International Order*. New Haven: Yale University Press, 2017.

Kendall, Gavin, Ian Woodward, and Zlatko Skrbis. *The Sociology of Cosmopolitanism: Globalization, Identity, Culture and Government*. London: Palgrave, 2009.

Kennan, George F. "Telegram from Moscow to the US Secretary of State ('Long Telegram'), February 22, 1946. https://www.trumanlibrary.gov/library/research-files/tel egram-george-kennan-james-byrnes-long-telegram

Kennan, George F. "To Prevent a World Wasteland: A Proposal." *Foreign Affairs* 48, no. 3 (1970): 401–13.

Kennedy, Paul. *The Parliament of Man: The United Nations and the Quest for World Government*. London: Penguin, 2006.

Keohane, Robert O., and David G. Victor. "The Regime Complex for Climate Change." *Perspectives on Politics* 9, no. 1 (2011): 7–23.

Kinna, Ruth, Alex Prichard, and Thomas Swann. "Occupy and the Constitution of Anarchy." *Global Constitutionalism* 8, no. 2 (2019): 357–90.

Kissinger, Henry A. *World Order: Reflections on the Character of Nations*. New York: Penguin, 2015.

Kleingeld, Pauline. *Kant and Cosmopolitanism: The Philosophical Ideal of World Citizenship*. Cambridge: Cambridge University Press, 2013.

Koenig-Archibugi, Mathias. "Can There Be a Global Demos? An Agency-Based Approach." *Philosophy & Public Affairs* 38, no. 1 (2010): 76–110.

Koenig-Archibugi, Mathias. "Is Global Democracy Possible?" *European Journal of International Relations* 17, no. 3 (2011): 519–42.

Koestler, Arthur. *Darkness at Noon*. London: Penguin, 1946.

Koestler, Arthur. *The Invisible Writing: An Autobiography, 1931–1953*. London: Collins with Hamish Hamilton, 1954.

Koestler, Arthur. *The Sleepwalkers: A History of Man's Changing Vision of the Universe*. London: Macmillan, 1959.

Koestler, Arthur. *The Yogi and the Commissar*. London: Jonathan Cape, 1945.

Kornprobst, Markus, and T. V. Paul. "Globalization, Deglobalization and the Liberal International Order." *International Affairs* 97, no. 5 (2021): 1305–16.

Kramers, Robert P. "The Development of the Confucian Schools." In *The Cambridge History of China*, Vol. 1, *The Ch'in and Han Empires, 221 B.C.–A.D. 220*, edited by Denis Twitchett and John K. Fairbank. Cambridge: Cambridge University Press, 1986.

Kratochwil, Friedrich. "Global Governance and the Emergence of World Society." In *The Puzzles of Politics: Inquiries into the Genesis and Transformation of International Relations*, 262–80. London: Routledge, 2011.

Kurki, Milja. *International Relations in a Relational Universe*. Oxford: Oxford University Press, 2020.

Lamb, Peter. *Harold Laski: Problems of Democracy, the Sovereign State, and International Society*. London: Palgrave, 2004.

Lang, Anthony F., Jr., and Antje Wiener, eds. *Handbook on Global Constitutionalism*, 2nd ed. Cheltenham, UK: Edward Elgar, 2023.

Lascurettes, Kyle M. *Orders of Exclusion: Great Powers and the Strategic Sources of Foundational Rules in International Relations*. Oxford: Oxford University Press, 2020.

Laski, Harold J. *Communism*. London: Frank Cass & Co., 1968.

Laski, Harold J. *Reflections on the Revolution of Our Time*. London: Frank Cass & Co., 1968.

Latour, Bruno. "Agency at the Time of the Anthropocene." *New Literary History* 45, no. 1 (2014): 1–18.

Latour, Bruno. *Down to Earth: Politics in the New Climatic Regime*. Cambridge: Polity, 2018.

Latour, Bruno. *Facing Gaia: Eight Lectures on the New Climatic Regime*. Cambridge: Polity Press, 2017.

Latour, Bruno. "From Realpolitik to Dingpolitik: Or How to Make Things Public." In *Making Things Public: Atmospheres of Democracy*, 4–31. Cambridge, MA: MIT Press, 2005.

Latour, Bruno. *An Inquiry into Modes of Existence: An Anthropology of the Moderns*. Cambridge, MA: Harvard University Press, 2013.

Latour, Bruno. *The Nature of Politics: How to Bring the Sciences into Democracy*. Cambridge, MA: Harvard University Press, 2004.

Latour, Bruno. "Onus Orbis Terrarum: About a Possible Shift in the Definition of Sovereignty." *Millennium: Journal of International Studies* 44, no. 3 (2016): 305–20.

Latour, Bruno. *Reset Modernity!* Cambridge, MA: MIT Press, 2016.

Latour, Bruno. *Reassembling the Social: An Introduction to Actor-Network-Theory*. Oxford: Oxford University Press, 2012.

Latour, Bruno. *We Have Never Been Modern*. Cambridge, MA: Harvard University Press, 1993.

Latour, Bruno. "The Whole Is Always Smaller Than Its Parts: A Digital Test of Gabriel Tardes' Monads." *British Journal of Sociology* 63, no. 4 (2012): 590–615.

Latour, Bruno. "Whose Cosmos, Which Cosmopolitics?" *Common Knowledge* 10, no. 3 (2004): 450–62.

Lawson, George. *Anatomies of Revolution*. Cambridge: Cambridge University Press, 2019.

Leinen, Jo, and Andreas Brummel. *A World Parliament: Governance and Democracy in the 21st Century*. Berlin: Democracy Without Borders, 2018.

Lem, Stanislaw. *Memoirs Found in a Bathtub*. Translated by Michael Kandel and Christine Rose. San Diego: Harcourt Brace, 1973.

Leonard, Mark. *The Age of Unpeace: How Connectivity Causes Conflict*. London: Penguin, 2021.

Leonard, Mark. "China Is Ready for a World of Disorder: America Is Not." *Foreign*

Affairs, June 20, 2023. https://www.foreignaffairs.com/united-states/china-ready-wo rld-disorder

Levy, Daniel, and Natan Sznaider. "The Institutionalization of Cosmopolitan Morality: The Holocaust and Human Rights." *Journal of Human Rights* 3, no. 2 (2004): 143–57.

Lewis, Mark Edward. *China's Cosmopolitan Empire: The Tang Dynasty*. Cambridge, MA: Harvard University Press, 2009.

Lewis, Mark Edward. *The Early Chinese Empires: Qin and Han*. Cambridge, MA: Harvard University Press, 2007.

Lieven, Dominic. *Russia against Napoleon: The True Story of the Campaigns of War and Peace*. New York: Penguin, 2009.

Linklater, Andrew. *Men and Citizens*. London: Palgrave, 1982.

Linklater, Andrew. *The Transformation of Political Community: Ethical Foundations of the Post-Westphalian Era*. Cambridge: Polity Press, 1998.

Linklater, Andrew. "Transforming Political Community: A Response to the Critics." *Review of International Studies* 25, no. 1 (1999): 165–75.

Loewe, Michael. *Divination, Mythology and Monarchy in Han China*. Cambridge: Cambridge University Press, 1994.

Loewe, Michael. *The Men Who Governed Han China*. Leiden: Brill, 2004.

Lovelock, James. *The Revenge of Gaia: Why the Earth Is Fighting Back—and How We Can Still Save Humanity*. New York: Penguin, 2006.

Lu, Catherine. *Just and Unjust Interventions in World Politics: Public and Private*. London: Palgrave, 2006.

Lu, Catherine. *Justice and Reconciliation in World Politics*. Cambridge: Cambridge University Press, 2017.

Lu, Catherine. "The One and Many Faces of Cosmopolitanism." *Journal of Political Philosophy* 8, no. 2 (2000): 244–67.

Lu, Catherine. 'World Government." *Stanford Encyclopedia of Philosophy*, 2006. https:// plato.stanford.edu/entries/world-government/

MacMillan, Margaret. *Paris 1919: Six Months That Changed the World*. New York: Random House, 2003.

Malloch-Brown, Mark. *The Unfinished Global Revolution: The Pursuit of a New International Politics*. New York: Penguin, 2011.

Mann, Michael. *The Sources of Social Power*, Vol. 1, *A History of Power from the Beginning to AD 1760*. New ed. Cambridge: Cambridge University Press, 2012.

Mann, Michael. *The Sources of Social Power*, Vol. 2, *The Rise of Classes and Nation-States, 1760–1914*. New ed. Cambridge: Cambridge University Press, 2012.

Marchetti, Raffaele. "Global Governance or World Federalism? A Cosmopolitan Dispute on Institutional Models." *Global Society* 20, no. 3 (2006): 287–305.

Marx, Karl, and Friedrich Engels. *The Communist Manifesto*. Translated by Samuel Moore. London: Penguin, 2015.

Mathews, Jessica T. "Power Shift." *Foreign Affairs* 76 (1997): 50–66.

Mattingly, D. J. *Imperialism, Power, and Identity: Experiencing the Roman Empire*. Princeton: Princeton University Press, 2011.

Mayall, James. *Nationalism and International Society*. Cambridge: Cambridge University Press, 1990.

Mayall, James. *World Politics: Progress and Its Limits*. Cambridge: Polity, 2000.

Mazower, Mark. *Dark Continent: Europe's Twentieth Century*. London: Penguin, 1998.

Mazower, Mark. *Hitler's Empire: How the Nazis Ruled Europe*. New York: Penguin, 2008.

Mazower, Mark. *No Enchanted Palace: The End of Empire and the Ideological Origins of the United Nations*. Princeton: Princeton University Press, 2009.

Mazower, Mark. "Review Essay: Keeping the World at Bay: Does Globalism Subvert Democracy—or Strengthen It?" *Foreign Affairs*, April 18, 2023. https://www.foreigna ffairs.com/reviews/democracy-globalization-keeping-world-bay

Mazrui, Ali A. *A World Federation of Cultures: An African Perspective*. New York: Free Press, 1976.

Mbembe, Achille. *Critique of Black Reason*. Durham: Duke University Press, 2017.

Mbembe, Achille. *On the Postcolony*. London: University of California Press, 2001.

McConaughey, Meghan, Paul Musgrave, and Daniel Nexon. "Beyond Anarchy? Logics of Political Organization, Hierarchy, and International Structure." *International Theory* 10, no. 2 (2018): 181–218.

McCourt, David M. "Practice Theory and Relationalism as the New Constructivism." *International Studies Quarterly* 60, no. 3 (2016): 475–85.

McKeil, Aaron. "Global Disorder: A Blindspot or Distinct Concept of the International Society Approach?" *Global Studies Quarterly* 2, no. 4 (2022).

McKeil, Aaron. "Global Societies Are Social Things: A Conceptual Reassessment." *Global Society* 31, no. 4 (2017): 551–66.

McKeil, Aaron. "Hegemonic Orders and the Idea of History." *International Politics* (2023): 1–14.

McKeil, Aaron. "The Limits of Realism after Liberal Hegemony." *Journal of Global Security Studies* 7, no. 1 (2022).

McKeil, Aaron. "The Modern 'International' Imaginary: Sketching Horizons and Enriching the Picture." *Social Imaginaries* 4, no. 2 (2018): 159–80.

McKeil, Aaron. "On the Concept of International Disorder." *International Relations* 35, no. 2 (2021): 197–215.

McKeil, Aaron. "Order without Victory: International Order Theory before and after Liberal Hegemony." *International Studies Quarterly* 67, no. 1 (2023).

McKeil, Aaron. "Revisiting the World Order Models Project: A Case for Renewal?" *Global Policy* 13, no. 4 (2022): 417–26.

McKeil, Aaron. "A Silhouette of Utopia: A Comparative Assessment of English School and Constructivist Conceptions of World Society." *International Politics* 55, no. 1 (2018): 41–56.

McKeil, Aaron. "The Sources of International Disorder." *Oxford Research Encyclopedia of International Studies*, 2023. https://doi.org/10.1093/acrefore/9780190846626.013 .695

Mearsheimer, John J. "Bound to Fail: The Rise and Fall of the Liberal International Order." *International Security* 43, no. 4 (2019): 7–50.

Mearsheimer, John J. *The Great Delusion: Liberal Dreams and International Realities*. New Haven: Yale University Press, 2018.

Mendlovitz, Saul H. *On the Creation of a Just World Order: Preferred Worlds for the 1990s*. New York: Institute for World Order, 1975.

Mendlovitz, Saul H. "A Perspective on the Cutting Edge of World Order Inquiry: The Past, Present and Future of WOMP." *International Interactions* 8, no. 1 (1981): 151–60.

Michael, Michalis S., and Fabio Petito. *Civilizational Dialogue and World Order: The Other Politics of Cultures, Religions, and Civilizations in International Relations*. London: Palgrave, 2009.

Mignolo, Walter D. "The Many Faces of Cosmo-Polis: Border Thinking and Critical Cosmopolitanism." In *Cosmopolitanism*, edited by Carole A. Breckenridge, Sheldon Pollock, Homi K. Bhabha, and Dipesh Chakrabarty, 157–88. Durham: Duke University Press, 2002.

Mitrany, David. *A Working Peace System: An Argument for the Functional Development of International Organization*. London: Royal Institute of International Affairs, 1943.

Montani, Guido. *Supranational Political Economy: The Globalisation of the State-Market Relationship*. London: Routledge, 2019.

Morin, Marie-Eve. "The Spacing of Time and the Place of Hospitality: Living Together according to Bruno Latour and Jacques Derrida." *Parallax* 2, no. 1 (2015): 26–41.

Morgenthau, Hans J. *Politics among Nations: The Struggle for Power and Peace*. 1st ed. New York: Alfred A. Knopf, 1948.

Morsink, Johannes. *The Universal Declaration of Human Rights: Origins, Drafting, and Intent*. Philadelphia: University of Pennsylvania Press, 1999.

Moyn, Samuel. *Humane: How the United States Abandoned Peace and Reinvented War*. London: Verso, 2022.

Moyn, Samuel. *The Last Utopia: Human Rights in History*. Cambridge, MA: Belknap Press of Harvard University Press, 2010.

Moyn, Samuel. *Liberalism against Itself: Cold War Intellectuals and the Making of Our Times*. New Haven: Yale University Press, 2023.

Murithi, Tim. "Order of Oppression: Africa's Quest for a New International System." *Foreign Affairs*, April 18, 2023. https://www.foreignaffairs.com/africa/global-south -un-order-oppression

Murray, Michelle. *The Struggle for Recognition in International Relations: Status, Revisionism, and Rising Powers*. Oxford: Oxford University Press, 2019.

Nancy, Jean Luc. *Being Singular Plural*. Stanford: Stanford University Press, 2000.

Nancy, Jean Luc. "The Confronted Community." *Post-Colonial Studies* 6, no. 1 (2003): 23–36.

Nava, Mica. "Cosmopolitan Modernity: Everyday Imaginaries and the Register of Difference." *Theory, Culture & Society* 19, nos. 1–2 (2002): 81–99.

Naylor, Tristen. *Social Closure and International Society: Status Groups from the Family of Civilised Nations to the G20*. London: Routledge, 2018.

Nehru, Jawaharlal. *The Discovery of India*. New Delhi: Oxford University Press, 1985.

Neier, Aryeh. *The International Human Rights Movement: A History*. Princeton: Princeton University Press, 2020.

Neumann, Iver B. "International Relations as a Social Science." *Millennium: Journal of International Studies* 43, no. 1 (2014): 330–50.

Neumann, Iver B. "Returning Practice to the Linguistic Turn: The Case of Diplomacy." *Millennium: Journal of International Studies* 31, no. 3 (2002): 627–51.

Neumann, Iver B., and Ole Jacob Sending. *Governing the Global Polity: Practice, Mentality, Rationality*. Ann Arbor: University of Michigan Press, 2010.

Newfang, Oscar. *World Government*. New York: Barnes & Noble, 1942.

Nexon, Daniel H. "The Balance of Power in the Balance." *World Politics* 61, no. 2 (2009): 330–59.

Nexon, Daniel H. *The Struggle for Power in Early Modern Europe: Religious Conflict, Dynastic Empires, and International Change.* Princeton: Princeton University Press, 2009.

Nexon, Daniel H., and Thomas Wright. "What's at Stake in the American Empire Debate?" *American Political Science Review* 101, no. 2 (2007): 253–71.

Nkrumah, Kwame. *Neo-Colonialism: The Last Stage of Imperialism.* New York: International Publishers, 1965.

Norris, Pippa, and Ronald Inglehart. *Cultural Backlash: Trump, Brexit, and Authoritarian Populism.* Cambridge: Cambridge University Press, 2019.

Nussbaum, Martha C. *The Cosmopolitan Tradition: A Noble but Flawed Ideal.* Cambridge, MA: Belknap Press of Harvard University Press, 2019.

Nussbaum, Martha C. *Creating Capabilities: The Human Development Approach.* Cambridge: Belknap Press of Harvard University Press, 2011.

Nussbaum, Martha. *For Love of Country?* Boston: Beacon Press, 1996.

Nussbaum, Martha. *Frontiers of Justice: Disability, Nationality, Species Membership.* Cambridge: Belknap Press of Harvard University Press, 2006.

Nylan, Michael. "Confucian Piety and Individualism in Han China." *Journal of the American Oriental Society* 116, no. 1 (1996): 1–27.

Nylan, Michael. *The Five "Confucian" Classics.* Oxford: Oxford University Press, 2001.

O'Hagan, Jacinta. "Martin Wight and the Problem of Difference." *Millennium: Journal of International Studies* 44, no. 1 (2015): 137–40.

O'Neill, Onora. *Bounds of Justice.* Cambridge: Cambridge University Press, 2004.

Orwell, George. *Notes on Nationalism.* London: Penguin, 1984.

Orwell, George. "Wells, Hitler and the World State." In *Critical Essays.* London: Secker and Warburg, 1946.

Osgood, Josiah. *Rome and the Making of a World State: 150 BCE–20 CE.* Cambridge: Cambridge University Press, 2018.

Osterhammel, Jurgen. *The Transformation of the World: A Global History of the Nineteenth Century.* Princeton: Princeton University Press, 2014.

Padmore, George. *Pan-Africanism or Communism? The Coming Struggle for Africa.* New York: Roy Publishers, 1956.

Panke, Diana, and Soren Stapel. "Exploring Overlapping Regionalism." *Journal of International Relations and Development* 21 (2018): 635–62.

Pardesi, Manjeet S. "Mughal Hegemony and the Emergence of South Asia as a 'Region' for Regional Order-Building." *European Journal of International Relations* 25, no. 1 (2019): 276–301.

Pardesi, Manjeet S. "Region, System, and Order: The Mughal Empire in Islamic Asia." *Security Studies* 26, no. 2 (2017): 249–78.

Parent, Joseph M. *Uniting States: Voluntary Union in World Politics.* Oxford: Oxford University Press, 2011.

Paris, Roland. "The Right to Dominate: How Old Ideas about Sovereignty Pose New Challenges for World Order." *International Organization* 74, no. 3 (2020): 453–89.

Parrat, Charlotta Friedner. "On the Evolution of Primary Institutions of International Society." *International Studies Quarterly* 61 (2017): 623–30.

Patomaki, Heikki. *World Statehood: The Future of World Politics.* Cham, Switzerland: Springer, 2023.

Pearce, Jenny. *Politics without Violence? Towards a Post-Weberian Enlightenment.* London: Palgrave, 2020.

Pedersen, Susan. *The Guardians: The League of Nations and the Crisis of Empire.* Oxford: Oxford University Press, 2015.

Perkins, Judith. *Roman Imperial Identities in the Early Christian Era.* London: Routledge, 2009.

Phạm, Quỳnh N., and Robbie Shilliam, eds. *Meanings of Bandung: Postcolonial Orders and Decolonial Visions.* London: Rowman & Littlefield, 2016.

Phillips, Andrew. *How the East Was Won: Barbarian Conquerors, Universal Conquest and the Making of Modern Asia.* Cambridge: Cambridge University Press, 2021.

Phillips, Andrew. "International Systems." In *The Globalization of International Society,* edited by Tim Dunne and Christian Reus-Smit, 43–62. Oxford: Oxford University Press, 2017.

Phillips, Andrew. *War, Religion and Empire: The Transformation of International Orders.* Cambridge: Cambridge University Press, 2011.

Phillips, Andrew, and Christian Reus-Smit. *Culture and Order in World Politics.* Cambridge: Cambridge University Press, 2020.

Piketty, Thomas. *Capital and Ideology.* Cambridge, MA: Harvard University Press, 2020.

Piketty, Thomas. *Capital in the Twenty-First Century.* Cambridge, MA: Harvard University Press, 2014.

Pines, Yuri. *The Everlasting Empire: The Political Culture of Ancient China and Its Imperial Legacy.* Princeton: Princeton University Press, 2013.

Pinker, Steven. *The Better Angels of Our Nature: Why Violence Has Declined.* London: Viking, 2011.

Plokhy, S. M. *Yalta: The Price of Peace.* London: Viking, 2010.

Pogge, Thomas. "Cosmopolitanism and Sovereignty." *Ethics* 103, no. 1 (1992): 48–75.

Pogge, Thomas. *Realizing Rawls.* Ithaca: Cornell University Press, 1989.

Polasky, Janet. *Revolutions without Borders: The Call to Liberty in the Atlantic World.* New Haven: Yale University Press, 2015.

Popper, Karl. *The Open Society and Its Enemies,* Vol. 1, *The Spell of Plato.* London: George Routledge & Sons, 1945.

Porter, Patrick. *The False Promise of Liberal Order: Nostalgia, Delusion and the Rise of Trump.* Cambridge: Polity, 2020.

Prashad, Vijay. *The Darker Nations: A People's History of the Third World.* New York: New Press, 2007.

Prozorov, Sergei. "Generic Universalism in World Politics: Beyond International Anarchy and the World State." *International Theory* 1, no. 2 (2009): 215–47.

Ralph, Jason. *Defending the Society of States: Why America Opposes the International Criminal Court and Its Vision of World Society.* Oxford: Oxford University Press, 2007.

Rao, Rahul. "Postcolonial Cosmopolitanism: Making Place for Nationalism." In *The Democratic Predicament: Cultural Diversity in Europe and India,* edited by Jyotirmaya Tripathy and Sudarsan Padmanabhan, 165–87. New Delhi: Routledge, 2012.

Rawls, John. *The Law of Peoples: With the Idea of Public Reason Revisited.* Cambridge, MA: Harvard University Press, 1999.

Rawls, John. *A Theory of Justice.* London: Belknap Press of Harvard University Press, 1971.

Reagan, Ronald. "Statement at the First Plenary Session of the International Meeting on Cooperation and Development in Cancun, Mexico." October 22, 1981. Reagan Library, https://www.reaganlibrary.gov/archives/speech/statement-first-plenary-session-international-meeting-cooperation-and-development

Reeves, Emery. *The Anatomy of Peace*. London: Penguin, 1947.

Reilly, Niamh. "Cosmopolitan Feminism and Human Rights." *Hypatia* 22, no. 4 (2007): 180–98.

Rengger, Nicholas. "Between Transcendence and Necessity: Eric Voegelin, Martin Wight and the Crisis of Modern International Relations." *Journal of International Relations and Development* 22 (2019): 327–45.

Revell, Louise. *Roman Imperialism and Local Identities*. Cambridge: Cambridge University Press, 2009.

Richter, Daniel S. *Cosmopolis: Imagining the Community in Late Classical Athens and the Early Roman Empire*. Oxford: Oxford University Press, 2011.

Ringmar, Erik. "Performing International Systems: Two East-Asian Alternatives to the Westphalian Order." *International Organization* 66, no. 1 (2012): 1–25.

Risse, Mathias. *On Global Justice*. Princeton: Princeton University Press, 2012.

Roach, Steven C. *Governance, Order, and the International Criminal Court: Between Realpolitik and a Cosmopolitan Court*. Oxford: Oxford University Press, 2009.

Romero, Federico. "Cold War Anti-Communism and the Impact of Communism on the West." In *The Cambridge History of Communism*, Vol. 2, *The Socialist Camp and World Power, 1941–1960s*, edited by Norman Naimark, Silvio Pons, and Sophie Quinn-Judge, 291–314. Cambridge: Cambridge University Press, 2017.

Roosevelt, Franklin D. "Fourth Inaugural Address." January 20, 1945. https://avalon.law.yale.edu/20th_century/froos4.asp

Rorty, Richard. "Cosmopolitanism without Emancipation: A Response to Jean-Francois Lyotard." In *Objectivity, Relativism, and Truth: Philosophical Papers*, 211–22. Cambridge: Cambridge University Press, 1991.

Rorty, Richard. *Contingency, Irony, and Solidarity*. Cambridge: Cambridge University Press, 1989.

Rorty, Richard. Human Rights, Rationality, and Sentimentality." In *On Human Rights*, edited by S. Shute, 112–34. New York: Basic Books, 1993.

Rorty, Richard. "Justice as a Larger Loyalty." *Ethical Perspectives* 4, no. 2 (1997): 139–51.

Rorty, Richard. *What Can We Hope For? Essays on Politics*. Princeton: Princeton University Press, 2022.

Rorty, Richard. "Who Are We? Moral Universalism and Economic Triage." *Diogenes* 173, no. 44/1 (1996): 5–15.

Rosenberg, Justin. "International Relations in the Prison of Political Science." *International Relations* 30, no. 2 (2016): 127–53.

Rosenboim, Or. *The Emergence of Globalism: Visions of World Order in Britain and the United States, 1939–1950*. Princeton: Princeton University Press, 2017.

Rousseau, Jean-Jacques. *The Plan for Perpetual Peace*. Lebanon, NH: University Press of New England, 2005.

Ruggie, J. G. *Constructing the World Polity: Essays on International Institutionalization*. London: Routledge, 1998.

Ruggie, J. G. "Continuity and Transformation in the World Polity: Towards a Neorealist Synthesis." *World Politics* 35, no. 2 (1983): 261–85.

Ruggie, J. G. "Human Rights and the Future International Community." *Daedalus* 112, no. 4 (1983): 93–110.

Ruggie, J. G. "Territoriality and Beyond: Problematizing Modernity in International Relations." *International Organization* 47, no. 1 (1993): 139–74.

Sagan, Carl. *The Cosmic Connection: An Extraterrestrial Perspective*. New York: Dell, 1973.

Sagan, Carl. *Cosmos*. London: Macdonald & Co, 1981.

Saint-Simon, Henri. *Selected Writings on Science, Industry and Social Organisation*. Translated by Keith Taylor. London: Croom Helm, 1975.

Salter, Mark B., and William Walters. "Bruno Latour Encounters International Relations: An Interview." *Millennium: Journal of International Studies* 44, no. 3 (2016): 1–23.

Sandel, Michael. *The Tyranny of Merit: What's Become of the Common Good?* New York: Penguin, 2020.

Scheuerman, William E. "The (Classical) Realist Vision of Global Reform." *International Theory* 2, no. 2 (2010): 246–82.

Scheuerman, William E. "Cosmopolitanism and the World State." *Review of International Studies* 40, no. 3 (2014): 419–41.

Scheuerman, William E. "Deudney's Neorepublicanism: One-World or America First?" *International Politics* 47, no. 5 (2010): 523–34.

Scheuerman, William E. "Realism and the Kantian Tradition: A Revisionist Account." *International Relations* 26, no. 4 (2012): 453–77.

Scheuerman, William E. *The Realist Case for Global Reform*. Cambridge: Polity Press, 2011.

Schimmelfennig, Frank. "Regional Integration Theory." *Oxford Research Encyclopedia of Politics*, 2018. https://doi.org/10.1093/acrefore/9780190228637.013.599

Schlesinger, Arthur M., Jr. *The Vital Center: The Politics of Freedom*. New York: Routledge, 1998.

Schroeder, Paul W. *The Transformation of European Politics, 1763–1848*. Oxford: Oxford University Press, 1994.

Schuman, Frederick. *The Commonwealth of Man: An Inquiry into Power Politics and World Government*. London: Hale, 1954.

Schweller, Randall L. "The Balance of Power in World Politics." *Oxford Research Encyclopedia of Politics*, 2016. https://doi.org/10.1093/acrefore/9780190228637.013.119

Schweller, Randall L. "Fantasy Theory." *Review of International Studies* 25, no. 1 (1999): 147–50.

Service, Robert. *Comrades: Communism: A World History*. London: Pan Books, 2008.

Shelley, Percy Bysshe. *Shelley: Poetical Works*. Oxford: Oxford University Press, 1971.

Shani, Giorgio. *Religion, Identity and Human Security*. London: Routledge, 2014.

Shapcott, Richard. *Justice, Community and Dialogue in International Relations*. Cambridge: Cambridge University Press, 2001.

Shaw, Martin. *Theory of the Global State: Globality as an Unfinished Revolution*. New York: Cambridge University Press, 2000.

Siemann, Wolfram. *Metternich: Strategist and Visionary*. Cambridge, MA: Belknap Press of Harvard University Press, 2019.

Sikkink, Kathryn. *Evidence for Hope: Making Human Rights Work in the 21st Century*. Princeton: Princeton University Press, 2017.

Sikkink, Kathryn. *The Justice Cascade: How Human Rights Prosecutions Are Changing World Politics*. New York: W.W. Norton, 2011.

Simpson, Gerry. *Law, War, and Crime: War Crimes Trials and the Reinvention of International Law*. Cambridge: Polity, 2007.

Singer, Peter. *One World: The Ethics of Globalization*. New Haven: Yale University Press, 2002.

Slate, Nico. *Colored Cosmopolitanism: The Shared Struggle for Freedom in the United States and India*. Cambridge: Harvard University Press, 2012.

Slobodian, Quinn. *The Globalists: End of Empire and the Birth of Neoliberalism*. Cambridge, MA: Harvard University Press, 2018.

Sluga, Glenda. *The Invention of International Order: Remaking Europe after Napoleon*. Princeton: Princeton University Press, 2021.

Somers, Margaret R. "The Narrative Constitution of Identity: A Relational and Network Approach." *Theory and Society* 23, no. 5 (1994): 605–49.

Spalding, Elizabeth Edwards. *The First Cold Warrior: Harry Truman, Containment, and the Remaking of Liberal Internationalism*. Lexington: University Press of Kentucky, 2006.

Spohr, Kristina. *Post Wall, Post Square: Rebuilding the World after 1989*. London: William Collins, 2019.

Spruyt, Hendrik. *The World Imagined: Collective Beliefs and Political Order in the Sino-centric, Islamic and Southeast Asian International Societies*. Cambridge: Cambridge University Press, 2020.

Starr, Chester G. *The Roman Empire, 27 B.C.-A.D. 476*. Oxford: Oxford University Press, 1982.

Steffek, Jens. "Fascist Internationalism." *Millennium: Journal of International Studies* 44, no. 1 (2015): 3–22.

Steffek, Jens. "The Legitimation of International Governance: A Discourse Approach." *European Journal of International Relations* 9, no. 2 (2003): 249–75.

Stengers, Isabella. "The Cosmopolitical Proposal." In *Making Things Public*, edited by Bruno Latour and Peter Weibel, 994–1003. Cambridge, MA: MIT Press, 2005.

Stern, S. M. *Aristotle on the World-State*. Columbia: University of South Carolina Press, 1968.

Stivachtis, Yannis A., and Aaron McKeil. "Conceptualizing World Society." *International Politics* 55, no. 1 (2018): 1–10.

Stroikos, Dimitrios. "Engineering World Society? Scientists, Internationalism, and the Advent of the Space Age." *International Politics* 55 (2018): 73–91.

Stroikos, Dimitrios. "Introduction: Rethinking the Standard(s) of Civilization(s) in International Relations." *Millennium: Journal of International Studies* 42, no. 3 (2014): 546–56.

Suganami, Hidemi. *The Domestic Analogy and World Order Proposals*. Cambridge: Cambridge University Press, 1989.

Suganami, Hidemi. "On Wendt's Philosophy: A Critique." *Review of International Studies* 28, no. 1 (2002): 23–37.

Suganami, Hidemi, Madeline Carr, and Adam Humphreys, eds. *The Anarchical Society at 40: Contemporary Challenges and Prospects*. Oxford: Oxford University Press, 2017.

Sweet, Alec Stone. *A Cosmopolitan Legal Order: Kant, Constitutional Justice, and the European Convention on Human Rights*. Oxford: Oxford University Press, 2018.

Sznaider, Natan. *Jewish Memory and the Cosmopolitan Order*. Cambridge: Polity, 2011.

Tagore, Saranindranath. "Tagore's Conception of Cosmopolitanism: A Reconstruction." *University of Toronto Quarterly* 77, no. 4 (2008): 1070–84.

Taylor, Charles. *Dilemmas and Connections: Selected Essays*. Cambridge, MA: Harvard University Press, 2011.

Taylor, Charles. *Modern Social Imaginaries*. Durham: Duke University Press, 2004.

Taylor, Charles. "The Plurality of Goods." In *The Legacy of Isaiah Berlin*, edited by Mark Lilla, Ronald Dworkin, and Robert B. Silvers, 113–20. New York: New York Review of Books, 2001.

Taylor, Charles. "The Politics of Recognition." In *Multiculturalism*, edited by Amy Gutmann, 25–74. Princeton: Princeton University Press, 1994.

Taylor, Charles. *A Secular Age*. Cambridge, MA: Belknap Press of Harvard University Press, 2007.

Tennyson, Alfred Lord. *Alfred Lord Tennyson: Selected Poems*. London: Penguin, 1991.

Tilly, Charles. "The Analysis of a Counter-Revolution." *History and Theory* 3, no. 1 (1963): 30–58.

Tilly, Charles. "International Communities, Secure or Otherwise." In *Security Communities*, edited by Emanuel Adler and Michael Barnett, 397–412. Cambridge: Cambridge University Press, 1992.

Tilly, Charles. "Ties That Bind . . . and Bound." In *Identities, Boundaries, and Social Ties*, 3–12. Boulder: Paradigm, 2005.

Toulmin, Stephen. *Cosmopolis: The Hidden Agenda of Modernity*. Chicago: University of Chicago Press, 1990.

Toynbee, Arnold J. *Change and Habit: The Challenge of Our Time*. Oxford: Oxford University Press, (1966) 1992.

Toynbee, Arnold J. *A Study of History: Abridgement of Volumes VII–X*. London: Oxford University Press, 1957.

Toynbee, Arnold J. "World Sovereignty and World Culture: The Trend of International Affairs since the War." *Pacific Affairs* 4, no. 9 (1931): 753–78.

Trotsky, Leon. *The History of the Russian Revolution*. London: Pluto Press, 1977.

Trubowitz, Peter, and Brian Burgoon. *Geopolitics and Democracy: The Western Liberal Order from Foundation to Fracture*. Oxford: Oxford University Press, 2023.

Trueblood, Benjamin F. *The Federation of the World*. Boston: Houghton, Mifflin and Company, 1899.

Tucker, Paul. *Global Discord: Values and Power in a Fractured World Order*. Princeton: Princeton University Press, 2022.

Twitchett, Denis, and John K. Fairbank, eds. *The Cambridge History of China*, Vol. 1, *The Ch'in and Han Empires, 221 B.C.–A.D. 220*. Cambridge: Cambridge University Press, 1986.

Urpelainen, Johannes, and Thijs Van de Graaf. "United States Non-Cooperation and the Paris Agreement." *Climate Policy* 18, no. 7 (2018): 839–51.

Valentini, Laura. "No Global Demos, No Global Democracy? A Systemization and Critique." *Perspectives on Politics* 12, no. 4 (2014): 789–807.

Vattel, Monsieur de. *The Law of Nations; or Principles of the Law of Nature, applied to the Conduct and Affairs of Nations and Sovereigns.* Philadelphia: T&J.W. Johnson & Co., 1863.

Vertovec, Steven, and Robin Cohen, eds. *Conceiving Cosmopolitanism: Theory, Context, and Practice.* Oxford: Oxford University Press, 2002.

Vincent, R. J. *Human Rights and International Relations.* Cambridge: Cambridge University Press, 1986.

Vincent, R. J. "Western Conceptions of a Universal Moral Order." *British Journal of International Studies* 4, no. 1 (1978): 20–46.

Vinjamuri, Leslie. "Why Multilateralism Still Matters: The Right Way to Win Over the Global South." *Foreign Affairs*, October 2, 2023. https://www.foreignaffairs.com/world/why-multilateralism-still-matters

Vitalis, Robert. "The Midnight Ride of Kwame Nkrumah and Other Fables of Bandung (Ban-doong)." *Humanity: An International Journal of Human Rights, Humanitarianism, and Development* 4, no. 2 (2013): 261–88.

Voegelin, Eric. "World-Empire and the Unity of Mankind." *International Affairs* 38, no. 2 (1962): 170–88.

Vogt, Katja Maria. *Law, Reason, and the Cosmic City: Political Philosophy in the Early Stoa.* Oxford: Oxford University Press, 2008.

Waldron, Jeremy. "What Is Cosmopolitan?" *Journal of Political Philosophy* 8, no. 2 (2000): 227–43.

Walker, R. B. J. *After the Globe, before the World.* London: Routledge, 2010.

Walker, R. B. J. *One World, Many Worlds: Struggles for a Just World Peace.* London: Zed, 1987.

Walt, Stephen M. *Revolution and War.* Ithaca: Cornell University Press, 1996.

Waltz, Kenneth N. "Kant, Liberalism, and War." *American Political Science Review* 56, no. 2 (1962): 331–40.

Waltz, Kenneth N. *Theory of International Politics.* Reading: Addison Wesley, 1979.

Wapner, Paul. "The Changing Nature of Nature: Environmental Politics in the Anthropocene." *Global Environmental Politics* 14, no. 4 (2014): 36–54.

Ward, Barbara. *Space Ship Earth.* New York: Columbia University Press, 1966.

Ward, Barbara, and Rene Jules Dubos. *Only One Earth: The Care and Maintenance of a Small Planet: An Unofficial Report Commissioned by the Secretary-General of the United Nations Conference on the Human Environment.* New York: Penguin, 1972.

Watson, Adam. *The Evolution of International Society: A Comparative Historical Analysis.* London: Routledge, 1992.

Watson, Adam. *Hegemony & History.* London: Routledge, 2007.

Watson, Matthew C. "Derrida, Stengers, Latour, and Subalternist Cosmopolitics." *Theory, Culture & Society* 31, no. 1 (2014): 75–98.

Webb, Adam K. "Can the Global South Take Over the Baton? What Cosmopolitanism in 'Unlikely' Places Means for Future World Order." *Third World Quarterly* 37, no. 6 (2016): 1016–34.

Webb, Adam K. *Deep Cosmopolis: Rethinking World Politics and Globalization.* London: Routledge, 2015.

Webb, Sydney, and Beatrice Webb. *Soviet Communism: A New Civilization.* 3rd ed. London: Longmans, Green, 1944.

Weber, Elisabeth, ed. *Living Together: Jacques Derrida's Communities of Violence and Peace.* New York: Fordham University Press, 2013.

Webster, Charles. *The Congress of Vienna: 1814–1815.* London: G. Bell & Sons, 1950.

Weinert, Matthew S. *Making Human World Order and the Governance of Human Dignity.* Ann Arbor: University of Michigan Press, 2015.

Weinert, Matthew S. "Reframing the Pluralist-Solidarist Debate." *Millennium: Journal of International Studies* 40 no. 1 (2011): 21–41.

Weiss, Thomas G. "What Happened to the Idea of World Government?" *International Studies Quarterly* 53, no. 2 (2009): 253–71.

Weldes, Jutta. "Globalisation Is Science Fiction." *Millennium: Journal of International Studies* 30, no. 3 (2001): 647–67.

Wells, H. G. *The Open Conspiracy and Other Writings.* London: Walterlow & Sons, 1933.

Wells, H. G. *The Outline of History: Being a Plain History of Life and Mankind.* New York: Garden City Publishing, 1931.

Welsh, Jennifer. *The Return of History: Conflict, Migration, and Geopolitics in the Twenty-First Century.* Toronto: Anansi Press, 2016.

Wendt, Alexander. "Anarchy Is What States Make of It: The Social Construction of Power Politics." *International Organization* 46, no. 2 (1992): 391–425.

Wendt, Alexander. "The State as Person in International Theory." *Review of International Studies* 30, no. 2 (2004): 289–316.

Wendt, Alexander. "Why a World State Is Inevitable." *European Journal of International Relations* 9, no. 4 (2003): 491–542.

Werbner, Pnina. *Anthropology and the New Cosmopolitanism.* Oxford: Berg, 2008.

Wheeler, Nicholas. *Saving Strangers: Humanitarian Intervention in International Society.* Oxford: Oxford University Press, 2000.

White, E. B. *The Wild Flag.* Boston: Houghton Mifflin, 1943.

Wiener, Antje, Tanja Borzel, and Thomas Risse. *European Integration Theory.* 3rd ed. Oxford: Oxford University Press, 2019.

Wight, Martin. "The Apostasy of Christendom." LSE Martin Wight Archives, 1948–50.

Wight, Martin. "The Balance of Power and International Order." In *The Bases of International Order: Essays in Honour of C.A.W. Manning,* edited by Alan James, 85–115. London: Oxford University Press, 1973.

Wight, Martin. "The Church, Russia and the West." *Ecumenical Review* 1, no. 1 (1948): 25–45.

Wight, Martin. "The Disunity of Mankind." *Millennium: Journal of International Studies* 44, no. 1 (2015): 129–33.

Wight, Martin. *Foreign Policy and Security Strategy.* Edited by David S. Yost. Oxford: Oxford University Press, 2023.

Wight, Martin. *International Relations and Political Philosophy.* Edited by David S. Yost. Oxford: Oxford University Press, 2022.

Wight, Martin. *International Theory: The Three Traditions.* New York: Holmes & Meier for the Royal Institute of International Affairs, 1992.

Wight, Martin. *Power Politics.* New York: Holmes & Meier for the Royal Institute of International Affairs, 1978.

Wight, Martin. "Some Reflections on the Historic Antichrist." LSE Martin Wight Archives, 1971.

Wight, Martin. *Systems of States.* Leicester: Leicester University Press, 1977.

Williams, Huw Lloyd. *On Rawls, Development and Global Justice*. London: Palgrave, 2011.

Williams, John. "Pluralism, Solidarism and the Emergence of World Society in English School Theory." *International Relations* 19, no. 1 (2005): 19–38.

Wilson, Peter. "Retrieving Cosmos: Gilbert Murray's Thought on International Relations." In *Gilbert Murray Reassessed: Hellenism, Theatre, and International Politics*, edited by Christopher Stray, 239–60. Oxford: Oxford University Press, 2007.

Woolf, Greg. *Becoming Roman: The Origins of Provincial Civilization in Gaul*. Cambridge: Cambridge University Press, 1998.

Wright, Quincy, ed. *The World Community*. Chicago: University of Chicago Press, 1948.

Wyne, Aly. *America's Great Power Opportunity: Revitalizing U.S. Foreign Policy to Meet the Challenges of Strategic Competition*. Cambridge: Polity, 2022.

Yasuaki, Onuma. *A Transcivilizational Perspective on International Law: Questioning Prevalent Cognitive Frameworks in the Emerging Multi-Polar and Multi-Civilizational World of the Twenty-First Century*. Boston: Martinus Nijhoff, 2010.

Yu, Ying-Shih. *Chinese History and Culture*, Vol. 1, *Sixth Century B.C.E. to Seventeenth Century*. New York: Columbia University Press, 2016.

Yunker, James A. *The Idea of World Government: From Ancient Times to the Twenty-First Century*. London: Routledge, 2011.

Zaalberg, Thijs Brocades, and Bart Luttikhuis, eds. *Empire's Violent End: Comparing Dutch, British, and French Wars of Decolonization, 1945–1962*. Ithaca: Cornell University Press, 2022.

Zachmann, Urs Matthias, ed. *Asia after Versailles: Asian Perspectives on the Paris Peace Conference and the Interwar Order, 1919–33*. Edinburgh: Edinburgh University Press, 2017.

Zahra, Tara. *Against the World: Anti-Globalism and Mass Politics between the World Wars*. New York: W.W. Norton, 2023.

Zarakol, Ayse. *Before the West: The Rise and Fall of Eastern World Orders*. Cambridge: Cambridge University Press, 2022.

Zarakol Ayse, ed. *Hierarchies in World Politics*. Cambridge: Cambridge University Press, 2017.

Zhang, Yongjin. "Early Cultural Orientations and Ancient International Thought." *Millennium: Journal of International Studies* 44, no. 1 (2015): 144–46.

Zhdanov, Andrei. "New Aspects of the World Conflict: The International Situation." 1947. https://soviethistory.msu.edu/1947-2/cold-war/cold-war-texts/zhdanov-on-the-international-situation/

Zipp, Samuel. *The Idealist: Wendell Wilkie's Wartime Quest to Build One World*. Cambridge, MA: Belknap Press of Harvard University Press, 2020.

Zurn, Michael. "Global Governance and Legitimacy Problems." *Government and Opposition* 39, no. 2 (2004): 260–87.

Zurn, Michael. *A Theory of Global Governance: Authority, Legitimacy, and Contestation*. Oxford: Oxford University Press, 2018.

Index